3/2

ECONOMIC JUSTICE

Economic Justice

Selections from Distributive Justice *and* A Living Wage

John A. Ryan

Edited and Introduced by
Harlan R. Beckley

 Westminster John Knox Press
Louisville, Kentucky

Distributive Justice: The Right and Wrong of Our Present Distribution of Wealth originally published by The Macmillan Co., 1916, 1927, 1942.

A Living Wage: Its Ethical and Economic Aspects originally published by The Macmillan Co., 1906.

Book design by Publishers' WorkGroup

First edition

Published by Westminster John Knox Press
Louisville, Kentucky

This book is printed on acid-free paper that meets the American National Standards Institute Z39.48 standard. ♾

PRINTED IN THE UNITED STATES OF AMERICA

96 97 98 99 00 01 02 03 04 05 — 10 9 8 7 6 5 4 3 2 1

Library of Congress Cataloging-in-Publication Data

Ryan, John Augustine, 1869–1945.
    [Distributive justice. Selections]
    Economic justice : selections from Distributive justice and A living
wage / John A. Ryan ; edited and introduced by Harlan R. Beckley.
        p.   cm. — (Library of theological ethics)
    Includes bibliographical references (p.   ).
    ISBN 0-664-25660-0 (alk. paper)
    1. Economics—Religious aspects. 2. Economics—Moral and ethical
aspects. 3. Distribution (Economic theory) 4. Wages.   I. Beckley,
Harlan R., date.   II. Ryan, John Augustine, 1869–1945. A living
wage. Selections. 1996.   III. Title.   IV. Series.
HB72.R9325   1996
330.1′6—dc20
                                          96-398

CONTENTS

LIBRARY OF THEOLOGICAL ETHICS
General Editors' Introduction

The field of theological ethics possesses in its literature an abundant inheritance concerning religious convictions and the moral life, critical issues, methods, and moral problems. The Library of Theological Ethics is designed to present a selection of important texts that would otherwise be unavailable for scholarly purposes and classroom use. The series will engage the question of what it means to think theologically and ethically. It is offered in the conviction that sustained dialogue with our predecessors serves the interests of responsible contemporary reflection. Our more immediate aim in offering it, however, is to enable scholars and teachers to make more extensive use of classic texts as they train new generations of theologians, ethicists, and ministers.

The volumes included in the Library will comprise a variety of types. Some will make available English-language texts and translations that have fallen out of print; others will present new translations of texts previously unavailable in English. Still others will offer anthologies or collections of significant statements about problems and themes of special importance. We hope that each volume will encourage contemporary theological ethicists to remain in conversation with the rich and diverse heritage of their discipline.

ROBIN W. LOVIN
DOUGLAS F. OTTATI
WILLIAM SCHWEIKER

INTRODUCTION: CATHOLIC SOCIAL ETHICIST AND ADVOCATE FOR REFORM

John Augustine Ryan developed and promoted moral arguments for reforming the economy of the United States throughout much of the first half of the twentieth century. He published his first book, *A Living Wage,* in 1906 and his last article, "Roosevelt and Social Justice," in 1945. Although he never gained the national recognition granted leaders of the Social Gospel or Christian realism, Ryan's public career overlapped all of Walter Rauschenbusch's leadership as the foremost proponent of the Social Gospel, as well as much of Reinhold Niebuhr's Christian realist criticism of the Social Gospel and the American economic system. Virtually ignored by his Protestant contemporaries, Ryan's primary influence was among Roman Catholics and within the Roosevelt Administration. He was much more closely connected with the makers of national economic policy than was either Rauschenbusch or Niebuhr.

FORMATION AND ACHIEVEMENTS

Ryan's interest in economic reform emerged quite naturally from his upbringing in an Irish Catholic farm family in Minnesota during the period following the Civil War. Monetary deflation coupled with high interest rates—Ryan's father paid 12 percent interest on one of his farm mortgages—made many farm families painfully aware of the debilitating effects of unjust economic structures. Ryan was among those attracted to populist politics, and he sought to become informed on matters of economic injustice at a very early age. At the age of eleven, he began to read the *Irish World and American Industrial Liberator,* which according to Ryan one could not read week after week "without acquiring an interest in and a love of economic justice." At age thirteen, he was "stimulated" to "sympathy with the weaker economic classes" by reading Henry

George's *Progress and Poverty,* which his family had borrowed from a neighboring farmer.[1]

By the time Ryan traveled the short distance to St. Paul for post-secondary education, he was receptive to an interpretation of Catholic moral theology aligned with American progressivism and with the cause of economic justice for labor in the United States. Ryan later remembered being impressed on his first reading of Pope Leo XIII's encyclical *Rerum novarum* ("On the Condition of Labor") by the fact that the Pope approved state intervention to secure justice for the working class; more important, however, for Ryan's career was what he described as Pope Leo's application of "the commonplaces of Catholic moral theology" to the "facts of present-day industry."[2] Ryan's principal contribution to the Christian ethics of his day was his application of neo-Thomist moral theology, invigorated by Pope Leo's efforts, to the American economy, which Ryan examined critically on the basis of his prodigious reading in economic theory and analysis. The result was a melding of Catholic moral theology with American reform traditions,[3] an intellectual accomplishment that enabled Ryan, and many other Catholics who joined him, to become participants at the center of political reform of the American economy. Hence Ryan's particular brand of economic ethics brought him into a close relationship with leading figures in the New Deal.

Ryan's serious study of economics began at St. Paul Seminary. He supplemented the economics and sociology recently added to St. Paul's curriculum with an in-depth study of texts in economics, to which he devoted the entire summer of 1894.[4] During Ryan's four years of graduate study at the Catholic University of America, Thomas J. Bouquillon, his principal mentor, insisted that moral theology was deficient because it remained largely uninformed by the social sciences. Ryan acted on this advice with alacrity. Although requirements forced him to study canon law as his secondary concentration, Ryan complemented his work in moral theology with courses in political economy and sociology, essential preparation for his dissertation on the right to a living wage. When Ryan finished his dissertation in 1905, he had laid the essential intellectual groundwork for his lifelong vocation as a social ethicist and advocate for reforming the economy. This uniting of Catholic moral theology and economic studies provided the tools Ryan needed to criticize injustices in the economy and propose policies to remedy them. A complete theory of distributive justice (i.e., one applied to land, capital, and entrepreneurship, as well as to labor) awaited the publication of *Distributive Justice* in 1916, but the canons of justice that anchored that volume were already scattered throughout Ryan's dissertation.

Following publication of his dissertation (as *A Living Wage*) in 1906, Ryan committed significant time and energy to stating his moral arguments for just economic policies, especially for a minimum wage. He addressed these arguments to the Catholic hierarchy and lay organizations, to labor groups, and directly to politicians. Ryan took this vocational pattern with him to Washington, D.C., in 1915. As a member of the faculty at Catholic University and of the Social Action Department of the National Catholic Welfare Conference, Ryan was positioned to "populariz[e] his ideas" in what his biographer, Francis Broderick, calls an "active apostolate for social justice." Broderick adds that with the publication of *Distributive Justice*, Ryan's "program for social justice was set": "No major scholarly work followed."[5]

From 1915, when he came to teach at Catholic University, until Roosevelt's election, Ryan's influence was largely confined to the most progressive forces in the Catholic hierarchy. A proposal Ryan had written for postwar reconstruction was adopted as the Bishops' Program for Social Reconstruction, issued in 1919 by the forerunner to the National Catholic Welfare Council (NCWC—later Conference). Ryan then became head of the Social Action Department when the NCWC was first formed in 1919. These connections, however, did not spare him from scathing criticism by influential forces in the church. Cardinal O'Connell of Boston, angered by Ryan's public support for a constitutional amendment to restrict child labor, wrote to Ryan's archbishop demanding that he reprimand Ryan. Cardinal O'Connell characterized Ryan and Jane Addams as "socialistic teachers and writers."[6] Ryan's proposals were even less popular with the government during this period, the lowest point occurring when, in 1923, the Supreme Court declared minimum-wage legislation unconstitutional in *Adkins* v. *Children's Hospital.* Ryan's popular arguments for economic reform, especially for a minimum wage, held little sway in Washington prior to the 1930s. The moral theologian who sought to produce political reform through ethical argument was effectively isolated from political power.

Ryan, nonetheless, continued undeterred in his labors to gain the approval of the church and the government for his moral and political arguments for reform, a tactic that produced a plentiful harvest in the 1930s. Pope Pius XI's designation of Ryan as a Right Reverend in 1933 officially affirmed the orthodoxy of his teaching on the economic question and enhanced his stature among American Catholics. Ryan called this recognition "authoritative testimony to the soundness of my social teaching."[7] This new ecclesiastical title enabled Father Charles Coughlin to chide Ryan as the "Right Reverend spokesman for the New Deal" following a 1936 radio address in which Ryan, at the behest of the Democratic National Committee, defended Roosevelt against charges Coughlin had made that Roosevelt was a Communist. Ryan must have secretly relished Coughlin's sarcastic sobriquet as it publicized and exaggerated Ryan's role in the Roosevelt Administration. When the changing political climate of the 1930s brought Ryan's legal and economic arguments into vogue in the Supreme Court and Congress,[8] he exulted in his newfound status, as evidenced by his autobiographical account of the celebration of his seventieth birthday in 1939. Ryan fondly remembered that the party at the Willard Hotel, which he called "one of the most distinguished banquets ever held in Washington," was attended by many dignitaries from all three branches of government.[9] The banquet was a testimony to Ryan, but more significantly, it symbolized his success in bringing Catholic moral theology into the center of public debate about economic justice in the United States.

KEY ETHICAL CONCEPTS

The intellectual basis for Ryan's historical achievement is revealed through his writings in this volume, but there is a greater reward for us in engaging Ryan's theory of rights and justice as he applied it to the economy. Ryan's theory and its application have continuing relevance for theological and social ethics. His understandings of human dignity, rights, economic "expediency" (i.e., prudential accounting for the circumstances and consequences of economic policies), the common good, and the canons of justice are informative in both their insights and their errors.[10]

Dignity and Rights

The theory of rights undergirding the canons of justice and economic policies Ryan advocated in these writings is distinctively Roman Catholic. Rights in Catholic social teaching are based on a concept of human dignity that differs from dignity as it is understood in much of Enlightenment ethics. The equal dignity of each person consists in the capacity to progress toward the telos of one's rational human nature, a teleological foundation for ethics formulated most comprehensively by Thomas Aquinas.[11]

Ryan's explicitly teleological understanding of dignity clearly and instructively distinguishes this Catholic use of the concept from Immanuel Kant's view. Kant associated dignity with individual autonomy, that is, with respect for the individual's right to legislate the moral law for oneself. This autonomy is intrinsically valuable, an end in itself not to be violated for any purpose. Ryan, like Kant, repeatedly insisted that every person possesses intrinsic worth and as such should be treated as an end, not merely as an instrument for the welfare of others or of society. For Ryan, however, the end to be respected is not autonomy but a person's privilege to seek the end of one's rational nature, an end that Ryan considered self-evident. Persons have a right to whatever means are instrumental to this end of human nature. They have no right to legislate for themselves a "moral law" that is incompatible with this end. Respect for the moral autonomy of others is not sufficient, nor is it always necessary to treat them as an end in themselves. When liberty alone does not assure the means to self-development (e.g., a decent livelihood in return for work, or a workplace that facilitates one's creative and directive capacities), autonomy is not sufficient; when the liberty is nonessential or detrimental for self-development (e.g., amassing wealth that is superfluous to achieving the end of our rational nature), it is not necessary.

Kant rejected any such determination of rights on the basis of a conception of the good for persons. Respect for persons' dignity as self-legislating (i.e., autonomous) rational wills prohibits reference to a telos of human rational nature. Binding persons' rights and obligations to a conception of the good constitutes a heteronomous imposition on their moral freedom. In contrast to Ryan, Kant held that justice should not be based on "the end that a person intends to accomplish by means of the object that he wills."[12] Kant's respect for dignity does not entail an individual's right to choose ends arbitrarily; one has no right to violate the universal moral maxims that all rational beings necessarily legislate for themselves. Nevertheless, justice requires neither more nor less than respect for an individual's moral autonomy.[13] According to Ryan, on the other hand, the formula that respects human dignity is "that the individual has a right to all things that are essential to the reasonable development of his personality," a formula that he explicitly juxtaposes to Kant's respect for the right to individual autonomy. Ryan held that Kant was among those moral philosophers who fail to "set the limits of individual rights."[14]

This concept of dignity had enormous consequences for Ryan's justifications for economic rights, their relation to what he called economic "expediency," and his canons of justice. According to Ryan, "All rights are means, . . . by which the individual attains the end appointed to him by nature."[15] No rights are intrinsic.[16] They are justified by their instrumental value as means to development toward an appointed end in which satisfaction of sensual desires is merely instrumental to the development of the intellectual, moral, and spiritual faculties. Based on his understanding of this end, Ryan arrived at the content of rights such as liberty, equality, and property by determining whether specific formulations of these rights foster self-development. Liberty is "merely a means to right and reasonable self-development."[17] "Equality and natural rights . . . are not ends in themselves. They are means to human welfare."[18] Private ownership is "not an intrinsic good, but merely a means to human welfare."[19] These natural rights are, according to Ryan, absolute and equal, but these terms must be carefully qualified. What is absolute is only the liberty or claims to property that are needed for proper self-development, not all liberties and claims to use and dispose of property. What is equal is only claims on what one needs for self-development, not claims on the distribution of all the goods a society produces.

Two important conclusions follow. First, Ryan's Catholic rights theory maximizes neither individual liberties nor distributive equality. Ryan's writings here reflect his persistent battles with those who sought to absolutize individual property rights or individual liberties in forming contracts. They also demonstrate his willingness to tolerate inequalities that do not jeopardize individuals' privilege to perfect themselves, and to affirm inequalities that further the common good or permit a higher level of development for persons who possess superior capacities. Second, the absolute and equal rights to the means for self-perfection are independent of what Ryan called "social welfare," the good of the whole considered without regard for its contribution to the satisfaction of individual rights. Ryan was not a utilitarian or unmitigated consequentialist in his economic ethics. Distributive justice should consider the common good of the economy only insofar as the common good serves the absolute rights of individuals as ends in themselves. The common good never overrides any individual's right to self-development.[20]

Economic Consequences and the Common Good

Consequences, nevertheless, play a significant role in Ryan's economic ethics. In a debate with the well-known socialist Morris Hillquit, Ryan claimed that "in the matter of social institutions, moral values and genuine expediency are in the long run identical,"[21] a claim applied and tested throughout the pages of this volume. *Distributive Justice* demonstrates the importance Ryan attributed to economic studies in determining just economic policies. The consequences of economic policies should be measured as accurately as possible before the ethicist advocates a policy to secure particular natural rights. Ryan judged rights to rent, interest, and profits merely presumptive rights because they are not directly essential for an individual's self-development. The consequences of these rights for promoting absolute economic rights were determinative for Ryan's justification for them. Ryan also examined the economic consequences of minimum wage legislation to test whether this policy would maintain a vibrant economy capable of delivering in the long run on the absolute right to a living wage. In none of these cases did he consider the consequences of a particular policy for economic or social welfare alone. To him, just policies are not determined by their consequences for some conception of the common good considered independently from individual rights. In all instances, Ryan asked about the economic consequences only insofar as they ultimately redounded to the benefit of the individual measured in terms of opportunities or means for self-perfection. Ryan called this end "human welfare," the common good of a society insofar as it safeguards and advances the dignity and rights of each individual. Human welfare, one of Ryan's six canons of justice, requires that policies will in the long run be expedient or prudent in securing rights. This moral impulse persuaded Ryan to become the most thorough student of economics among theological ethicists in the first half of the twentieth century.[22]

Ryan's claim in the Hillquit debate also maintained that promoting economic expediency will in the long run advance moral values. Economic realities never led Ryan to compromise satisfying some moral rights in order to meet others. He never doubted the feasibility of fulfilling the absolute and equal rights necessary for every person's self-perfection. Ryan's examination of presumptive rights (i.e., those only indirectly related to securing the absolute rights to self-development) reveals a willingness to alter these rights in light of changed circumstances and newly foreseen consequences. Absolute rights, however, are not subject to such revision. Ryan viewed the workers' right to a decent livelihood as unalterable and enforceable without compromise, though the means for satisfying the right might change. In *A Living Wage,* Ryan conjectured that the mere existence of the right to a decent livelihood supposes a sufficiency of goods to secure it for all persons.[23] The rights that secure dignity do not conflict with one another; God has ordered creation so that persons can have the means to achieve the end that God has appointed them. Ryan suggested only rarely that some temporary compromise, such as very limited unemployment, might have to be tolerated in the short run in order to provide a living wage to most workers, and he never, so far as I know, argued that individuals must sacrifice an absolute right in order to achieve a common good or justice for all.

Justice

Ryan expressed his regard for how economics can further human welfare in his use of the three levels of justice commonly referred to in Catholic moral theology: commutative, distributive, and social justice. Though he did not discuss these terms in *Distributive Justice,* he used them, and readers should be alert to how they informed his thinking. Ryan considered commutative justice (i.e., equity in exchange relations between individuals or entities) necessary but insufficient. Commutative justice does not take account of moral factors extrinsic to an exchange relationship, for example, the needs of the wage earner that might not be satisfied by such contract-intrinsic factors as consent, productivity, or equality in the things exchanged. Distributive justice (i.e., what society owes to individuals) is largely determined by individual needs whose satisfaction is requisite for the privilege of self-perfection. Hence distributive justice accounts for the extrinsic factor that renders commutative justice alone deficient. Social justice examines what is due to the common good in order that the whole may perform its distributive function to deliver the means individuals need for self-perfection. Ryan began to use this term after the publication of Pope Pius XI's *Quadragesimo anno* in 1931, observing that it expressed "better and more accurately" what he, Ryan, had previously referred to as "human welfare."[24] Readers will want to note how human welfare and social justice widened Ryan's perspective in order to consider how economic practices serve individual needs in the long run. To determine distributive justice according to need is inadequate because it does not account for how social and economic policies affect the permanent satisfaction of the requirements of distributive justice. Prudence or economic expediency requires this larger perspective, which accounts for production as well as distribution as part of a just economic system.[25]

The six canons of justice (equality, needs, efforts and sacrifices, scarcity, productivity, and human welfare or social justice) that Ryan set forth in *Distributive Justice* reflect the interrelation among these three levels of justice. Though Ryan calls these canons of distributive justice, they take into account his concepts of commutative and social justice as well. Human needs, defined as the means for self-perfection, stipulate the primary claim on the goods of society. Though equality precedes needs in Ryan's list of canons, equality refers to persons' equal claims on the basic needs for self-perfection. It does not stipulate a pattern of distribution distinct from a needs-based distribution. Ryan followed Aristotle and Thomas in the view that distributive justice is proportional to what is due to persons and not, as is commutative justice, an arithmetic equality of goods. For Ryan, the proportion of goods due each individual is equal insofar as all persons have the same basic needs to be met in order to exercise their privilege for normal development. Beyond that minimal level of distributive equality, individuals are due different amounts of goods. The capabilities of some persons for a more sophisticated level of self-perfection constitute one basis for discrepancies in what is due. For example, some individuals who possess special abilities for intellectual excellence deserve goods commensurate with their needs for achieving this extraordinary level of development.

In addition, people differ in the contributions they are willing and able to make to the economy. These inequalities in contributions to the economy do not in their own right warrant inequalities of distribution; the canons of efforts and sacrifices, scarcity, and productivity are all subservient to meeting individuals' needs, the moral purpose of any economic system. Nevertheless, the canon of needs alone is insufficient to determine a just distribution. It fails to account for how distribution affects production and thereby the long-term satisfaction of needs. Neither individual liberty to pursue material gains in the marketplace nor any measure of individual productivity in and of itself justifies inequalities that restrict the satisfaction of others' needs. Commutative justice is not determined by liberty in contracts nor by productivity alone, but by how exchanges meet needs in the long run. Nevertheless, when inequalities in efforts and sacrifice, relative scarcity of a skill, or productivity can be demonstrated to increase the likelihood of satisfying the needs of all persons, they justify inequalities in distribution from the perspective of human welfare or social justice.

This sixth canon of justice does not constitute a separate criterion for distribution; it is, rather, a requirement that a just distribution account for economic welfare insofar as it serves long-run distribution according to needs. Human welfare required Ryan to weigh how distribution according to productive contributions to the economy can be the most expedient method for achieving the moral end of economic systems and activity: the meeting of every individual's needs.

Ryan observed in *Distributive Justice* that these canons of justice apply only to profits and wages, but a careful reading will show that he applied most of them (needs and efforts excepted) to his justifications for rent and interest as well. Indeed, the canons of justice, as they are informed by his concepts of dignity, rights, and expediency, express the criteria by which Ryan made judgments about all the economic policies he advocated, an aspect of his life that was an ingredient to his self-understanding of his vocation as a Catholic moral theologian.

ADVOCATE FOR SOCIAL REFORM

A Living Wage

Even this brief exposition of his most crucial moral concepts indicates why Ryan was committed to a nearly incessant lifelong effort to satisfy the right to a living wage through minimum wage legislation. Among those absolute and equal rights necessary for the privilege of self-perfection, none was more chronically abused in practice than the right to a living wage. In 1906, Ryan estimated the sum of $600 to be the minimal income required for the full development of a reasonably sized family, and he calculated that 60 percent of the adult male workers in the cities of the United States received less than this minimum amount.[26] He believed that a remedy to this injustice could be obtained by legislating a minimum wage. A minimum wage, Ryan proclaimed, would secure for the laboring class "substantially all that was due by any of the canons of distributive justice."[27] Minimum-wage legislation was tantamount to a panacea for economic injustice. Ryan supported other remedial efforts to provide the means for self-development (e.g., housing, compulsory insurance programs, and so forth), but he insisted that if the workers received a decent livelihood, they would themselves solve the problems for which the reformers were trying to provide remedies through other means.[28] Although *Distributive Justice,* in all three editions, devotes considerable space to other rights—rent, interest, profits, and wages above what one needs for self-perfection—these are merely presumptive rights. As such, they are based on their economic expediency in securing what each person normally needs for self-perfection, or on the uncertain claims of greater needs for persons with superior abilities and of the special efforts and sacrifices by some individuals. Ryan observed in *Distributive Justice* that a concern for wage justice beyond a right to a decent livelihood is "devoid of practical interest" until a decent livelihood is achieved for all wage earners.[29] He then proceeded, in the next chapter, to argue that the best way to secure this centerpiece of economic justice is through minimum wage legislation.

Redistribution and Industrial Reorganization

By the time Ryan repeated this conclusion in his third edition of *Distributive Justice,* other policies, in addition to minimum wage legislation, occupied a large portion of his efforts as a moral advocate for economic reforms. Ryan's policy agenda changed as he factored his economic analysis of the Depression into his judgments about policies, and it was emboldened by Pope Pius XI and the New Deal. First, he began to call on the Roosevelt Administration to take initiatives that would redistribute income and wealth for the purpose of restoring a prosperous economy, ending unemployment, and securing a decent livelihood for labor. These redistributive proposals complemented living wage legislation in the face of economic conditions that Ryan, under the influence of a theory of underconsumption proposed by British economist John A. Hobson, believed caused the Depression. Ryan held that insufficient demand for consumer goods from low-paid farmers and wage earners depressed the economy. Transfers of income to these groups and to the dwindling middle class, he thought, would promote economic recovery. Economic recovery was necessary in order to end unemployment and assure a living wage through minimum wage laws. These redistributive policies were warranted by economic expediency, not by a principle of equality or a new moral rights claim. They did make Ryan's reforms much more egalitarian than those that he had advocated in the previous two decades, a feature of his thought that is not adequately revealed in the writings of this volume.[30]

Second, Ryan began, during the Roosevelt era, to speak out persistently for two interrelated policies that were based on the absolute and equal right to the means for self-development. The first of these policies Ryan called the "occupational group system," following the terminology of Pope Pius XI in *Quadragesimo anno*. It proposed planning councils composed of owners, managers, and laborers in a particular industry. Ryan believed this organizational structure would facilitate a cooperative spirit and safeguard the workers' dignity, independence, and security—attributes essential for their self-development. He hoped the National Recovery Administration of the Roosevelt Administration could, *mutatis mutandis*, achieve the purpose of the occupational group system. After the Schechter case of 1935, in which the Supreme Court declared the NRA unconstitutional, Ryan called for resurrecting it as an occupational group system, even though the Roosevelt Administration had abandoned this method of industrial planning. As he began to champion this reorganization for industry, Ryan simultaneously emphasized a proposal for reorganizing firms internally that he had proffered earlier. He called this a proposal for industrial democracy. His version of economic democracy sought to have labor share in management, profits, and ownership. Sharing in profits was primarily another means of providing for a decent livelihood and full equity in the payment of wages, but Ryan considered sharing in ownership and management essential means for fostering the laborers' complete development. The laborer needs, Ryan argued, a sense of independence and control that sharing in ownership would nurture, and an opportunity to exercise "directive" and "creative" faculties through sharing in the management of business.[31]

Moral Theology Informed Advocacy

This new policy agenda was spurred on by the influence of the Depression, Pope Pius XI, and Roosevelt, but it also reflects Ryan's increasing reliance on social justice to correct deficiencies in distributive justice. Distributive justice concerns the distribution of goods persons can possess and control for their own purposes. Taken alone, it neglects what individuals owe to the common good so that it might serve the rights of all. As Ryan conceived social justice, it considers how the health of the whole affects the long-term distribution of goods that satisfy rights, as well as with how social institutions might nourish opportunities for self-development. Ryan believed that redistributive policies were necessary for a healthy economy that could deliver on the right of every laborer to a living wage. He thought that the occupational group system and industrial democracy would install economic institutions and practices that could engender and support the very qualities of character workers need in order to attain the full development of their rational nature. In neither case was he concerned with the direct distribution of goods to fulfill rights claims, the focus of distributive justice; his intention was to promote the kind of social institutions that would advance and preserve the long-term means for self-development, the purpose of human welfare or social justice.

These revisions in Ryan's policy agenda did not displace his earlier concern for minimum wage legislation, and the new policies, though reflecting an increased emphasis on social justice, were all solidly backed by the theory of rights and justice Ryan had formulated two decades earlier. The extent to which his policy arguments during the '30s rely on the ethics he developed in *Distributive Justice* confirms Broderick's judgment that Ryan offered no major scholarly work after 1916. This observation is further confirmed by the republication of revised editions of *Distributive Justice* in 1927 and again in 1942, and by the nearly verbatim republication in 1940 of the chapter from *A Living Wage* reprinted in this volume.[32] Ryan's speeches and shorter popular writings after 1916 may be appropriately characterized as the work of an advocate for reform. They applied the ethics presented in this volume to the changing political and economic conditions of the day.

Moreover, Ryan perceived this quest for reform as a task of using moral arguments to persuade political decision makers to advance justice. God orders human social life through the eternal and natural law, which rational agents, even outside a state of grace, are able to comprehend and act on. Ryan's hope for justice rests on the ability of rational persons to understand and implement the moral law in relation to current economic circumstances. In this perception, Ryan differed markedly from his leading Protestant contemporaries. Rauschenbusch's hope for justice resided in the forces of redemption that he discerned in the labor and socialist movements and in the "democratization" of politics, the family, and the churches. The fulfillment of this hope depended principally on a conversion of the forces that controlled the economic system, and not in moral suasion.[33] Reinhold Niebuhr founded his chastened hope for an approximation of justice on wise compromises of the highest ideals of morality in order to achieve a balance of political power that could cope with the realities of intractable and conflicting, sinful self-interests. He did not share Ryan's confidence that human reason could arrive at true or agreed-upon standards of justice, let alone effect those standards through political action. The theological notions of sin, grace, redemption, and God's acting in history were not relevant to Ryan's struggle for reform. There is no need for grand strategies of compromise, or to produce profound changes in the cultural ethos, when rational agents can comprehend and apply the natural law to economic affairs. Although Ryan concluded all three editions of *Distributive Justice* with an observation that a revival of genuine religion is a requisite for progress in the pursuit of justice,[34] and offered a similar observation in a few other instances, he clearly had in mind the need to persuade persons that their true human welfare lay in pursuing the end of their rational human nature.

Ryan sought to teach at Catholic University in Washington and took pride in the celebration of his seventieth birthday with important persons from official Washington because these facets of his life emerged naturally from this theologically and ethically informed understanding of his vocation. He felt called to make reasoned moral arguments to those in a position to serve the cause of economic justice for the laboring class. Ryan did not tire of this calling, even as he savored the attention at his seventieth birthday party. After acknowledging the "progress toward social justice in [his] lifetime," Ryan took the occasion to plead with his audience for solutions to two remaining problems: a redistribution of purchasing power to remedy chronic unemployment and an occupational group system to give labor a "new status' in economic activities.[35] Ethical argument, especially the argument set forth in this book, is the method Ryan employed to promote economic reform.

THE PRESENT TEXT

The edited version of *Distributive Justice* in this volume is intended to present the crucial elements of Ryan's ethical argument without requiring introductory readers to trudge through highly technical arguments that are time-bound by the events and debates in the first half of this century or that are supplemental to the core of his ethics and economics. Editorial notes have been added to Ryan's original text to indicate where the deletions occur.

I have been most cautious in wielding the deleting ax in the section on wages, since that material is already a condensation of Ryan's earlier book on a living wage and constitutes the ethical argument that defines the center of his vocation as an ethicist and reformer. I have included Ryan's account of the best method for achieving a living wage (i.e., through legislation) because it reveals his ethical arguments against a form of strictly contractual justice and conveys the hope he placed in making moral arguments for legislative reforms. Admittedly, few of our contemporaries, of whatever moral or political persuasion, grant similar importance to the minimum wage legislation that Ryan proposed in this chapter. The section omitted from this chapter on methods of increasing wages includes a brief account of Ryan's views on labor unions. He was supportive of unions and union practices, but he often criticized union leaders for deemphasizing legislative remedies for injustices to labor and for contributing to conflict with management when the ultimate goal should be the cooperation he envisioned in the occupational group system and industrial democracy. Those interested in a fuller account of Ryan's views about labor unions will want to read the appropriate chapters in *Social Reconstruction* and *The Church and Socialism* and articles from *Declining Liberty*.[36]

In only one other case have I omitted part of a chapter. Short sections on the teachings of theologians and of Pope Leo XIII have been deleted from Ryan's argument for private ownership of land in the second chapter. They add little to his argument and are too short to contribute to historical interpretation. The operative rule of thumb was to retain whole chapters and delete whole chapters.

The chapter from *A Living Wage* at the end of this volume offers the justification for rights that informs all Ryan's thinking, but he did not include it in *Distributive Justice*. This chapter is the foundation for Ryan's arguments for the rights to a decent livelihood and a living wage, but I have located it here after the entirety of *Distributive Justice* in order to avoid confusing the flow of Ryan's argument. The combination of these selections presents the bulk of Ryan's innovative scholarly contributions to theologically informed economic ethics.

In accordance with the standards of his day, Ryan did not declare full bibliographical information in his footnotes. For those interested in more complete information regarding the sources Ryan used, the bibliography at the conclusion of Ryan's writings cites complete publication data for most of the sources to which Ryan refers.

This volume will have served one of its purposes if some readers finish slightly dissatisfied and are prompted to read on in Ryan's shorter and more popular essays. Even though Ryan did not revise substantially the moral theology and economic ethics presented here, his mode for joining rights and canons of justice with inductive economic analysis required that he continue to rethink the policy implications of his ethics. This way of joining ethics and economics for the purpose of arriving at judgments about policies may be his most distinctive and long-lasting contribution to theological and social ethics. Reading some of Ryan's later policy essays will further illustrate his rejection of an unfortunate tendency to separate ethics from prudence informed by empirical study.[37]

*Much of the work on this volume was completed during a sabbatical leave at the National Humanities Center in Research Triangle Park, North Carolina. Its library staff was indispensable in helping collect the publication facts for John Ryan's sources.

DISTRIBUTIVE JUSTICE

PREFACE

In the preface to the first edition of this book, I attributed to "the majority of the American people" the opinion that "the first cause of industrial unrest is unjust distribution of wealth and income," but added that there exists no general agreement concerning "the precise nature and extent of the injustice." These propositions are still true. The necessity still remains of reforming the bad distribution through a better understanding of its nature and causes.

The aim and method of the present edition are the same as those of the first. They are: "to discuss systematically and comprehensively the justice of the processes by which the product of industry is distributed. Inasmuch as the product is actually apportioned among landowners, capitalists, business men and laborers, the moral aspects of the distribution are studied with reference to these four classes. While their rights and obligations form the main subject of the book, the effort is also made to propose reforms that would remove the principal defects of the present system and bring about a larger measure of justice."

Some persons will question the value of such a study for the near and uncertain future. Within a few years, the war will somehow come to an end. After that, the prevailing economic order will probably be very different from the system known as capitalism. Therefore, a discussion of just distribution in terms of the landowner, the capitalist, the businessman and the laborer, will be outmoded and outdated. The ethical problems and judgments will become entirely different when the instruments of production are owned and operated by the state, under some form of collectivism. While the *principles* of justice will remain unchanged, their *application* to the structure and functioning of the new economic order will call for a vast amount of argument and discussion which are not found in this volume. And much of the material which it does contain will become superfluous and useless.

To this objection there are two ready replies: until the war does come to an

3

end, the system of private enterprise will probably continue in most countries essentially as it is at present; and I am not convinced that the post war economy will exemplify outright collectivism, at least in the United States. That the system of private capitalism will undergo considerable modifications is my expectation and, indeed, my hope; but they will not render the method of treatment or the conclusions in this book inappropriate and irrelevant. Therefore, it is highly probable that the work has still before it a considerable period of usefulness.

In the words of the title page, this edition is "completely revised." Two chapters of the previous editions have been omitted, two others have been combined and a new one has been added. Important changes have been made in almost every chapter, and the additions to many of them are considerable; particularly in vi, vii, xii, xvi, xix, xx, xxii, xxiii. The most important new matter is undoubtedly that which presents the doctrine of the encyclical of Pope Pius XI, *Quadragesimo Anno*. Altogether the additions comprise about one-sixth of the volume. The statistical material, the presentation of economic opinion, and the account of legislation have been brought down to date.*

Feb. 2, 1942.   JOHN A. RYAN

---

*Editor's Note: The chapters Ryan lists have been renumbered in this edited volume using arabic numbers. The original chapters xii and xvi have been omitted, and the remaining chapters are iv, v, xiii, xiv, xvi, and xvii in this book. Chapter xvii actually appeared for the first time in the third edition.

INTRODUCTION: THE ELEMENTS
AND SCOPE OF THE PROBLEM

Distributive justice is primarily a problem of incomes rather than of possessions. It is not immediately concerned with John Brown's railway stock, John White's house, or John Smith's automobile. It deals with the morality of such possessions only indirectly and under one aspect; that is, in so far as they have been acquired through income. Moreover, it deals only with those incomes that are derived from participation in production. For example, it considers the laborer's wages, but not the subsidies that he may receive through charity or friendship. Its province is not the distribution of all the goods of the country among all the people of the country, but only the distribution of the products of industry among the classes that have taken part in making them.

These classes are four, designated as landowners, capitalists, undertakers or business men, and laborers or wage earners. The individual member of each class is an *agent* of production, while the instrument or energy that he owns and contributes is a *factor* of production. Thus, the landowner is an agent of production because he contributes the factor known as land, and the capitalist is an agent of production because he contributes the factor called capital, while the business man and the laborer are agents not only in the sense that they contribute factors but because their contributions involve the continuous expenditure of human energy. Now the product of industry is distributed among these four classes precisely because they are agents of production; that is, because they own and put at the disposal of industry the indispensable factors of production. We say that the agents of production "put the factors of production at the disposal of industry" rather than "exercise or operate the factors," because neither the landowner nor the capitalist, as such, expends continuous energy in the productive process.

This chapter is reprinted from *Distributive Justice: The Right and Wrong of Our Present Distribution of Wealth*, 3d ed., rev. (New York: Macmillan Co., 1942), 3–6.

The product distributed in any country during a single year is variously denoted by economists as the national product, the national income, the national dividend. It consists not merely of material goods, such as houses, food, clothing and automobiles, but also of those non-material goods known as services. Such are the tasks performed by the domestic servant, the barber, the chauffeur, the public official, the physician, the teacher, or any other personal performance "that is valued, as material commodities are valued, according to their selling prices." Even the services of the clergyman are included in the national income or product, since they are paid for and form a part of the annual supply of good things produced and distributed within the country. In the language of the economist, anything that satisfies a human want is a utility, and forms part of the national wealth; hence there can be no sufficient reason for excluding from the national income those goods which minister to spiritual or intellectual wants. The services of the clergyman, the actor, the author, the painter, and the physician are quite as much a part of the utilities of life as the services of the cook, the chambermaid, or the barber; and all are as clearly utilities as bread, hats, houses, or any other material thing. In a general way, therefore, we say that the national product which is available for distribution among the different productive classes comprises all the utilities, material and non-material, that are produced through human agents and satisfy human desires.

In the great majority of instances the product is not distributed in kind. The wheat produced on a given farm is not directly apportioned among the farmers, laborers and landowners who have cooperated in its production; nor are the shoes issuing from a given factory divided among the cooperating laborers and capitalists; and it is obvious that personal services cannot be returned to the persons who have rendered them. Cases of partial direct distribution do, indeed, occur; as when the tenant takes two-thirds and the landowner one-third of the crop raised by the former on land belonging to the latter; or when the miller receives his compensation in a part of the flour that he grinds. To-day, however, such instances are relatively insignificant. By far the greater part of the material product is sold by the undertaker or business man, and the price is then divided between himself and the other agents of production. All personal services are sold, and the price is obtained by the performers thereof. The farmer sells his wheat, the miller his flour, and the barber his services. With the money received for his part in production each productive agent obtains possession of such kinds and amounts of the national product as his desires dictate and his income will procure. Hence the distribution of the product is effected through the conversion of producers' claims into money, and the exchange of the latter for specific quantities and qualities of the product.

While the national product as a whole is divided among the four productive classes, not every portion of it is distributed among actually distinct representatives of these classes. When more than one factor of production is owned by the same person, the product will obviously not go to four different persons. For example; the crop raised by a man on his own unmortgaged land, with his own instruments, and without any hired assistance; and the products of the small shopkeeper, tailor, and barber who are similarly self-sufficient and independent,—are in each case obtained by one person, and do not undergo any actual distribution. Even in these instances, however, there occurs what may be called *virtual* distribution, inasmuch as the single agent owns more than one factor, and performs more than one productive function. And the problem of distributive justice in such cases is to determine whether all these productive functions are properly rewarded through the total amount which the individual has received. Where the factors are owned by distinct groups of persons, the problem is to determine whether each group is properly remunerated for the function that it has performed.

SECTION 1

The Morality
of Private Landownership and Rent

CHAPTER 1

The Landowner's Share
of the National Product

That part of the national product which represents land, and is attributed specifically to land, goes to the landowner. It is called economic rent, or simply rent. We say that rent "is attributed specifically to land," rather than "is produced specifically by land," because we do not know what proportion of the joint product of the different factors of production exactly reflects the productive contribution of any factor. Economic rent represents the productivity of land in so far as it indicates what men are willing to pay for land-use in the productive process. In any particular case rent comes into existence because the land makes a commercially valuable contribution to the product; and it goes to the landowner because this is one of the powers or rights included in the institution of private ownership. And the landowner's share is received by him precisely in his capacity as landowner, and not because he may happen to be laborer, farmer, or proprietor of agricultural capital.

It is perhaps superfluous to observe that not all land produces rent. While most land is useful and productive, at least potentially, there is in almost every locality some land which in present conditions does not warrant men in paying a price for its use. If the crop raised on very sandy soil is so small as to cover merely the outlay for labor and capital, men will not pay rent for the use of that soil. Yet the land has contributed something to the product. Herein we have another indication that rent is not an adequate measure of land productivity. It represents land value.

This chapter is reprinted from *Distributive Justice: The Right and Wrong of Our Present Distribution of Wealth,* 3d ed., rev. (New York: Macmillan Co., 1942). 9–12.

ECONOMIC RENT ALWAYS GOES TO THE LANDOWNER

All land that is in use and for the use of which men are willing to pay a price yields rent, whether it is used by a tenant or by the owner. In the latter case the owner may not call the rent that he receives by that name; he may not distinguish between it and the other portions of the product that he gets from the land; he may call the entire product profits, or wages. Nevertheless the rent exists as a surplus over that part of the product that he can regard as the proper return for his labor, and for the use of his capital-instruments, such as horses, buildings, and machinery. If a farmer employs the same amount and kind of labor and capital in the cultivation of two pieces of land, one of which he owns, the other being hired from some one else; if his net product is the same in both cases, say 1,000 dollars; and if he must pay 200 dollars to the owner of the hired land, then, 200 of the 1,000 dollars that he receives from his own land is likewise to be attributed specifically to his land rather than to his capital or labor. It is rent. While the whole product is due in some degree to the productive power of land, 200 dollars of it represents land value in the process of production, and goes to him solely in his capacity as landowner.

The rent that arises on land used for building sites is of the same general character, and goes likewise to the owner of the land. The owner of the site upon which a factory is located may hire it to another for a certain sum annually, or he may operate the factory himself. In either case he receives rent, the amount that the land itself is worth for use, independently of the return that he obtains for his expenditure of capital and labor. Even when a person uses his land as a site for a dwelling which he himself occupies, the land still brings him economic rent, since it affords him something for which he would be obliged to pay if his house were located on land of the same value owned by some one else.

ECONOMIC RENT AND COMMERCIAL RENT

It will be observed that the landowner's share of the product, or economic rent, is not identical with commercial rent. The latter is a payment for land and capital, or land and improvements combined. When a man pays nine hundred dollars for the use of a house and lot for a year, this sum contains two elements, economic rent for the lot and interest on the money invested in the house. Assuming that the house is worth ten thousand dollars, and that the usual return on such investments is eight per cent, we see that eight hundred dollars goes to the owner as interest on his capital, and only one hundred dollars as rent for his land. Similarly the price paid by a tenant for the use of an improved farm is partly interest on the value of the improvements, and partly economic rent.

In both cases the owner may reckon the land as so much capital value, and the economic rent as interest thereon, just as the commercial rent for the buildings and other improvements is interest on their capital value; but the economist distinguishes between them because he knows that they are determined by different forces, and that the distinction is of importance. He knows, for example, that the supply of land is fixed, while the supply of capital is capable of indefinite increase. In many situations, therefore, rent increases, but interest remains stationary or declines. Sometimes, though more rarely, the reverse occurs. As we shall see later, this and some other specific characteristics of land and rent have important moral aspects; consequently the moralist cannot afford to confuse rent with interest.

THE CAUSE OF ECONOMIC RENT

The cause of economic rent is the fact that land is limited relatively to demand. If land were as plentiful as air mere ownership of some portion of it would not enable the owner to collect rent. As landowner his return therefrom would not exceed normal compensation for his labor, and normal interest on his capital. Since no one would be compelled to pay for the use of land, competition among the different cultivators would keep the price of their product so low that it would merely reimburse them for their expenditures of capital and labor. In similar conditions no rent would arise on building sites.

The cause of the *amount* of rent may also be stated in terms of scarcity. At any given time and place, the rent of a piece of land will be determined by the supply of that kind of land relatively to the demand for it. However, the demand itself will be modified by the fertility or by the location of the land in question. Two pieces of agricultural land equally distant from a city, but of varying fertility, will yield different rents because of this difference in natural productiveness. Two pieces of ground of equal natural adaptability for building sites, but at unequal distances from the center of a city, will produce different rents on account of their difference of location. The absolute scarcity of land is, of course, fixed by nature; its relative scarcity is the result of human activities and desires.

The definition of rent adopted in these pages, "what men are willing to pay for the use of land," or, "what land is worth for use," is simpler and more concrete, though possibly less scientific, than those ordinarily found in manuals of economics, namely: "that portion of the product that remains after all the usual expenditures for labor, capital, and directive ability have been deducted;" or, "the surplus which any piece of land yields over the poorest land devoted to the same use, when the return from the latter is only sufficient to cover the usual expenses of production."

The statement that all rent goes to the landowner supposes that, in the case of hired land, the tenant pays the full amount that would result from competitive bidding. Evidently this was not the case under the feudal system, when rents were fixed by custom and remained stationary for centuries. Even to-day, competition is not perfect, and men often obtain the use of land for less than they or others might have been willing to give. But the statement in question does describe what tends to happen in a system of competitive rents.*

---

*Editor's Note: Ryan followed this chapter with a chapter discussing the socialist and single-tax objections to private ownership of land and a chapter containing rebuttals to these objections that Ryan believed demonstrated private ownership is justified. The single tax, proposed by Henry George in *Progress and Poverty,* was a 100 percent tax on land rent. It permitted rent for improvement on the land and allowed for private titles to possess, use, and dispose of the land.

CHAPTER 2

Private Landownership
a Natural Right

The conclusions of the preceding chapter include the statement that individuals are morally justified in becoming and remaining landowners. May we take a further step and assert that private landownership is a natural right of the individual? If it is, the abolition of it by the State, even with compensation to the owners, would be an act of injustice. The doctrine of natural rights is so prominent in the arguments of both the advocates and the opponents of private landownership that it deserves specific treatment. Moreover, the claim that private landownership is a natural right rests upon precisely the same basis as the similar claim with regard to the individual ownership of capital; and the conclusions pertinent to the former will be equally applicable to the latter.

A natural right is a right derived from the nature of the individual, and existing for his welfare. Hence it differs from a political right, which is derived from society or the State, and is intended for a political purpose. Such, for example, is the right to vote, or the right to hold a public office. Between natural rights and civil rights there are some resemblances and some differences. They are alike, inasmuch as civil rights are intended primarily for the benefit of the individual himself and many, if not most, of them are also natural rights; for example, our own "Bill of Rights," as found in the first ten amendments to the Federal Constitution. Civil rights differ from natural rights, inasmuch as they are formally conferred and guaranteed by the State. Since a natural right neither proceeds from nor is primarily designed for a civil or political end, it cannot be annulled, and it may not be ignored, by the State. For example, the right to life and the right to liberty are so sacred to the individual, so necessary to his welfare, that the State cannot rightfully kill an innocent man, nor sentence him to a term in prison.

This chapter is reprinted from *Distributive Justice: The Right and Wrong of Our Present Distribution of Wealth,* 3d ed., rev. (New York: Macmillan Co., 1942), 45–49.

THREE PRINCIPAL KINDS OF NATURAL RIGHTS

Although natural rights are all equally valid, they differ in regard to their basis and their urgency or importance. From this point of view we may profitably distinguish three principle types.

The first is exemplified in the right to live. The object of this right, life itself, is intrinsically good, good for its own sake, an end in itself. It is the end to which even civil society is a means. Since life is good intrinsically, the right to life is also valid intrinsically, and not because of consequences. Since there is no conceivable equivalent for life, the right thereto is immediate and direct in all possible circumstances.

Among the natural rights of the second class, the most prominent are the right to marry, to enjoy personal freedom, and to own consumption-goods, such as food and clothing. The objects of these rights are not ends in themselves, but means to human welfare. Confining our attention to marriage, we see that membership in the conjugal union is an indispensable means to reasonable life and self-development for the majority of persons. The only conceivable substitutes are free love and celibacy. Of these the first is inadequate for any person, and the second is adequate only for a minority. Marriage is, therefore, *directly* and *per se* necessary for the majority of individuals; for the majority it is an *individual* necessity. If the State were to abolish marriage it would deprive the majority of an indispensable means of right and reasonable life. Consequently the majority have a *direct* natural right to the legal power to marry.

In the case of the minority who do not need to marry, who can live as well or better as celibates, the legal opportunity of marriage is evidently not directly necessary. But it is necessary indirectly, inasmuch as individuals need the *power of choice* between marriage and celibacy. No argument is required to show that the State could not decide this matter consistently with individual welfare or social peace. Whence it follows that even the minority who do not wish or do not need to marry, have a natural right to embrace or reject the conjugal condition. In their case the right to marry is indirect, but inviolable.[1]

Private ownership of land belongs in a third class of natural rights. Inasmuch as it is not an intrinsic good, but merely a means to human welfare, it differs from life and resembles marriage. On the other hand, it is unlike marriage in that it is not *directly* necessary for any individual whatever.[2] The alternative to marriage, namely, celibacy, would not even under the best social administration enable the majority to lead right and reasonable lives. The alternative to private landownership (and to private ownership of capital as well), namely, some form of employment as wage receiver, salary receiver, or fee receiver enables the individual to attain all the vital ends of private ownership: food, clothing, shelter, security of livelihood and residence, and the means of mental, moral, and spiritual development. None of these vital ends or needs is essentially dependent upon private ownership of land; for millions of persons satisfy them every day without becoming landowners. Nor are they exceptions, as those who can get along without marriage are exceptions. The persons who live reasonable lives without owning land are average persons. What they do any other person could do if placed in the same circumstances. Therefore, private landownership is not directly necessary for any individual.

PRIVATE LANDOWNERSHIP INDIRECTLY NECESSARY

In our present industrial civilization, however, private landownership is *indirectly* necessary for the welfare of the individual. It is said to be indirectly necessary because it is necessary as a *social institution,* rather than as something immediately connected with individual needs as such. It is not, indeed, so necessary that society would promptly go to pieces under any other form of land tenure. It is necessary in the sense that it is capable of promoting the welfare of the average person, of the majority of persons, to a much greater degree than State ownership. It is necessary for the same reason and in the same way as a civil police force. As the State is obliged to maintain a police force, so it is obliged to maintain a system of private landownership. As the citizen has a right to police protection, so he has a right to the social and economic advantages which are connected with the system of private ownership of land. These rights are natural, derived from the needs of the individual in society, not dependent upon the good pleasure of the city or the State. They are individual rights to the presence and benefits of these social institutions.

But man's rights in the matter of land tenure are more extensive than his rights with regard to a police force. They are not restricted to the presence and functioning of a social institution. Every citizen has a natural right to police protection, but no citizen has a natural right to become a policeman. The welfare of the citizen is sufficiently looked after when the members of the police are selected by the authorities of the city. On the contrary, his welfare would not be adequately safeguarded if the State were to decide who might and who might not become landowners. In the first place, the ideal condition is that in which *all* persons can easily become actual owners. In the second place, the mere legal opportunity of becoming owners is a considerable stimulus to the energy and ambition of all persons, even of those who are never able to convert it into an economic opportunity. Therefore, only a very powerful reason of social utility would justify the State in excluding any person or any class from the legal power to own land. No such reason exists; and there are many reasons why the State should not attempt anything of the sort.[3] As a consequence of these facts, every person, whether an actual owner or not, has a natural right to acquire property in land. This right is evidently a necessary condition of a fair and efficient system of private ownership, which is in turn a necessary condition of individual welfare. The right of private landownership is, therefore, an indirect right; but it is quite as valid and quite as certain as any other natural right.

Now this right is certainly valid as against complete Socialism, which includes State management and use, as well as State ownership. It is valid against the Single Tax system, or against such modified forms of Socialism as would allow the individual to rent and use the land as an independent cultivator with security of tenure? Would the introduction of some such scheme in a country in which only a small minority of the population were actual owners, constitute a violation of individual rights? While we cannot with any feeling of certainty return an affirmative answer to these questions, we can confidently affirm that reform within the lines of private ownership would in the long run be more effective, and, therefore, that the right of private ownership is *probably* valid even against these modified forms of common ownership.[4]*

---

*Editor's Note: I have omitted two short sections—the church fathers and theologians on property ownership and Pope Leo XIII on property ownership—that completed this chapter.

CHAPTER 3

Defects of the Existing Land System

Starting from the principle that the rightness or wrongness of any system of land tenure is determined not by metaphysical and intrinsic considerations, but by the effects of the institution upon human welfare, we arrived at the conclusion that private landownership is not unjust, so long as no better system is available. By the same test of human welfare we found that it would be wrong to substitute a better system through the process of confiscating rent and the commercial value of land. A further step brought us to the conclusion that complete Socialism would certainly, and the complete Single Tax probably, be inferior to the present system. As a sort of corollary, the social and moral superiority of private landownership was stated in terms of natural rights. Finally, the question was raised whether the landowner has a right to take rent.

In stating the superiority of the present system, we explicitly noted that we had in mind the system as capable of improvement. This implied that there are defects in the present form of land tenure, and that these can be eliminated in such a way as to make the system more beneficial and more in harmony with the principles of justice. In the present chapter we shall give a summary review of the principal defects, and in the following chapter we shall suggest some methods of reform. All the defects and abuses may conveniently be grouped under three heads: Monopoly; Excessive Gains; and Exclusion from the Land.

LANDOWNERSHIP AND MONOPOLY

In the literature of the Single Tax movement the phrase, "land monopoly," is constantly recurring. The expression is inaccurate, for the system of individual

This chapter is reprinted from *Distributive Justice: The Right and Wrong of Our Present Distribution of Wealth,* 3d ed., rev. (New York: Macmillan Co., 1942), 55–63.

landownership does not conform to the requirements of a monopoly. There is, indeed, a certain resemblance between the control exercised by the owner of land and that possessed by the monopolist. As the proprietor of every superior soil or site has an economic advantage over the owner of the poorest soil or site, so the proprietor of a monopolist business obtains larger gains than the man who must operate in conditions of competition. In both cases the advantage is based upon scarcity and the extent of the advantage is measured by the degree of scarcity.

Nevertheless, there is an important difference between landownership and monopoly. The latter is usually defined as that degree of unified control which enables its possessors arbitrarily to limit supply and raise price. As a rule, no such power is attainable with regard to land. The pecuniary advantage possessed by the landowner, that is, the power to take rent, is conferred and determined by influences outside of himself, by the natural superiority of his land, or by its favorable location. He can neither diminish the amount of land in existence nor raise the price of his own. The former result is inhibited by nature; the latter by the competition of persons who own the same kind of land. To be sure, there are certain kinds of land which are so scarce and so concentrated that they can fall under true monopolistic control. Such are the anthracite coal mines of Pennsylvania, and some peculiarly situated plots in a few great cities, for example, land that is desired for a railway terminal. But these instances are exceptional. The general fact is that the owners of any kind of land are in competition with similar owners. While the element of scarcity is common to landownership and to monopoly, it differs in its operation. In the case of monopoly it is subject, within limits, to the human will. This difference is sufficiently important, both theoretically and practically, to forbid the identification or confusion of landownership with monopoly.

Certain kinds of land are liable, in varying degrees, to become monopolies or a contributory cause thereof. They are usually denominated "natural resources." Concerning some of these the Federal Trade Commission declares that the available data "indicate a distinct concentration of control in the hands of a few large companies. Six companies are shown as controlling about a third of the total developed water power; eight companies as controlling over three-quarters of the anthracite coal reserves; thirty companies as controlling over a third of the immediate bituminous coal reserves; two companies as controlling well over half of the iron ore reserves; four companies controlling nearly half of the copper reserves; and thirty companies controlling over twelve per cent of the petroleum reserves."[1]

The existence and menace of monopolies in the field of electric power were thus described by Governor Pinchot of Pennsylvania in his Message of Transmittal of the Report of the Giant Power Survey Board to the State Legislature: "No one who studies the electrical developments already achieved and those planned for the immediate future can doubt that a unified electrical monopoly extending into every part of this Nation is inevitable in the very near future. The question before us is not whether there shall be such a monopoly. That we cannot prevent. The question is whether we shall regulate it or whether it shall regulate us. . . . Nothing like this gigantic monopoly has ever appeared in the history of the world. Nothing has ever been imagined before that even remotely approaches it in the thoroughgoing, intimate, unceasing control it may exercise over the daily life of every human being within the web of its wires. It is immeasurably the greatest industrial fact of our time. If uncontrolled it will be a plague without previous example."

Speaking generally, we may say that when a great corporation controls a large proportion of the raw material required for its manufactures, such control will supplement and reinforce other factors which make for monopoly.[2]

EXCESSIVE GAINS
FROM PRIVATE LANDOWNERSHIP

The second evil of private landownership to be considered here, is the general fact that it enables some men to take a larger share of the national product than is consistent with the welfare of their neighbors and of society as a whole. As in the matter of monopoly, however, so here, Single Tax advocates are chargeable with a certain amount of overstatement. They contend that the landowner's share of the national product is constantly increasing, that rent advances faster than interest or wages, nay, that all of the annual increase in the national product tends to be gathered in by the landowner, while wages and interest remain stationary, if they do not actually decline.[3]

The share of the product received by any of the four agents of production depends upon the relative scarcity of the corresponding factor. When undertaking ability becomes scarce in proportion to the supply of land, labor, and capital, there is a rise in the remuneration of the business man; when labor decreases relatively to undertaking ability, land, and capital, there is an increase in wages. Similar statements are true of the other two agents and factors. All these propositions are merely particular illustrations of the general rule that the price of any commodity is immediately governed by the movement of supply and demand. Hence, it is not impossible that rent might increase to the extent described in the preceding paragraph. All that is necessary is that land should become sufficiently scarce, and the other factors sufficiently plentiful.

As a fact, the supply of land is strictly limited by nature, while the other factors can and do increase. There are, however, several forces which neutralize or retard the tendency of land to become scarce, and of rent to rise. Modern methods of transportation, of drainage, and of irrigation have greatly increased the supply of available land, and of commercially profitable land. During the nineteenth century, the transcontinental railroads of the United States made so much of our Western territory accessible that the value and rent of New England lands actually declined; and there are still many millions of acres throughout the country which can be made productive through drainage and irrigation. In the second place, every increase of what is called the "intensive use" of land gives employment to labor and capital which otherwise would have to go upon new land. As a consequence the demand for additional land is checked, and the rise in land values and rents correspondingly diminished. Finally, the proportion of capital and labor that is absorbed in the manufacturing, finishing and distributive operations of modern industry is constantly increasing. These processes call for very little land in comparison with that required for the extractive operations of agriculture and mining. An increase of one-fifth in the amount of capital and labor occupied in growing wheat or in taking out coal, implies a much greater demand for land than the same quantity employed in factories, stores and railroads.[4]

There is one devastating refutation of the contention that the share of the national product taken by landowners tends to increase or has increased. It is provided by authoritative estimates and official reports. According to Dr. Willford I. King, the portion of the national income received in 1910 as rent was 8.8 per cent whereas it was 8 per cent in 1850.[5] The reports of the U.S. Department of Commerce show that the net income from "rents and royalties," in 1929, was 4.2 per cent of the total income paid out; in the five years, 1935–1939, it was only 3 per cent annually. "Net rents and royalties are considered as payments for the loan of land and improvements thereto. 'Land' as thus used includes all natural resources."[6] Consequently the share paid out and received for the use of land alone was even less than that denoted by the meager figures just cited. The total amount of rents and royalties in 1939 was only $2,050,000,000. So far as farm lands are concerned, the distribution of this sum is, indeed, far from satisfactory. In 1880, tenants constituted only 25.6 per cent of all farm operators; in 1935, their percentage had increased to 42.1 per cent.[7]

When we consider the amount of gains accruing to the average member of the landowning class, we do not find that it is unreasonably large. The great majority of landed proprietors have not received, nor are they likely to receive, from their holdings income sufficiently large to be called excessive shares of the national product. Their gross returns from land have not exceeded the equivalent of fair interest on their actual investment, and fair wages for their labor. The landowners who have been enabled through their holdings to rise above the level of moderate living constitute a comparatively small minority. And these statements are true of both agricultural and urban proprietors.

It is true that a considerable number of persons, absolutely speaking, have amassed great wealth out of land. It is a well-known fact that land was the principal source of the great mediaeval and post-mediaeval fortunes, down to the end of the eighteenth century. "The historical foundation of capitalism is rent."[8] Capitalism had its beginning in the revenue from agricultural lands, city sites, and mines. A conspicuous example is that of the great Fugger family of the sixteenth century, whose wealth was mostly derived from the ownership and exploitation of rich mineral lands.[9] In the United States very few large fortunes have been obtained from agricultural land, but the same is not true of mineral lands, timber lands, or urban sites. "The growth of cities has, through real estate speculation and incremental income, made many of our millionaires."[10] "As with the unearned income of city land, our mineral resources have been conspicuously prolific producers of millionaires."[11] The most striking instance of great wealth derived from urban land is the fortune of the Astor family. While gains from trading ventures formed the beginning of the riches of the original Astor, John Jacob, these were "a comparatively insignificant portion of the great fortune which he transmitted to his descendants."[12] At his death in 1848, John Jacob Astor's real estate holdings in New York City were valued at eighteen or twenty million dollars. To-day the Astor estate in that city is estimated at between 450 and 500 millions, and within a quarter of a century will not improbably be worth one billion dollars.[13] According to an investigation made in 1892 by the *New York Tribune,* 26.4 per cent of the millionaire fortunes of the United States at that time were traceable to landownership, while 41.5 per cent were derived from competitive industries which were largely assisted by land possessions.[14]

EXCLUSION FROM THE LAND

One of the most frequent charges brought against the present system of land tenure is that it keeps a large proportion of our natural resources out of use. It is contended that this evil appears in three principal forms: Owners of large estates refuse to break up their holdings by sale; many proprietors are unwilling to let the use of their land on reasonable terms; and a great deal of land is held at speculative prices, instead of at economic prices. So far as the United States are concerned, the first of these charges does not seem to represent a condition that is at all general. Although many holders of large mineral and timber tracts seem to be in no hurry to sell portions of their holdings, they are probably moved by a desire to obtain higher prices rather than to continue as large landowners. As a rule, the great landholders of America are without those sentiments of tradition, local attachment, and social ascendancy which are so powerful in maintaining intact the immense estates of Great Britain. On the contrary, one of the common facts of to-day is the persistent effort carried on by railroads and other holders of large tracts to dispose of their land to settlers. While the price asked by these proprietors is frequently higher than that which corresponds to the present productiveness of the land, it is generally as low as that which is demanded by the owners of smaller parcels. To be sure, this is one way of unreasonably hindering access to the land, but it falls properly under the head of the third charge enumerated above. There is no sufficient evidence that the *large* landholders are exceptional offenders in refusing to sell their holdings to actual settlers.

The assertion that unused land cannot be rented on reasonable terms is in the main unfounded, so far as it refers to land which is desired for agriculture. As a rule, any man who wishes to cultivate a portion of such land can fulfill his desire if he is willing to pay a rent that corresponds to its productiveness. After all, landowners are neither fools nor fanatics: while awaiting a higher price than it is now obtainable for their land, they would prefer to get from it some revenue rather than none at all. In so far as new land might profitably be improved and cultivated, and in so far as the owners are unwilling or unable to provide the improvements, the present system does keep out of use agricultural land that could be cultivated by tenants. Mineral and timber lands are sometimes withheld from tenants because the owners wish to limit the supply of the product or because they fear that a long-term lease would prevent them from selling the land to the best advantage. As to urban sites, the practice of leasing land to persons who wish to build thereon does not, with the exception of a very few cities, obtain in the United States for other than very large business structures. As a rule, it does not apply to sites for residences. The man who wants a piece of urban land for a dwelling or for a moderately sized business building cannot obtain it except by purchase.

The third evil noted above applies, of course, to vacant land which owners refuse to sell at its current economic value. They are awaiting a rise in price within what they regard at a reasonable time.[15] Such persons are frequently denounced for "holding land out of use." In this facile charge there are much exaggeration and superficial analysis. Rarely do *all* the owners of any kind of land obstinately hold it for higher prices. In most localities enough land is purchasable at current economic values to supply all those who want to buy it at that price level. Some of the complaints under this head imply that if all land were obtainable at prices corresponding to its present rental value; or, at any rate, if it were subject to the operation of the Single Tax, *all* land would be promptly occupied! None would be "held out of use," particularly in cities. Obviously this could not happen until the demand for land products and land uses had enormously increased relatively to the total supply. The strongest criticism that can reasonably be made of the situation under discussion is that in some central areas of some cities, enough land is held for speculative prices to compel an otherwise unnecessary and premature movement to suburban areas. But that is not an unmixed evil. Incidentally it emphasizes the reality of competition in land transactions and the unreality of land monopoly.

In any case, this alleged evil is not nearly so great or so menacing as it was a quarter of a century ago. Instead of a tendency to continuous value increases, almost all land now exhibits a contrary tendency. One cause of the reversed trend is improvement in the arts of agriculture, mining and manufacturing; more important and more portentous is the sharp and devastating decline in the birthrate.

CHAPTER 4

Methods of Reforming
Our Land System

In economic and social discussion the word reform is commonly opposed to the word revolution. It implies modification rather than abolition, gradual rather than violent change. Hence reforms of the system of land tenure do not include such radical proposals as those of land nationalization or the Single Tax. On the other hand, some extension of State ownership of land, and some increase in the proportion of taxes imposed upon land, may quite properly be placed under the head of reform, inasmuch as they are changes in, rather than a destruction of, the existing system.

In general, the reform measures needed are such as will meet the defects described in the last chapter; namely, Monopoly, Excessive Gains and Exclusion from the Land. Obviously they can be provided only by legislation; and they may all be included under public ownership and taxation.

By far the greater part of the more valuable lands of the country are no longer under the ownership of the State. Urban land is practically all in the hands of private proprietors. While many millions of acres of land suitable for agriculture are still under public ownership, almost all of this area requires a considerable outlay for irrigation, clearing, and draining before it can become productive. Sixty years ago, three-fourths of the timber now standing was public property; at present about four-fifths of it is owned by private persons or corporations.[1] The bulk of our mineral deposits, coal, copper, gold, silver, etc., have likewise fallen under private ownership, with the exception of those of Alaska. The undeveloped water power remaining under government ownership has been roughly estimated at fourteen million horse power in the national forests, and considerably less than that amount in other parts of the public domain.[2] This is a gratifying proportion

This chapter is reprinted from *Distributive Justice: The Right and Wrong of Our Present Distribution of Wealth,* 3d ed., rev. (New York: Macmillan Co., 1942), 64–81.

of the whole supply, developed and undeveloped, of this national resource, which was estimated by the United States Geological Survey in 1924 at about 35 million horse power available 90 per cent of the time and an additional 20 million available 50 per cent of the time.

THE LEASING SYSTEM

In many countries of Europe it has long been the policy of governments to retain ownership of all lands containing timber, minerals, oil, natural gas, phosphate, and water power. The products of these lands are extracted and put upon the market through a leasing system. That is, the user of the land pays to the State a rental according to the amount and quality of raw material which he takes from the storehouse of nature. Theoretically, the State could sell such lands at prices that would bring in as much revenue as does the leasing system; practically, this result has never been attained. The principal advantages of the leasing arrangement are: To prevent the premature destruction of forests, the private monopolization of limited natural resources and the private acquisition of exceptionally valuable land at ridiculously low prices; and to enable the State to secure just treatment for the consumer and the laborer by stipulating that the former shall obtain the product at fair prices, and that the latter shall receive fair wages.

Public grazing lands should remain government property until such time as they become available for agriculture. Cattle owners could lease the land from the State on equitable terms, and receive ample protection for money invested in improvements.

The leasing system cannot well be applied to agricultural lands. In order that they may be continuously improved and protected against deterioration, they must be owned by the cultivators. The temptation to wear out a piece of land quickly, and then move to another piece, and all the other obstacles that stand in the way of the Single Tax as applied to agricultural land, show that the government cannot with advantage assume the function of landlord in this domain. In the great majority of cases the State would do better to sell the land in small parcels to genuine settlers. There are, indeed, many situations, especially in connection with government projects of irrigation, clearing and drainage, in which the leasing arrangement could be adopted temporarily. It should not be continued longer than is necessary to enable the tenants to become owners.

PUBLIC OWNERSHIP OF URBAN LAND

No city should part with the ownership of any land that it now possesses. Since capitalists are willing to erect costly buildings on sites leased from private owners, there is no good reason why any one should refuse to put up or purchase any sort of structure on land owned by the municipality. The situation differs from that presented by agricultural land, for the value of urban land can easily be distinguished from that of improvements, the owner of the latter can sell them even if he is not the owner of the land, and he cannot be deprived of them without full compensation. While the lessee paid his annual rent his control of the land would be as complete and certain as that of the landowner who continues to pay his taxes. On the other hand, the leaseholder could not permit or cause the land to deteriorate if he would. Finally, the official activities involved in the collection of the rent and the periodical revaluation of the land, would not differ essentially from those now required to make assessments and gather taxes.

The benefits of this system would be great and manifest. Persons who were unable to own a home because of their inability to purchase land, could get secure possession of the necessary land through a lease from the city. Instead of spending all their lives in rented houses, thousands upon thousands of families could become the owners and occupiers of homes. The greater the amount of land thus owned and leased by the city, the less would be the power of private owners to hold land for exorbitant prices. Competition with the city would compel them to sell the land at its revenue-producing value instead of at its speculative value. Finally, the city would obtain the benefit of every increase in the value of its land by means of periodical revaluation, and periodical readjustment of rent.

Unfortunately the amount of municipal land available for such an arrangement in our American cities is negligible. If they are to establish the system they must first purchase the land from private owners. Undoubtedly this ought to be done by all large cities in which the housing problem has become acute, and the value of land is constantly rising. This policy has been adopted with happy results by many of the municipalities of France and Germany.[3] At the State election of 1915 the voters of Massachusetts adopted by an overwhelming majority a constitutional amendment authorizing the cities of the commonwealth to acquire land for prospective home builders. In Savannah, Georgia, no extension of the municipal limits is made until the land to be embraced has passed into the ownership of the city. Another method is to refrain from opening a new street in a suburban district until the city has become the proprietor of the abutting land. Whatever be the particular means adopted, the objects of municipal purchase and ownership of land are definite and obvious: To check the congestion of population in the great urban centers, to provide homes for the homeless, and to secure for the whole community the socially occasioned increases in land values. Indeed, it is probable that no comprehensive scheme of housing reform can be realized without a considerable amount of land purchase by the municipalities. Cities must be in a position to provide sites for those home builders who cannot obtain land on fair conditions from private proprietors.[4]

Turning now from the direct method of public ownership to the indirect method of reform through taxation, we reject the thoroughgoing proposals of the

Single Taxers. To appropriate all economic rent for the public treasury would be to transfer all the value of land without compensation from the private owner to the State. For example: A piece of land that brought to the owner an annual revenue of one hundred dollars would be taxed exactly that amount; if the prevailing rate of interest were five per cent the proprietor would be deprived of wealth to the amount of two thousand dollars, for the value of all productive goods is determined by the revenue that they yield, and benefits the person who receives the revenue. Thus the State would become the beneficiary and the virtual owner of the land. Inasmuch as we do not admit that the so-called social creation of land values gives the State a moral right to these values, we must regard the complete appropriation of economic rent through taxation as an act of pure and simple confiscation.

APPROPRIATING FUTURE INCREASES
OF LAND VALUE

Let us examine, then, the milder suggestion of John Stuart Mill, that the State should impose of tax upon land sufficient to absorb all future increases in its value.[5] This scheme is commonly known as the appropriation of future unearned increment. It is expected to obtain for the whole community future increases in land values, and to wipe out the speculative, as distinguished from the revenue-producing value of land. Consequently it would make land cheaper and more accessible. Before discussing its moral character, let us see briefly whether the ends that it seeks may properly be sought by the method of taxation. For these ends are mainly social rather than fiscal.

To use the taxing power for a social purpose is neither unusual nor unreasonable. "All governments," says Professor Seligman, "have allowed social considerations in the wider sense to influence their revenue policy. The whole system of protective duties has been framed not merely with reference to revenue considerations, but in order to produce results which should directly affect social and national prosperity. Taxes on luxuries have often been mere sumptuary laws designed as much to check consumption as to yield revenue. Excise taxes have as frequently been levied from a wide social, as from a narrow fiscal, standpoint. From the very beginning of all tax systems these social reasons have often been present."[6] Our Federal taxes on imports, on oleomargarine, and on white phosphorus matches, and many of the license taxes in our municipalities, as on peddlers and dog owners, are in large part intended to meet social as well as fiscal ends. They are in the interest of domestic production, public health and public safety. The reasonableness of effecting social reforms through taxation cannot be seriously questioned. While the maintenance of government is the primary object of taxation, its ultimate end, the ultimate end of government itself, is the welfare of the people. Now if the public welfare can be promoted by certain social changes, and if these in turn can be effected through taxation, this use of the taxing power will be quite as normal and legitimate as though it were employed for the upkeep of government. Hence the morality of taxing land for purposes of social reform will depend upon the tax that is imposed.

MORALITY OF THE PROPOSAL

The tax that we are now considering can be condemned as unjust on only two possible grounds; first, that it would be injurious to society; and, second, that it would wrong the private landowner. If it were fairly adjusted and efficiently administered it could not prove harmful to the community. In the first place, landowners could not shift the tax to the consumer. All the authorities on the subject admit that taxes on land stay where they are put, and are paid by those upon whom they are levied in the first instance.[7] The only way in which the owners of a commodity can shift a tax to the users or consumers of it, is by limiting the supply until the price rises sufficiently to cover the tax. By the simple device of refusing to erect more buildings until those in existence have become scarce enough to command an increase in rent equivalent to the new tax, the actual and prospective owners of buildings can pass the tax on to the tenants thereof. By refusing to put their money into, say, shoe factories, investors can limit the supply of shoes until any new tax on this commodity is shifted upon the wearers of shoes in the form of higher prices. Until these rises take place in the rent of buildings and the price of shoes, investors will put their money into enterprises which are not burdened with equivalent taxes. But nothing of this sort can follow the imposition of a new tax upon land. The supply of land is fixed, and cannot be affected by any action of landowners or would-be landowners. The users of land and the consumers of its products are at present paying all that competition can compel them to pay. They would not pay more merely because they were requested to do so by landowners who were laboring under the burden of a new tax. If all landowners were to carry out an agreement to refrain from producing, and to withhold their land from others until rents and prices had gone up sufficiently to offset the tax, they could, indeed, shift the latter to the renters of land and the consumers of its products. Such a monopoly, however, is not within the range of practical achievement. In its absence, individual landowners are not likely to withhold land nor to discontinue production in sufficient numbers to raise rents or prices. Indeed, the tendency will be all the other way; for all landowners, including the proprietors of land now vacant, will be anxious to put their land to the best use in order to have the means of paying the tax. Owing to this increased production, and the increased willingness to sell and let land, rents and prices must fall. It is axiomatic that new taxes upon land always make it cheaper than it would have been otherwise, and are beneficial to the community as against the present owners.

In the second place, the tax in question could not injure the community on account of discouraging investment in land. Once men could no longer hope to sell land at an advance in price, they would not seek it to the extent that they now do as a field of investment. For the same reason many of the present owners would sell their holdings sooner than they would have sold them if the tax had not been levied. From the viewpoint of the public the outcome of this situation would be wholly good. Land would be cheaper and more easy of access to all who desired to buy or use it for the sake of production, rather than for the sake of speculation. Investments in land which have as their main object a rise in value are an injury rather than a benefit to the community; for they do not increase the products of land, while they do advance its price. Hence the State should discourage instead of encourage mere speculators in land. Whether it is or is not bought and sold, the supply of land remains the same. The supreme interest of the community is that it should be put to use and made to supply the wants of the people. Consequently the only land investments that help the community are those that tend to make the land productive. Under a tax on future increases in value, such investments would increase for the simple reason that land would be cheaper than it would have been without the tax. Men who desired land for the sake of its rent or its product would continue as now to pay such prices for it as would enable them to obtain the prevailing rate of interest on their investment after all charges, including taxes, had been paid. Men who wanted to rent land would continue as now to get it at a rental that would give them the usual return for their capital and labor.

So much for the effect of the tax upon the community. Would it not, however, be unjust to the landowners? Does not private ownership of its very nature demand that increases in the value of the property should go to the owners thereof? *Res fructificat domino*: a thing fructifies to its owner; and value-increases are a kind of fruit.

In the first place, this formula was originally a dictum of the civil law merely, the law of the Roman Empire. It was a legal rather than an ethical maxim. Whatever validity it has in morals must be established on moral grounds, by moral arguments. It cannot forthwith be pronounced morally sound on the mere authority of legal usage. In the second place, it was for a long time applied only to natural products, to the grain grown in a field, to the offspring of domestic animals. It simply enunciated the policy of the law to defend the owner of the land in his claim to such fruits, as against any outsider who should attempt to set up an adverse title through mere appropriation or possession. Thus far, the formula was evidently in conformity with reason and justice. Later on it was extended, both by lawyers and moralists, to cover commercial "fruits," such as rent from lands and houses and interest from loans and investments. Its validity in this field will be examined in connection with the justification of interest. More recently the maxim has received the still wider application which we are now considering. Obviously increases in value are quite a different thing from the concrete fruit of the land, its natural product. A right to the latter does not necessarily and forthwith imply a right to the former. In the third place, the formula in question is not a self-evident, fundamental principle. It is merely a summary conclusion drawn from the consideration of the facts and principles of social and industrial life. Consequently its validity as applied to any particular situation will depend on the correctness of these premises, and on the soundness of the reasoning process.

Would the increment tax inflict undue hardship upon individuals? Here we must make a distinction between those persons who own land at the time that, and those who buy land after, the law is enacted.

The only inconvenience falling upon the latter class would be deprivation of the power to obtain future increases in value. The law would not cause the value of the lands to decline below their purchase price. Other forces might, indeed, bring about such a result; but, as a rule, such depreciation would be relatively insignificant, for the simple reason that it would already have been "discounted" in the reduction of value which followed the law at the outset. The very knowledge that they could not hope to profit by future increases in the value of the land would impel purchasers to lower their bids accordingly. While abolishing the possibility of gaining, the law would enable the buyers to take the ordinary precautions against losing. Therefore, it does not, as sometimes objected, lessen the "gambler's chances."

On the other hand, the tax does not deprive the owners of any value that they may add to the land through the expenditure of labor or money, nor in any way discourage productive effort. Now it is, as a rule, better for individuals as well as for society that men's incomes should represent labor, expenditure, and saving instead of being the result of "windfalls," or other fortuitous and conjunctural circumstances. And the power to take future value increments is not an intrinsically essential element of private property in land. Like every other condition of ownership, its morality is determined by its effects upon human welfare. But human welfare in the sense of the social good is better promoted by a system of landownership which does not include this element, and which causes no undue hardship to the individual who buys land subsequently.

Such is the answer to the contention that the landowner has a right to future increments of value because they are a kind of fruit of his property. It is more reasonable that he should not enjoy this particular and peculiar "fruit." Were the increment tax introduced into a new community before any one had purchased land, it would clearly be a fair and valid limitation on the right of ownership. Those who should become owners after the regulation went into effect in an old community would be in exactly the same moral and economic position.

Those persons who are landowners when the increment tax goes into effect are in a very different situation from those that we have just been considering. Many of them would undoubtedly suffer injury through the operation of the measure, inasmuch as their land would reach and maintain a level of value below the price that they had paid for it. The immediate effect of the increment tax would be a decline in the value of all land, caused by men's increased desire to sell and decreased desire to buy. In all growing communities a part of the present value of land is speculative; that is, it is due to demand for the land by persons who want it mainly to sell at an expected rise, and also to the disinclination of present owners to sell until this expectation is realized. The practical result of the attitude of these two classes of persons is that the demand for, and therefore the value of land is considerably enhanced. Let a law be enacted depriving them of all hope of securing the anticipated increases in value, and the one group will cease to buy, while the other will hasten to sell, thus causing a decline in demand relatively to supply, and therefore a decline in value and price.

All persons who had paid more for their land than the value which it attained as a result of the increment tax law, would lose the difference. No matter how much the land might rise in value subsequently, the increase would all be taken by the State. All owners of vacant land the value of which after the law was passed did not remain sufficiently high to provide accumulated interest on the purchase price, would also lose accordingly. To be sure, both these kinds of losses would exist even if the law should cause no decline in the value of land, but they would not be so great either in number or in volume.

Landowners who should suffer either of these sorts of losses in consequence of a tax appropriating future value increases, would have a valid moral claim against the State for compensation. Through its silence on the subject of increment-tax legislation, the State virtually promised them at the time of their purchases that it would not thus interfere with the ordinary course of values. Had it given any intimation that it would enact such a law at a future time, these persons would not have paid as much for their land as they actually did pay. When the State passes the law, it violates its implicit promise, and consequently is under obligation to make good the losses.

In the foregoing pages we have been considering a law which would from the beginning of its operation take *all* the future increments of land value. There is, however, no likelihood that any such measure will soon be enacted in any country, least of all in the United States. What we may see is legislation designed to take a part, and a gradually growing part, of value increases, after the example of Germany.

A MILDER FORM OF THE PLAN

The first increment tax (Werthzuwachssteuer) was established in the year 1898 in the German colony of Kiautschou, China. In 1904, the principle of the tax was adopted by Frankfurt-am-Main, and in 1905 by Cologne. By April, 1910, it had already been enacted in 457 cities and towns of Germany, some twenty of which had a population of more than 100,000 each, in 652 communes, several districts, one principality, and one grand duchy. While these laws are all alike in certain essentials, they vary greatly in details. They agreed in taking only a per cent of the value increases, and in imposing a higher rate on the more rapid increases. Inasmuch as the highest rate in any of the laws was 25 per cent; inasmuch as all the laws allowed deductions from the tax to cover the interest that was not obtained while the land was unproductive; and inasmuch as only those increases were taxed which were measured from the value that the land had when it came into the possession of the present owner,—it is clear that landowners were not obliged to undergo any positive loss, and that they were permitted to retain the lion's share of the "unearned increment."[8]

No good reason, from the side of ethics, economics or politics, can be urged against a moderate increment tax, whenever and wherever it would yield a significant amount of revenue. However, its importance is much smaller to-day than twenty-five years ago, when land was steadily rising in value and seemed likely to continue in that course for an indefinite period. The proportion of agricultural land to which the tax could now be profitably applied is insignificant. In certain areas of some large American cities, the tax would be worthwhile; in other areas of the same cities, it would bring in practically no revenue.

TRANSFERRING OTHER TAXES TO LAND

Complete application of this measure would be identical with the Single Tax. All public revenues would be derived from land. The ethical objections to this scheme have been sufficiently described in chapter ii.* Economically and fiscally it would prove ridiculously inadequate and impossible.[9] According to a report published by the Census Bureau, March 26, 1941, the total amount of money collected in taxes by all our governments, federal, state, county, and municipal in the fiscal year 1940, was $14,300,000,000.[10] As we have seen above, all the rents and royalties paid out in the calendar year, 1939, amounted to only $2,050,000,000. In other words, if all the rent had been taken in taxes it would have provided only one-seventh of the revenue required by our federal, state, and local governments.[11]

Nevertheless, Professor Broadus Mitchell makes this assertion: "The adequacy of ground rents as a general thing to supply needed public revenue seems to be established."[12] Franchises to railways, pipe lines, and radio should, Professor Mitchell contends, be classified as ground rents, thereby swelling considerably their total amount. The propriety and usefulness of this classification are questionable, and the conception is misleading. The profit-yielding powers of railways, pipe lines, and radio—and, indeed, of public utilities generally—are due in only a slight degree to their control and use of land. Without land they could

---

*Editor's Note: Omitted in this volume. See editor's note on p. 14.

not function, indeed; nevertheless, land is only a *condition,* not the efficient cause, of their profitableness and profits. To the extent that they are monopolies, the real cause is the law of increasing returns, combined with the corporate privileges granted them by government.

In any case, the amount of additional revenue, whatever it may be called, which the government could extract from these concerns would be only a slight fraction of the twelve billion dollars needed by our governments over and above the two billion dollars yielded by rents and royalties in 1939. Moreover, the charges to the patrons of railroads and pipe lines could be kept so low by the regulatory authorities that the potentially fruitful franchises would yield neither rent nor taxes. On the other hand, if the public authority permits the imposition of charges sufficiently high to produce enormous profits, the latter cannot without a confusing misuse of language be called "ground rents." They are one form of differential gains. As such, they may prudently be taxed.

The utmost feasible and ethically lawful exercise of the transfer process would comprise a gradual shift to land of the existing taxes upon buildings and other improvements. Measures of this nature have been adopted in varying but moderate degrees and with varying results, in Canada, Australia, and in our own cities of Scranton and Pittsburgh. A transfer of all the improvement taxes to land at one time would produce a fall in land values amounting on the average to between twenty-five and fifty per cent. Obviously, this would be unjust and impracticable. Wherever the arrangement is adopted it ought to be extended over a period of several years.

Under any rate of transfer, the change would bear unequally upon different classes of owners. Proprietors of real estate whose land values stood in the same ratio to the improvement values as the general ratio for the entire taxing jurisdiction (city, county, or state) would experience no net gain nor any net loss. Their gains through the abolition or diminution of taxes on improvements would be offset by their losses on account of the higher taxes on land. Those whose land value ratio exceeded the general average would find their taxes proportionally increased. Those in the opposite position would pay correspondingly less than at present. Those who owned buildings or other improvements but no land, would be relieved of all taxes on real estate. Those who owned land but no improvements, would find their taxes increased and the value of their land lowered in proportion to the rapidity of the shifting process. The foregoing considerations suggest an additional reason why the change should be made gradually.[13]

SUPERTAXES

Every estate containing more than a maximum number of acres, or having more than a maximum total value, could be compelled to pay a special tax in addition to the ordinary tax levied on land of the same value. The rate of this supertax should increase with the size of the estate above the fixed maximum. Through this device large holdings could be broken up and divided among many owners and occupiers. For several years it has been successfully applied for this purpose in New Zealand and Australia.[14] Inasmuch as this tax exemplifies the principle of progression, it is in accord with the principles of justice; for relative ability to pay is closely connected with relative sacrifice. Other things being equal, the less the sacrifice involved the greater is the ability of the individual to pay the tax. Thus, the man with an income of ten thousand dollars a year makes a smaller sacrifice in giving up two per cent of it than the man whose income is only one thousand dollars; for in the latter case the twenty dollars surrendered represent a deprivation of the necessaries or the elementary comforts of life, while the two hundred dollars taken from the rich man would have been expended for luxuries or converted into capital. While the incomes of both are reduced in the same proportion, their satisfactions are not diminished to the same degree. The wants that are deprived of satisfaction are much less important in the case of the richer than in that of the poorer man. Hence the only way to bring about anything like equality of sacrifice between them is to increase the proportion of income taken from the former. This means that the rate of taxation would be progressive.[15] It would increase with the increase of income.

At the Hearings conducted by the Select Committee of the House of Representatives to Investigate the Interstate Migration of Destitute Citizens, much testimony was offered concerning the recent trend toward larger farm units and mechanized farming.[16] Undoubtedly this development reduces the cost of agricultural production and promotes "efficiency." It raises, however, at least two questions: First, do these advantages outweigh the social evil involved in a reduction in the number of persons who get their living on farms? second, can they not be obtained on farms of moderate size? Some competent witnesses before the Committee answered the latter question in the affirmative; for example, one farmer stated that all the economies of mechanization could be realized on a farm of 320 acres. In that case, the social argument against the trend would lose some of its force, but the argument for the supertax would remain applicable to holdings above a reasonable maximum.

A particularly appropriate subject for the supertax would seem to be certain great holdings of mineral, timber, and water power lands. "There are many great combinations in other industries whose formation is complete. In the lumber industry, on the other hand, the Bureau now finds in the making a combination caused, fundamentally, by a long standing public policy. The concentration already existing is sufficiently impressive. Still more impressive are the possibilities for the future. In the last forty years concentration has so proceeded that 195 holders, many interrelated, now have practically one-half of the privately owned timber in the investigation area (which contains eighty per cent of the whole). This formidable process of concentration, in timber and in land, clearly involves grave future possibilities of impregnable monopolistic conditions, whose far-reaching consequences to society it is now difficult to anticipate fully or to overestimate."[17]

In order to check the growth of absentee ownership and tenancy it has been suggested that a supertax be imposed upon all agricultural land which is not cultivated by the owner. This would tend to increase the owner's desire to sell and to hasten the process of converting tenants into operating owners. In those States where tenancy has steadily and rapidly increased and where the increase shows signs of continuing indefinitely, this measure would undoubtedly be justified on grounds of social welfare. Of course, the supertax should be so restricted that when combined with the general land tax it would not amount to actual or virtual confiscation.

The conclusion of this chapter may be summed up as follows: Exceptionally valuable public lands, such as those containing timber, minerals, metals, oil, gas, phosphate, and water power should remain under public ownership. Municipalities should lease instead of sell their lands and should strive to increase their holdings. To take all future increases in the value of land would be morally lawful if owners were compensated for positive losses of interest and principal. To take a small part of the increase and to transfer very gradually the taxes on improvements and on personal property to land would be likewise free from moral censure. The same judgment may be pronounced upon moderate supertaxes on large holdings of exceptionally valuable land and on certain agricultural land not cultivated by the owners.

SECTION 2

The Morality of Private Capital and Interest

CHAPTER 5

The Nature and the Rate of Interest

Interest denotes that part of the product of industry which goes to the capitalist. As the ownership of land commands rent, so the ownership of capital commands interest; as rent is a price paid for the use of land, so interest is a price paid for the use of capital.

However, the term capital is less definite and unambiguous, both in popular and in economic usage, than the word land. The farmer, the merchant, and the manufacturer often speak of their land, buildings, and chattels as their capital, and reckon the returns from all these sources as equivalent to a certain per cent of interest or profit. This is not technically correct; when we use the terms capital and interest we should exclude the notions of land and rent.

MEANING OF CAPITAL AND CAPITALIST

Capital is ordinarily defined as, wealth employed directly for the production of new wealth. According as it is considered in the abstract or the concrete, it is capital-value or capital-instruments. For example, the owner of a factory may describe his capital as having a value of $100,000, or as consisting of certain buildings, machines, tools, office furniture, etc. In the former case he thinks of his capital as so much abstract value which, through a sale, he could take out of the factory, and put into other concrete capital forms, such as a railroad or a jobbing house. In the latter case he has in mind the particular instruments in which his capital is at present embodied. The capital-value concept is the more convenient, and is usually intended when the word capital is used without qualification. It is

This chapter is reprinted from *Distributive Justice: The Right and Wrong of Our Present Distribution of Wealth,* 3d ed., rev. (New York: Macmillan Co., 1942), 85–91.

also the basis upon which interest is reckoned; for the capitalist does not measure his share of the product as so many dollars of rent on his capital-instruments, but as so many per cent on his capital-value.

Capitalists are of two principal kinds: Those who employ their own money in their own enterprises; and those who lend their money to others for use in industry. The former may be called active capitalists, the latter loan-capitalists. Perhaps a majority of active capitalists use some borrowed money in their business. To the lenders they turn over a part of the product in the form of interest. When, therefore, interest is defined as the share of the product that goes to the capitalist, it is the owner of capital-value rather than of capital-instruments that is meant. For the man who has loaned $50,000 at five per cent to the manufacturer is not, except hypothetically, the owner of the buildings which have been erected with that money. These are owned (subject possibly to a mortgage) by the borrower, the active capitalist. But the abstract value which has gone into them continues to be the property of the lender. As owner thereof, he, instead of the active capitalist, receives the interest that is assigned to this portion of the total capital. Hence interest is the share of the product that is taken by the owner of capital, whether he employes it himself or lends it to some one else. While the fundamental reason of interest is the fact that certain concrete instruments are necessary for making product, interest is always *reckoned* on capital-value, and goes to the owner of the capital-value, to the man whose money has been put into the instruments, whether or not he is their owner.

MEANING OF INTEREST

Interest is the share of the capitalist as capitalist. The man who employs his own capital in his own business receives therefrom in addition to interest other returns. Let us suppose that some one has invested $100,000 of borrowed money and $100,000 of his own money in a grocery business. At the end of the year, after defraying the cost of labor, materials, rent, repairs, and replacement, his gross returns are $15,000. Out of this sum he must pay five thousand dollars as interest on the money that he has borrowed. This leaves him ten thousand dollars as his share of the product of the industry. Since he could command a salary of three thousand dollars if he worked for some one else, he regards his labor of directing his own business as worth at least this sum. Deducting it from ten thousand dollars, he has left seven thousand dollars, which must in some sense be accredited as payment for the use of his own capital.

However, it is not all pure interest; for he runs the risk of losing his capital, and also of failing to get the normal rate of interest on it during future unprosperous years. Hence he will require a part of the seven thousand dollars as insurance against these two contingencies. Two per cent of his capital, or two thousand dollars, is not an excessive allowance. If the business did not provide him with this amount of insurance he would probably regard it as unsafe, and would sell it and invest his money elsewhere. Subtracting two thousand dollars from seven thousand, we have five thousand left as pure interest on the director's own capital. This is equivalent to five per cent, which is the rate that he is paying on the capital that he has borrowed. If he could not get this rate on his own money he would probably prefer to become a lender himself, a loan capitalist instead of an active capitalist. This part of his total share, then, and only this part, is pure interest. The other two sums that he receives, the three thousand dollars and the two thousand dollars, are respectively wages for his labor and insurance against his risks. Sometimes they are classified together under the general name of profits.

Let us suppose, however, that the gross returns are not $15,000 but $17,000. How is the additional sum to be denominated? In strict economic language it would probably be called net profits, as distinguished from normal or necessary profits, which comprise wages of direction and insurance against loss. Sometimes it is called interest. In that case the owner of the store would receive seven instead of five per cent on his own capital. Whether the extra two per cent be called net profits or surplus interest, is mainly a matter of terminology. The important thing is to indicate clearly that these terms designate the surplus which goes to the active capitalist in addition to necessary profits and necessary interest.

At the risk of wearisome repetition, one more example will be given to illustrate the distinction between interest and the other returns that are received in connection with capital. The annual income from a railway bond is interest on lender's capital, and consequently pure interest. Ordinarily the bondholder is adequately protected against the loss of his capital by a mortgage on the railroad. On the other hand, the holder of a share of railway stock is a part owner of the railroad, and consequently incurs the risk of losing his property. Hence the dividend that he receives on his stock comprises interest on capital plus insurance against loss. It is usually one or two per cent higher than the rate on the bonds. Since the officers and directors are the only share-holders who perform any labor in the management of the railroad, only they receive wages of management. Consequently the gross profits are divided into interest and dividends at fixed rates, and fixed salaries. When a surplus exists above these requirements it is not, as a rule, distributed among the stockholders annually. In railroads, therefore, and many other corporations, interest is easily distinguished from those other returns with which it is frequently confused in partnerships and enterprises carried on by individuals.

THE RATE OF INTEREST

"Even in the most advanced countries there is no one general interest rate and no one general money market, although there is a perfect market for certain securities dealt in by name and an approximation to a general market for loans of very short duration and unquestionable security."[1] United States bonds pay from two to three per cent, although the Treasury frequently obtains short term loans for as low as one-fourth of one per cent; banks, about the same; municipal bonds, three or four per cent; railway bonds, four or five per cent; the stocks of stable industrial corporations five or six per cent, net; real estate mortgages from five to seven per cent; promissory notes, somewhat higher rates; and pawnbrokers' loans from twelve per cent upward. Moreover, the same kinds of loans bring different rates in different places. For example, money lent on the security of farm mortgages yields only about six per cent in the States of the East, but seven or eight per cent on the Pacific coast.[2]

These and similar variations are differences not so much of interest as of security, cost of negotiation, and mental attitude. The farm mortgage pays a higher rate than the government bond partly because it is less secure, partly because it involves greater trouble of investment, and partly because it does not run for so long a time. For the same reasons a higher rate of interest is paid on a promissory note than on a bank deposit certificate. Again, the lower rates on government bonds and bank deposits are due in some degree to the attitudes of those investors whose savings are small in amount, who are not well aware of the range of investment opportunities, or to whom security and convenience are exceptionally important considerations. If such persons did not exist the rates on government bonds and savings deposits would be higher than they actually are. The higher rates in a new country on, say, farm mortgages are likewise due in part to psychical peculiarities. Where men are more speculative and more eager to borrow money for industrial purposes, the demand for loans is greater relatively to the supply than in long established and more conservative communities. Therefore, the price of the loans, the rate of interest, is higher.

In one sense it would seem that the lowest of the rates cited above, namely, that on United States bonds, represents pure interest, and that all the other rates are interest plus something else. Perhaps it is more convenient and more correct to regard as the standard rate of interest in any community that which is obtained on first class industrial security, such as the bonds of stable corporations, and mortgages on real estate. Loans to these enterprises are subject to what may properly be called the average or prevailing industrial risks, are negotiated in average psychical conditions, and embrace by far the greater part of all money drawing interest; consequently the rate that they command may be looked upon as in a very real and practical sense normal. While this conception of the normal rate is in a measure conventional, it accords with popular usage. It is what most men have in mind when they speak of the prevailing rate of interest.

What causes the rate to be five per cent, or six per cent, or any other per cent? Briefly stated, it is the interplay of supply and demand. Since interest is a price paid for the use of a thing, i.e., capital, its rate or level is determined by the same general forces that govern the price of wheat, or shoes, or hats, or any other commodity that is bought and sold in the market. The rate is five or six per cent because at that rate the amount of money offered by lenders equals the amount demanded by borrowers. Should the amount offered at that rate increase without a corresponding increase in the amount demanded, the rate would fall, just as it would rise under opposite conditions.

Supply and demand, however, are merely the immediate forces. They are themselves the outcome or resultant of factors more remote. On the side of supply, the principal remote forces which regulate the rate of interest are: the industrial resources of the community, and the relative strength of its habits of saving and spending. On the side of demand, the chief ultimate factors are: The productivity of capital-instruments, the comparative intensity of the social desires of investing and lending, and the supplies of land, business ability, and labor. Each of these factors exercises upon the rate of interest an influence of its own, and each of them may be assisted or counteracted by one or more of the others. Precisely what rate will result from any given condition of the factors cannot be stated beforehand, for the factors cannot be measured in such a way as to provide a basis for this kind of forecast. All that can be said is that, when changes occur on the side of either demand or supply, there will be a corresponding change in the rate of interest, provided that no neutralizing change takes place on the other side.*

---

*Editor's Note: Following this chapter on definitions, Ryan devoted a chapter to rejecting the laborer's right to the entire product of industry and a chapter to reasons for repudiating socialism. These chapters, containing largely negative and dated arguments, have been omitted.

CHAPTER 6

Alleged Intrinsic Justifications
of Interest

In his address as president of the American Sociological Society at the annual meeting, Dec. 27, 1913, Professor Albion W. Small denounced "the fallacy of treating capital as though it were an active agent in human processes, and crediting income to the personal representatives of capital, irrespective of their actual share in human service." According to his explicit declaration, his criticism of the modern interest-system was based primarily upon grounds of social utility rather than upon formally ethical considerations.

A German priest has attacked interest from the purely moral viewpoint.[1] In his view the owner of any sort of capital who exacts the return of anything beyond the principal violates strict justice.[2] The Church, he maintains, has never formally authorized or permitted interest, either on loans or on producing capital. She has merely tolerated it as an irremovable evil.

Is there a satisfactory justification of interest? If there is, does it rest on individual or on social grounds? That is to say: Is interest justified immediately and intrinsically by the relations existing between the owner and the user of capital? Or, is it rendered morally good by its effects upon social welfare? Let us see what light is thrown on these questions by the anti-usury legislation of the Catholic Church.

ATTITUDE OF THE CHURCH
TOWARD INTEREST ON LOANS

During the Middle Ages all interest on *loans* was forbidden under severe penalties by repeated ordinances of Popes and Councils.[3] Since the end of the

This chapter is reprinted from *Distributive Justice: The Right and Wrong of Our Present Distribution of Wealth*, 3d ed., rev. (New York: Macmillan Co., 1942), 121–33.

seventeenth century the Church has quite generally permitted interest on one or more extrinsic grounds, or "titles." The first of these titles was known as *lucrum cessans,* or relinquished gain. It came into existence whenever a person who could have invested his money in a productive object, for example, a house, a farm, or a mercantile enterprise, decided instead to lend the money. In such cases the interest on the loan was regarded as proper compensation for the gain which the owner might have obtained from an investment on his own account. The title created by this situation was called "extrinsic" because it arose out of circumstances external to the essential relations of borrower and lender. Not because of the loan itself, but because the loan prevented the lender from investing his money in a productive enterprise, was interest on the former held to be justified. In other words, interest on the loan was looked upon as the fair equivalent of the interest that might have been obtained on the investment. It took the place of the gain that was passed by.

During the seventeenth, eighteenth, and nineteenth centuries, another title or justification of loan-interest found some favor among Catholic moralists. This was the *praemium legale,* or legal rate of interest allowed by civil governments. Wherever the State authorized a definite rate of interest, the lender might, according to these writers, take advantage of it with a clear conscience.

To-day the majority of Catholic authorities on the subject prefer the title of virtual productivity as a justification. Money, they contend, has become virtually productive. It can readily be exchanged for income-bearing or productive property, such as, land, houses, railroads, machinery, and distributive establishments. Hence it has become the economic equivalent of productive capital, and the interest which is received on it through a loan is quite as reasonable as the annual return to the owner of productive capital. Between this theory and the theory connected with *lucrum cessans* the only difference is that the former shifts the justification of interest from the circumstances and rights of the lender to the present nature of the money itself. Not merely the fact that the individual will suffer if, instead of investing his money he loans it without interest, but the fact that money is generally and virtually productive, is the important element in the newer theory. In practice, however, the two explanations or justifications come to substantially the same thing. Nevertheless, the Church has given no positive approval to any of the foregoing theories. In the last formal pronouncement by a Pope on the subject, Benedict XIV[4] condemned anew all interest that had no other support than the intrinsic conditions of the loan itself. At the same time, he declared that he had no intention of denying the lawfulness of interest which was received in virtue of the title of *lucrum cessans,* nor the lawfulness of interest or profits arising out of investments in productive property. In other words, the authorization that he gave to both kinds of interest was negative. He refrained from condemning them.

In canon 1543 of the new and revised Code of Canon Law approved and promulgated by Pope Benedict XV, September 15, 1917, we find a reiteration of the traditional principle that it is unlawful to take interest on the intrinsic ground of the loan itself. On the other hand, we find a rather general, though negative, authorization of interest taking on extrinsic grounds. Indeed, one such title, legalization by the State, is mentioned specifically. The whole canon may be thus translated: "If a fungible thing [anything that is consumed at first use and is replaceable in kind] is transferred to a person so as to become his property and later returnable only in the same kind [not identically] no profit may be taken by reason of the contract itself; nevertheless it is not *per se* unlawful to contract for the legal rate of interest, unless that be clearly exorbitant; nor is it wrong to agree upon a higher rate if there is at hand a just and proportionate title."

In brief, interest is not necessarily wrong if it does not exceed a reasonable legal rate; nor even if it does exceed the legal rate, provided that it is based upon adequate external grounds. Undoubtedly such grounds would include greater risk and the opportunity of larger alternative gains through investment.

All the theological discussion on the subject, and all the authoritative ecclesiastical declarations indicate, therefore, that interest on loans is to-day regarded as lawful because a loan is the economic equivalent of an investment. Evidently this is good logic and common sense. If it is right for the stockholder of a railway to receive dividends, it is equally right for the bondholder to receive interest. If it is right for a merchant to take from the gross returns of his business a sum sufficient to cover interest on his capital, it is equally right for the man from whom he has borrowed money for the enterprise to exact interest. The money in a loan is economically equivalent to, convertible into, concrete capital. It deserves, therefore, the same treatment and the same rewards. The fact that the investor undergoes a greater risk then the lender, and the fact that the former often performs labor in connection with the operation of his capital, have no bearing on the moral problem; for the investor is repaid for his extra risk and labor by the profits which he receives, and which the lender does not receive. As a mere recipient of interest, the investor undergoes no more risk nor exertion than does the lender. His claim to interest is no better than that of the latter.

INTEREST ON PRODUCTIVE CAPITAL

On what ground does the Church or Catholic theological opinion justify interest on invested capital? on the shares of the stockholders in corporations? on the capital of the merchant and the manufacturer?

In the early Middle Ages the only recognized titles to gain from the ownership of property were labor and risk.[5] Down to the beginning of the fifteenth century substantially all the incomes of all classes could be explained and justified by one or other of these two titles; for the amount of capital in existence was inconsiderable, and the number of large personal incomes insignificant.

When, however, the traffic in rent charges and the operation of partnerships, especially the *contractus trinus,* or triple contract, had become fairly common, it was obvious that the profits from these practices could not be correctly attributed to either labor or risk. The person who bought, not the land itself, but the right to receive a portion of the rent thereof, and the person who became the silent member of a partnership, evidently performed no labor beyond that involved in making the contract. And their profits clearly exceeded a fair compensation for their risks, inasmuch as the profits produced a steady income. How then were they to be justified?

A few authorities maintained that such incomes had no justification. In the thirteenth century Henry of Ghent condemned the traffic in rent charges; in the sixteenth Dominicus Soto maintained that the returns to the silent partner in an enterprise ought not to exceed a fair equivalent for his risks; about the same time Pope Sixtus V denounced the triple contract as a form of usury. Nevertheless, the great majority of writers admitted that all these transactions were morally lawful, and the gains therefrom just. For a time these writers employed merely negative and *a pari* arguments. Gains from rent charges, they pointed out, were essentially as licit as the net rent received by the owner of the land; and the interest received by a silent partner, even in a triple contract, had quite as sound a moral basis as rent charges. By the beginning of the seventeenth century the leading authorities were basing their defense of industrial interest on positive grounds. Lugo, Lessius, and Molina adduced the productivity of capital goods as a reason for allowing gains to the investor. Whether they regarded productivity as in itself a sufficient justification of interest, or merely as a necessary prerequisite to justification, cannot be determined with certainty.

At present the majority of Catholic writers seem to think that a formal defense of interest on capital is unnecessary. Apparently they assume that interest is justified by the mere productivity of capital. However, this view has never been *explicitly* approved by the Church.

So much for the teaching of ecclesiastical and ethical authorities. What are the objective reasons in favor of the capitalist's claim to interest? In this chapter we consider only the intrinsic reasons, those arising wholly out of the relations between the interest-receiver and the interest-payer. Before taking up the subject it may be well to point out the source from which interest comes, the class in the community that pays the interest to the capitalist. From the language sometimes used by Socialists it might be inferred that interest is taken from the laborer, and that if it were abolished he would be the chief if not the only beneficiary. This is incorrect. At any given time interest on producing capital is paid by the consumer. Those who purchase the products of industry must give prices sufficiently high to provide interest in addition to the other expenses of production. Were interest abolished and the present system of private capital continued, the gain would be reaped mainly by the consumer in the form of lower prices; for the various capitalist directors of industry would bring about this result through their competitive efforts to increase sales. Only those laborers who were sufficiently

organized and sufficiently alert to make effective demands for higher wages before the movement toward lower prices had got well under way, would obtain
any direct benefit from the change. The great majority of laborers would gain far
more as consumers than as wage earners. Speaking generally, then, we may say
that the capitalist's gain is the consumer's loss, and the question of the justice of
interest is a question between the capitalist and the consumer.

The intrinsic or individual grounds upon which the capitalist's claim to interest has been defended are mainly three: Productivity, service, and abstinence.
They will be considered in this order.

THE CLAIMS OF PRODUCTIVITY

It is sometimes asserted that the capitalist has as good a right to interest as the
farmer has to the offspring of his animals. Both are the products of the owner's
property. In two respects, however, the comparison is inadequate and misleading. Since the owner of a female animal contributes labor or money or both toward her care during the period of gestation, his claim to the offspring is based
in part upon these grounds, and only in part upon the title of interest. In the second place, the offspring is the definite and easily distinguishable product of its
parent. But the sixty dollars derived as interest from the ownership of ten shares
of railway stock, cannot be identified as the exact product of one thousand dollars of railway property. No man can tell whether this amount of capital has contributed more or less than sixty dollars of value to the joint product, i.e., railway
services. The same is true of any other share or piece of concrete capital. All that
we know is that the interest, be it five, six, seven, or some other per cent, describes
the share of the product which goes to the owner of capital in the present conditions of industry. It is the conventional, not the actual and physical, product of
capital.

Another faulty analogy is that drawn between the productivity of capital and
the productivity of labor. Following the terminology of the economists, most
persons think of land, labor, and capital as productive in the same sense. Hence
the productivity of capital is easily assumed to have the same moral value as the
productive action of human beings; and the right of the capitalist to a part of the
product is put on the same moral basis as the right of the laborer. Yet the differences between the two kinds of productivity, and between the two moral claims
to the product, are more important than their resemblances.

In the first place, there is an essential physical difference. As an instrument of
production, labor is active, capital is passive. As regards its worth or dignity, labor is the expenditure of human energy, the output of a *person*, while capital is a
material thing, standing apart from a personality, and possessing no human quality or human worth. These significant intrinsic or physical differences forbid any

immediate inference that the moral claims of the owners of capital and labor are equally valid. We should expect to find that their moral claims are unequal.

This expectation is realized when we examine the bearing of the two kinds of productivity upon human welfare. In the exercise of productive effort the average laborer undergoes a sacrifice. He is engaged in a process that is ordinarily irk-some. To require from him this toilsome expenditure of energy without compensation, would make him a mere instrument of his fellows. It would subordinate him and his comfort to the aggrandizement of beings who are not his superiors but his moral equals. For he is a person; they are no more than persons. On the other hand, the capitalist as such, as the recipient of interest, performs no labor, painful or otherwise. Not the capitalist, but capital participates in the productive process. Even though the capitalist should receive no interest, the productive functioning of capital would not subordinate him to his fellows in the way that wageless labor would subordinate the laborer.

The precise and fundamental reason for according to the laborer his product is that this is the only rational rule of distribution. When a man makes a useful thing out of materials that are his, he has a strict right to the product simply because there is no other reasonable method of distributing the goods and opportunities of the earth. If another individual, or society, were permitted to take his product, industry would be discouraged, idleness fostered, and reasonable life and self-development rendered impossible. Direful consequences of this magnitude would not follow the abolition of interest.

Perhaps the most important difference between the moral claims of capitalist and laborer is the fact that for the latter labor is the sole means of livelihood. Unless he is compensated for his product he will perish. But the capitalist has in addition to the interest that he receives the ability to work. Were interest abolished he would still be in as good a position as the laborer. The product of the laborer means to him the necessaries of life; the product of the capitalist means to him goods in excess of a mere livelihood. Consequently their claims to the product are unequal in vital importance and moral value.

The foregoing considerations show that even the claim of the laborer to his product is not based upon merely intrinsic grounds. It does not spring entirely from the mere fact that he has produced the product, from the mere relation between producer and things produced. If this is true of labor-productivity we should expect to find it even more evident with regard to the productivity of capital; for the latter is passive instead of active, non-rational instead of human.

The expectation is well founded. Not a single objective argument can be brought forward to show that the productivity of capital directly and *per se* confers upon the capitalist a right to the interest-product. All the attempted arguments are reducible to two formulas: *Res fructificant domino* (a thing fructifies to its owner) and "the effect follows its cause." The first of these was originally a legal rather than an ethical maxim; a rule by which the title was determined in the civil law, not a principle by which the right was determined in morals. The second is an irrelevant platitude. As a juristic principle, neither is self-evident.

THE CLAIMS OF SERVICE

The second intrinsic ground upon which interest is defended, is the *service* performed by the capitalist when he permits his capital to be used in production. Without capital, laborers and consumers would be unable to command more than a fraction of their present means of livelihood. From this point of view we see that the service in question is worth all that is paid in the form of interest. Nevertheless, it does not follow that the capitalist has a claim in strict justice to my payment for this service. According to St. Thomas, a seller may not charge a buyer an extra amount merely because of the extra value attached to the commodity by the latter.[6] In other words, a man cannot justly be required to pay an unusual price for a benefit or advantage or service, when the seller undergoes no unusual deprivation. Father Lehmkuhl carries the principle further and declares that the seller has a right to compensation only when and to the extent that he undergoes a privation or undertakes a responsibility.[7] According to this rule, the capitalist would have no right to interest; for as mere interest-receiver he undergoes no privation. His risk and labor are remunerated in profits, while the responsibility of not withdrawing from production something that can continue in existence only by continuing in production, is scarcely deserving of a reward according to the canons of strict justice.

Whatever we may think of this argument from authority, we find it impossible to prove objectively that a man who renders a service to another has an intrinsic right to anything beyond compensation for the expenditure of money or labor involved in performing the service. The man who throws a life preserver to a drowning person may justly demand a payment for his trouble. On any recognized basis of compensation, this payment will not exceed a few dollars. Yet the man whose life is in danger will pay a million dollars for his service if he is extremely rich. He will regard the service as worth this much to him. Has the man with the life preserver a right to exact such a payment? Has he a right to demand the full value of the service? No reasonable person would answer this question otherwise than in the negative. If the performer of the service may not charge the full value thereof, as measured by the estimate put upon it by the recipient, it would seem that he ought not to demand anything in excess of a fair price for his labor.

It would seem, then, that the capitalist has no moral claim to pure interest on the mere ground that the use of his capital in production constitutes a service to laborers and consumers. It would seem that he has no right to demand a payment for a costless service.

THE CLAIMS OF ABSTINENCE

The third and last of the intrinsic justifications of interest that we shall consider is *abstinence*. This argument is based upon the contention that the person who saves his money and invests it in the instruments of production undergoes a sacrifice in deferring to the future satisfactions that he might enjoy to-day. One hundred dollars now is worth as much as one hundred and five dollars a year hence. That is, when both are estimated from the viewpoint of the present. This sacrifice of present to future enjoyment which contributes a service to the community in the form of capital, creates a just claim upon the community to compensation in the form of interest. If the capitalist is not rewarded for this inconvenience he is, like the unpaid laborer, subordinated to the aggrandizement of his fellows.

Against this argument we may place the extreme refutation attempted by Ferdinand Lassalle:

"But the profit of capital is *the reward of abstinence*. Truly a happy phrase! European millionaires are ascetics, Indian penitents, modern St. Simeon Stylites, who, perched on their columns, with withered features and arms and bodies thrust forward, hold out a plate to the passers-by that they may receive the wages of their privations! In the midst of this sacrosanct group, high above his fellow mortifiers of the flesh, stands the Holy House of Rothschild. That is the real truth about our present society! How could I have hitherto blundered on this point as I have?"[8]

Obviously this is a malevolently one-sided implication concerning the sources of capital. But it is scarcely less adequate than the explanation in opposition to which it has been quoted. Both fail to distinguish between the different kinds of savers, the different kinds of capital-owners. For the purposes of our inquiry savings may be divided into three classes.[9]

First, those which are accumulated and invested automatically. Very rich persons save a great deal of money that they have no desire to spend, since they have already satisfied or safeguarded all the wants of which they are conscious. Evidently this kind of saving involves no real sacrifice. To it the words of Lassalle are substantially applicable, and the claim to interest for abstinence decidedly inapplicable.

Second, savings to provide for old age and other future contingencies which are estimated as more important than any of the purposes for which the money might now be expended. Were interest abolished this kind of saving would be even greater than it is at present; for a larger total would be required to equal the fund that is now provided through the addition of interest to the principal. In a no-interest régime one thousand dollars would have to be set aside every year in order to total twenty-thousand dollars in twenty years; when interest is accumulated on the savings, a considerably smaller annual amount will suffice to produce the same fund. Inasmuch as this class of persons would save in an even greater degree without interest, it is clear that they regard the sacrifice involved as fully compensated in the resulting provision for the future. In their case sacrifice is amply rewarded by accumulation. Their claim to additional compensation in the form of interest does not seem to have any valid basis. In the words of Professor Devas, "there is ample reward given without any need of any interest or dividend. For the workers with heads or hands keep the property intact, ready for the owner to consume whenever convenient, when he gets infirm or sick, or when his children have grown up, and can enjoy the property with him."[10]

The third kind of saving is that which is made by persons who could spend, and have some desire to spend, more on present satisfactions, and who have already provided for all future wants in accordance with the standards of necessaries and comforts that they have adopted. Their fund for the future is already sufficient to meet all those needs which seem weightier than their present unsatisfied wants. If the surplus in question is saved it will go to supply future desires which are no more important than those for which it might be expended now. In other words, the alternatives before the prospective saver are to procure a given amount of satisfaction to-day, or to defer the same degree of satisfaction to a distant day. In this case the inducement of interest will undoubtedly be necessary to bring about saving. As between equal amounts of satisfaction in different times, the average person will certainly prefer those of the present to those of the future. He will not decide in favor of the future unless the satisfactions then obtainable are to be greater in quantity. To this situation the rule that deferred enjoyments are worth less than present enjoyments, is strictly applicable. The increased quantity of future satisfaction which is necessary to turn the choice from the present to the future, and to determine that the surplus shall be saved rather than spent, can be provided only through interest. In this way the accumulations of interest and savings will make the future fund equivalent to a larger amount of enjoyment or utility than could be obtained if the surplus were exchanged for the goods of the present. "Interest magnifies the distant object." Whenever this magnifying power seems sufficiently great to outweigh the advantage of present over future satisfactions, the surplus will be saved instead of spent.

Among the well-to-do there is probably a considerable number of persons who take this attitude toward a considerable part of their savings. Since they would not make these savings without the inducement of interest, they regard the latter as a necessary compensation for the sacrifice of present enjoyment. In a general way we may say that they have a strict right to this interest on the intrinsic ground of sacrifice. Inasmuch as the community benefits by the savings, it may quite as fairly be required to pay for the antecedent sacrifices of the savers as for the inconvenience undergone by the performer of any useful labor or service.

CHAPTER 7

Social and Presumptive Justifications of Interest

As we saw in the last chapter, interest cannot be conclusively justified on the ground of either productivity or service. It is impossible to demonstrate that the capitalist has a strict right to interest because his capital produces interest, or because it renders a service to the laborer or the consumer. A part, probably a small part, of the interest now received can be fairly justified by the title of sacrifice. Some present owners of capital would not have saved had they not expected to receive interest. In their case interest may be regarded as a just compensation for the sacrifice that they underwent when they decided to save instead of consume.

THE VALUE OF CAPITAL
IN A NO-INTEREST RÉGIME

The interest that we have in mind is pure interest, not undertaker's profit, nor insurance against risk, nor gross interest. Even if all pure interest were abolished the capitalist who loaned his money would still receive something from the borrower in addition to the repayment of the principal, while the active capitalist would get from the consumer more than the expenses of production. The former would require a premium of, say, one or two per cent to protect him against the loss of his loan. The latter would demand the same kind of insurance, and an additional sum to repay him for his labor and enterprise. None of these payments could be avoided in any system of privately directed production. The return considered here is that which the capitalist receives over and above these payments,

This chapter is reprinted from *Distributive Justice: The Right and Wrong of our Present Distribution of Wealth*, 3d ed., rev. (New York: Macmillan Co., 1942), 134–46.

and which in this country seems to be about three or four per cent. It is what the capitalist gets as capitalist.

Would capital still have value in a no-interest régime, and if so how would its value be determined? At present the lower limit of the value of productive capital, as of all other artificial goods, is fixed in the long run by the cost of production. Capital instruments that do not bring this price will not continue to be made. In other words, cost of production is the governing factor of the value of capital from the side of supply. It would likewise fix the lower limit of value in a no-interest régime; only, the cost of producing capital instruments would then be somewhat lower than to-day, owing to the absence of an interest charge upon the productive process.

But the cost of production is not a constant and accurate measure of the value of artificial capital. The true measure is found in the revenue or interest that a given piece of capital yields to its owners. If the current rate of interest is five per cent, a factory that brings in ten thousand dollars net return will have a value of about two hundred thousand dollars. This is the governing factor of value from the side of demand. In a no-interest economy the demand factor would be quite different. Capital instruments would be in demand, not as revenue producers, but as the concrete embodiments, the indispensable requisites, of saving and accumulation. For it is impossible that saving should in any considerable amount take the form of cash hoards. In the words of Sir Robert Giffen: "The accumulations of a single war, even taking it at one hundred and fifty million only, . . . would absorb more than the entire metallic currency of the country [Great Britain]. They cannot, therefore, be made in cash."[1] The instruments of production would be sought and valued by savers for the same reason that safes and safety deposit boxes are in demand now. They would be the only means of carrying savings into the future, and they would necessarily bring a price sufficiently high to cover the cost of producing them. One man might deposit his savings in a bank, whence they would be borrowed without interest by some director of industry. When the owner of the savings desired to recover them he could obtain from the bank the fund of some other depositor, or get the proceeds of the sale of the concrete capital in which his own savings had been embodied. Another man might prefer to invest his savings directly in a building, a machine, or a mercantile business, whence he could recover them later from the sale of the property. Hence the absence of interest would not change essentially the processes of saving or investment. Capital would still have value, but its valuation from the demand side would rest on a different basis. It would be valued not in proportion to its power to yield interest, but because of its capacity to become a receptacle for savings, and to carry consuming power into the future.

The question whether the abolition of interest by the State would be socially helpful or socially harmful is mainly, though not entirely, a question of the supply of capital. If the community would not have sufficient capital to provide for all its needs, actual and progressive, the suppression of interest would obviously be a bad policy.

WHETHER INTEREST IS NECESSARY

With interest abolished, those persons who were willing to subordinate present secondary satisfactions to the primary future needs of themselves and their families, would save at least as much for these purposes as when they could have obtained interest. Most of them would probably save more in order to render their future provision as nearly as possible equal to what it would have been had interest accrued on their annual savings. Whether a person intended to leave all his accumulations, or part of them, or none of them to posterity, he would still desire them to be as large as they might have been in a régime of interest. In order to realize this desire, he would be compelled to increase his savings. And it is reasonable to expect that this is precisely the course that would be followed by men of average thrift and foresight. Such men regard future necessaries and comforts, whether for themselves or their children, as more important than present non-essentials and luxuries. Interest or no interest, prudent men will subordinate the latter goods to the former, and will save money accordingly.

When, however, both future and present goods are of the same order and importance, the future is no longer preferred to the present. In that case the preference is reversed. The luxuries of to-day are more keenly prized than the luxuries of tomorrow. If the latter are to be preferred they must possess some advantage over the luxuries that might be obtained here and now. Such advantage may arise in various ways: For example, when a man decides that he will have more leisure for a foreign journey two years hence than this year; or when he prefers a large amount of future enjoyment at one time to present satisfactions taken in small doses. But the most general method of conferring advantage upon the secondary satisfactions of the future as compared with those of the present, is to increase the quantity. The majority of foreseeing persons are willing to pass by one hundred dollars' worth of enjoyment now for the sake of one hundred and five dollars' worth one year hence. This advantage of quantity is provided through interest. It affects all those persons whose saving, as noted in the last chapter, involves a sacrifice for which the only adequate compensation is interest, and likewise all those persons who are in a position to choose between present and future luxuries. Were interest suppressed, these classes of persons would cease to save for this kind of future goods.

According to Professor Taussig, "most saving is done by the well-to-do and the rich."[2] On this hypothesis it seems probable that the abolition of interest would diminish the savings and capital of the community very considerably; for the accumulations of the wealthy are derived mainly from interest rather than from salaries. On the other hand, the suppression of interest should bring about a much wider diffusion of wealth. The sums previously paid out as interest would be distributed among the masses of the population as increased wages and reduced costs of living.

To sum up the results of our inquiry concerning the necessity of interest: The fact that men now receive interest does not prove that they would not save without interest. The fact that many men would certainly save without interest does not prove that a sufficient amount would be saved to provide the community with the necessary supply of capital. Whether the savings of those classes that increased their accumulations would counteract the decreases in the saving of the richer classes, is a question that admits of no definite or confident answer.[3]

THE STATE IS JUSTIFIED
IN PERMITTING INTEREST

If we assume that the suppression of interest would cause a considerable decline in saving and capital, we must conclude that the community would be worse off than under the present system. To diminish greatly the instruments of production, and consequently the supply of goods for consumption, would create far more hardship than it would relieve. While "workless" incomes would be suppressed, and personal incomes more nearly equalized, the total amount available for distribution would probably be so much smaller as to cause a deterioration in the condition of every class. In this hypothesis the State would do wrong to abolish the system of interest.

If, however, we assume that no considerable amount of evil would follow, or that the balance of results would be favorable, the question of the proper action of the State becomes somewhat complex. In the first place, interest could not rightfully be suppressed while the private taking of rent remained. To adopt such a course would be to treat the receivers of property incomes inequitably. Landowners would continue to receive an income from their property, while capital owners would not; yet the moral claims of the former to income are no better than those of the latter. In the second place, the State would be obliged to compensate the owners of existing capital instruments for the decline in value which, as we have already seen, would occur when the item of interest was eliminated from the cost of reproducing such capital instruments. It would likewise be under moral obligation to compensate landowners for whatever decrease in value befell their property as a result of the extinction of rent.

Nevertheless, the practical difficulties confronting the legal abolition of interest are apparently so great as to render the attempt socially unwise and futile. In order to be effective the prohibition would have to be international. Were it enforced in only one or in a few countries, these would suffer far more through the flight of capital than they would gain through the abolition of interest. The technical obstacles would be well nigh insuperable. If the attempt were made to suppress interest on producing capital, as well as on loans, the civil authorities would be unable to determine with any degree of precision what part of the gross returns of a business was pure interest and what part was a necessary compensation for risk and the labor of management. The supervision of expenses, receipts, and other details of business that would be required to prevent evasion of the law, would not improbably cost more than the total amount now paid in the form of interest.

On the other hand, if the method of suppression were confined to loans it would probably prove only a little less futile than the effort to abolish interest on productive capital. The great majority of those who were prevented from lending at interest would invest their money in stocks, land, buildings, and other forms of productive property. Moreover, it is probable that a large volume of loans would be made despite the prohibition. In the Middle Ages, when the amount of money available for lending was comparatively small, and when State and Church and public opinion were unanimous in favor of the policy, the legal prohibition of loans was only partially effective. Now that the supply of and the demand for loans have enormously increased, and interest is not definitely disapproved by the Church or the public, a similar effort by the State would undoubtedly prove a failure. Even if it were entirely successful it would only decrease, not abolish, interest on productive capital.[4]

In view of the manifold and grave uncertainties of the situation, it is practically certain that modern States are justified in permitting interest.

CIVIL AUTHORIZATION NOT SUFFICIENT FOR THE INDIVIDUAL

This justification of the attitude of the State does not of itself demonstrate that the capitalist has a right to accept interest. The civil law tolerates many actions which are morally wrong in the individual; for example, the payment of starvation wages, the extortion of unjust prices, and the traffic in immorality. Obviously, legal toleration does not *per se* nor always exonerate the individual offender. How, then, shall we justify the individual receiver of interest?

As already pointed out more than once, those persons who would not save without interest are justified on the ground of sacrifice. So long as the community desires their savings, and is willing to pay interest on them, the savers may take interest as the fair equivalent of the inconvenience that they undergo in performing this social service. The precise problem before us, then, is the justification of those savers and capitalists who do not need the inducement of interest, and whose functions of saving are sufficiently compensated without interest.

It is a fact that the civil law can sometimes create moral right and obligations. For example: The statute requiring a person to repair losses that he has unintentionally inflicted upon his neighbor is held by the moral theologians to be binding *in conscience*, as soon as the matter has been adjudicated by the court. In other words, this civil regulation confers on the injured man property rights, and imposes on the morally inculpable injurer property obligations. The civil statutes also give moral validity to the title of prescription, or adverse possession. When the alien possessor has complied with the legal provisions that apply, he has a moral right to the property, even though the original owner should assert his claim at a later time. Several other situations might be cited in which the State admittedly creates moral rights of individual ownership which would have no definite existence in the absence of such legal action and authorization.[5]

This principle would seem to have received a particularly pertinent application for our inquiry in the doctrine of *praemium legale* as a title of interest on loans. In the *Opus Morale* of Ballerini-Palmieri can be found a long list of moral theologians living in the seventeenth and eighteenth centuries who maintained that the mere legal sanction of a certain rate of interest was a sufficient moral justification for the lender.[6] While holding to the traditional doctrine that interest was not capable of being justified on intrinsic grounds, these writers contended that by virtue of its power of eminent domain the State could transfer from the borrower to the lender the right to the interest paid on a loan. They did not mean that the State could arbitrarily take one man's property and hand it over to another, but only that, when it sanctioned interest for the public welfare, this extrinsic circumstance (like the other "extrinsic titles" approved by moralists) annulled the claim of the borrower in favor of the lender. In other words, they maintained that the money paid in loan-interest did not belong to either borrower or lender with certainty or definiteness until the matter was determined by economic conditions and extrinsic circumstances. Hence legal authorization for the common good was morally sufficient to award it to the lender. More than one authority declared that the State had the same right to determine this indeterminate property, to assign the ownership to the lender, that it had to transfer property titles by the device of prescription. As we have already seen, canon 1523 of the New Code of Canon Law explicitly declares that it is not necessarily wrong to bargain for and accept the legal rate of interest.

HOW THE INTEREST-TAKER IS JUSTIFIED

Although the interest received by the non-sacrifice savers is not clearly justifiable on intrinsic grounds, it is not utterly lacking in moral sanctions. As we have already seen, the right of the capital owner to a share in the product was affirmed by Pope Pius XI. Moreover, we have not contended that the intrinsic factors of productivity and service are *certainly* invalid morally. We have merely insisted that the moral worth of these titles has never been objectively demonstrated. Possibly they have a greater and more definite efficacy than has yet been shown by their advocates. In more concrete terms, we admit that the productivity of capital and the service of the capitalist to the community, are possible and doubtful titles to interest. A doubtful title to property is, indeed, insufficient by itself. In the case of the interest receiver, however, the doubtful titles of productivity and service are reinforced by the fact of possession. Thus supplemented, they are sufficient to justify the non-sacrifice saver in giving himself the benefit of the doubt as regards the validity of his right to take interest. To be sure, this indefinite and uncertain claim could be overthrown by a more definite and positive title. But no such antagonistic title exists. Neither the consumer nor the laborer can show any conclusive reason why interest should go to him rather than to the capitalist. Hence the latter has at least a presumptive title. In the circumstances this is morally sufficient.

To this justification by presumption must be added a justification by analogy. The non-sacrifice savers seem to be in about the same position as those other agents of production whose rewards are out of proportion to their sacrifices. For example: The laborer of superior native ability gets as much compensation for the same quality and quantity of work as his companion who has only ordinary ability; and the exceptionally intelligent business man stands in the same relation to his less efficient competitor; yet the sacrifice undergone by the former of each pair is less than that suffered by the latter. It would seem that if the more efficient men may properly take the same rewards as those who make larger sacrifices, the non-sacrifice capitalist might lawfully accept the same interest as the man whose saving involves some sacrifice. On this principle the lenders who would not have invested their money in a productive enterprise were nevertheless permitted by the moralists of the post-mediaeval period to take advantage of the title of *lucrum cessans*. Although they had relinquished no opportunity gain, nor made any sacrifice, they were put on the same moral level as sacrificing lenders and allowed to take interest.

As a determinant of ownership, possession is the feeblest of all factors, and yet it is of considerable importance for a large proportion of incomes and property. In the distribution of the national product, as well as in the division of the original heritage of the earth, a large part is played by the title of first occupancy. Much of the product of industry is assigned to the agents of production mainly on the basis of inculpable possession. That is, it goes to its receivers automatically, in exchange for benefits to those who hand it over. Just as the first arrival on a piece of land may regard it as a no-man's territory, and make it his own by the mere device of appropriation, so the capitalist may get morally valid possession of interest. Sometimes, indeed, this debatable share, this no-man's share of the product of industry, is secured in some part by the consumer or the laborer. In such cases their title to it is just as valid as the title of the capitalist, notwithstanding the doubtful titles of productivity and service which the latter has in his favor. First occupancy and possession are the more decisive factors. In the great majority of instances, however, the capitalist is the first occupant, and therefore the lawful possessor of the interest-share.

The general justification of interest set forth in the immediately preceding paragraphs is supplemented in the case of the great majority of capital owners by the fact that their income from this source is relatively insignificant. This is notoriously true of the vast majority of farmers. It is likewise the case with a very large proportion of small manufacturers and shopkeepers and of almost all wage earners who have investments. The interest received by all these classes can easily be justified as a necessary supplement to the inadequate return which they obtain for their labor.

Again, there is a large number of interest-receivers who are entirely dependent upon this kind of income, and who obtain therefrom only a moderate livelihood. They are mainly children, aged persons, and invalids. Unlike the classes just described, they cannot justify their interest as a fair supplement to wages; however, they may reasonably claim it as their equitable or charitable share of the common heritage of the earth. If they did not receive this interest-income they would have to be supported by their relatives or by the State. For many reasons this would be a much less desirable arrangement. Consequently their general claim to interest is supplemented by considerations of human welfare.

The difference between the ethical character of the interest discussed in the last two paragraphs and of that received by persons who possess large incomes, is too often overlooked in technical treatises. Every man owning any productive goods is reckoned as a capitalist, and assumed to receive interest. If, however, a man's total interest-income is so small that when combined with all his other revenues it merely completes the equivalent of a decent living, it is surely of very little significance as interest. It stands in no such need of justification as the interest obtained by men whose incomes amount to, say, ten thousand dollars a year and upward.

Still another confirmatory title of interest is suggested by the following well known declaration of St. Thomas Aquinas: "The possession of riches is not in itself unlawful if the order of reason be observed: that a man should possess justly what he owns and *use* it in a proper manner for himself and others."[7] Neither just acquisition nor proper use is alone sufficient to render private possessions morally good. Both must be present. As we have seen above, the capitalist can appeal to certain titles which justify practically his acquisition of interest; but his moral claim and his moral power of disposal are considerably strengthened when he puts his interest-income to a proper use. One way of so using it is exemplified in the case of the farmers, business men, and non-workers whom we considered above. Those persons who receive incomes in excess of their reasonable needs could devote the surplus to religion, charity, education, and a great variety of altruistic purposes. We shall deal with this matter specifically in the chapter on the "Duty of Distributing Superfluous Wealth." In the meantime it is sufficient to note that the rich man who makes a benevolent use of his interest-income has a special reason for believing that his receipt of interest is justified.

The decisive value attributed to presumption, analogy, possession, and doubtful titles in our vindication of the capitalist's claim to interest, is no doubt disappointing to those persons who desire clear-cut mathematical rules and principles. Nevertheless, they are the only factors that seem to be available. While the title that they confer upon the interest-receiver is not as definite nor as noble as that by which the laborer claims his wages or the business man his profits, it is morally sufficient. It will remain logically and ethically unshaken until more cogent arguments have been brought against it than have yet appeared in the denunciations of the income of the capitalist. And what is true of him is likewise true of the rent-receiver, and of the person who profits by the "unearned increment" of land values. In all three cases the presumptive justification of "workless" incomes will probably remain valid as long as the present industrial system endures.*

---

*Editor's Note: Ryan included a chapter, omitted here, on how cooperatives of various kinds could have several salutary effects for economic justice, including easing the amount of interest paid as "workless" income.

SECTION 3

The Moral Aspect of Profits

CHAPTER 8

The Nature of Profits

We have seen that rent goes to the landlord as the price of land use, while interest is received by the capitalist as the return for the use of capital. The two shares of the product which remain to be considered include an element which is absent from both rent and interest. The use for which profits and wages are paid comprises not merely the utilization of a productive factor, but the sustained exertion of the factor's owner. Like the landowner and the capitalist, the business man and the laborer put the productive factors which they control at the disposal of the industrial process; but they do so only when and so long as they exercise human activity. The shares that they receive are payments for the continuous output of human energy. No such significance attaches to rent or interest.

THE FUNCTIONS AND REWARDS
OF THE BUSINESS MAN

Who is the business man, and what is the nature of his share of the product of industry? Let us suppose that the salaried manager of a hat factory decides to set up a business of the same kind for himself. He wishes to become an entrepreneur, an undertaker, a director of industry, in more familiar language, a business man. Let us assume that he is without money, but that he commands extraordinary financial credit. He is able to borrow half a million dollars with which to organize, equip, and operate the new enterprise. Having selected a favorable site, he rents it on a long term lease, and erects thereon the necessary buildings. He installs all the necessary machinery and other equipment, hires capable labor,

This chapter is reprinted from *Distributive Justice: The Right and Wrong of Our Present Distribution of Wealth*, 3d ed., rev. (New York: Macmillan Co., 1942), 175–79.

and determines the kinds and quantities of hats for which he thinks that he can find a market. At the end of a year, he realizes that, after paying for labor of all sorts, returning interest to the capitalist and rent to the landowner, defraying the cost of repairs, and setting aside a fund to cover depreciation, he has left for himself the sum of ten thousand dollars. This is the return for his labor of organization and direction, and for the risk that he underwent. It constitutes the share called profits, sometimes specified as net profits.

This case is artificial, since it assumes that the business man is neither capitalist nor landowner in addition to his function as director of industry. It has, however, the advantage of distinguishing quite sharply the action of the business man as such. In point of fact, however, no one ever functions solely as business man. Always the business man owns some of the capital, and very often some of the land involved in his enterprise, and is the receiver not only of profits but of interest and rent. Thus, the farmer is a business man, but he is also a capitalist, and frequently a landowner. The grocer, the clothier, the manufacturer, and even the lawyer and the doctor own a part at least of the capital with which they operate, and sometimes they own the land. Nevertheless their rewards as business men can always be distinguished by finding out what remains after making due allowance for rent and interest.

It is a fact that many business men, especially those directing the smaller establishments, use the term profits to include rent and interest on their own property. In other words, they describe their entire income from the business as profits. In the present discussion, and throughout this book generally, profits are to be understood as comprising merely that part of the business man's returns which he takes as the reward of his labor, and as insurance against the risks affecting his enterprise. Deduct from the business man's total income a sum which will cover interest on his capital at the prevailing rate and rent on his land, and you have left his income as business man, his profits.

THE AMOUNT OF PROFITS

In a preceding chapter we have seen that where the conditions of capital are the same, there exists a fairly uniform rate of interest. No such uniformity obtains in the field of profits. Businesses subject to the same risks and requiring the same kind of management yield very different amounts of return to their directors. In a sense the business man may be regarded as the residual claimant of industry. This does not mean that he takes no profits until all the other agents of production have been fully remunerated, but that his share remains indeterminate until the end of the productive period, say, six months or a year, while the shares of the other agents are determined beforehand. At the end of the productive period, the business man may find that his profits are large, moderate, or small, while the landowner, the capitalist, and the laborer ordinarily obtain the precise amounts of rent, interest, and wages that they had expected to obtain. That there exists no definite upper limit to profits is proved by the history of modern millionaires. That there exists no rigid lower limit is proved by the large proportion of enterprises that meet with failure.

Nevertheless it would be wrong to infer that the volume of profits is governed by no law whatever, or that they show no tendency toward uniformity in any part of the industrial field. There is a calculated or preconceived minimum. No man will embark in business for himself unless he has reason to expect that it will yield him, in addition to protection against risks, an income as large as he could obtain by hiring his services to some one else. In other words, contemplated profits must be at least equal to the income of the salaried business manager. No tendency toward uniformity of profits exists among very large enterprises nor among industries which are constantly adopting new methods and new inventions. In businesses of small and moderate size, and in those whose methods have become standardized, such as a retail grocery store, or a factory that turns out staple kinds of shoes, profits tend to be about the same in the great majority of establishments. In such industries the profits of the business man do not often exceed the salary that he could command as general manager in the same kind of business.[1]

PROFITS IN THE JOINT-STOCK COMPANY

Up to this point we have been considering the independent business man, the undertaker who manages his enterprise either alone or as a member of a partnership. In all such concerns it is easy to identify the business man. Who or where is the business man in a joint-stock company? Where are the profits, and who gets them?

Strictly speaking, there is no undertaker or business man in a corporation. His functions of ownership, responsibility, and direction are exercised by the whole body of stockholders through the board of directors and other officers. It is true that in many corporations, one or a very few of the largest stockholders dominate the policies of the concern, and exercise almost as much power and authority as though they were the sole owners. Neither these, however, nor any other officer in a corporation receives profits in the same sense as the independent owner of a business. For their active services the officers of the corporation are given salaries; for the risks that they undergo as owners of the stock they are compensated in the same way as all the other stockholders, that is, through a sufficiently high rate of dividend. The bonds represent borrowed money, and are secured by a mortgage on the physical property. The stock represents the money invested by the owners, and is subject to all the risks of ownership; hence its holders require the protection which is afforded by a higher rate of interest.

While a corporation has no profits in the sense of a reward for directive activity or a protection against risk, it frequently possesses profits in the sense of a surplus which remains after costs and expenses of every kind have been defrayed. These profits are ordinarily distributed pro rata among the stockholders, either outright in the form of an extra dividend, or indirectly through enlargement of the property and business of the company. They are surplus gains or profits having the same intermittent and speculative character as the extra gains which the individual business man sometimes obtains in addition to those profits which are necessary to remunerate him for his labor and protect him against risks. They are not profits in the ordinary economic sense of the term.

CHAPTER 9

The Principal Canons of Distributive Justice

Before taking up the morality of profits, it will be helpful, if not necessary, to consider the chief rules of justice that have been or might be adopted in distributing the product of industry among those who participate actively in the productive process. While the discussion is undertaken with particular reference to the rewards of the business man, it will also have an important bearing on the compensation of the wage earner. The morality of rent and interest depends upon other principles than those governing the remuneration of human activity; and it has been sufficiently treated in chapters x and xi [Editor's note: chapters 6 and 7 in this edition]. The canons of distribution applicable to our present study are mainly six in number: arithmetical equality; proportional needs; efforts and sacrifices; comparative productivity; relative scarcity; and human welfare.

THE CANON OF EQUALITY

According to the rule of arithmetical equality, all persons who contribute to the product should receive the same amount of remuneration. No important writer defends this rule to-day. It is unjust because it would treat unequals equally. Although men are equal as moral entities, as human persons, they are unequal in desires, capacities, and powers. An income that would fully satisfy the needs of one man would meet only 75 per cent, or 50 per cent, of the capacities of another. To allot them equal amounts of income would be to treat them unequally with regard to the requisites of life and self-development, with regard to the ultimate purpose of property rights. That purpose is welfare. Hence the equal

This chapter is reprinted from *Distributive Justice: The Right and Wrong of Our Present Distribution of Wealth*, 3d ed., rev. (New York: Macmillan Co., 1942), 180–88.

moral claims of men which admittedly arise out of their moral equality must be construed as claims to equal degrees of welfare, not to equal amounts of external goods. To put the matter in another way, external goods are not welfare; they are only means to welfare; consequently their importance must be determined by their bearing upon the welfare of the individual.

Moreover, the rule of equal incomes is socially impracticable. It would deter the great majority of the more efficient from putting forth their best efforts and turning out their maximum product. As a consequence, the total volume of product would be so diminished as to render the share of the majority smaller than it would have been under a rational plan of unequal distribution.

THE CANON OF NEEDS

The second conceivable rule is that of proportional needs. It would require each person to be rewarded in accordance with his capacity to use goods reasonably. If the task of distribution were entirely independent of the process of production, this rule would be ideal; for it would treat men as equal in those respects in which they are equal; namely, as beings endowed with the dignity and the potencies of personality; and it would treat them as unequal in those respects in which they are unequal; that is, in their desires and capacities. But the relation between distribution and production cannot be left out of account. The product is distributed primarily among the agents of production only, and it must be so distributed as to give due consideration to the moral claims of the producer as such. The latter has to be considered not merely as a person possessing needs, but as a person who has contributed something to the making of the product. Whence arise the questions of relative efforts and sacrifices, and relative productivity.

Since only those who have contributed to the product participate in the distribution thereof, it would seem that they should be rewarded in proportion to the efforts and sacrifices that they exert and undergo. As an example of varying effort, let us take two men of equal needs who perform the same labor in such a way that the first expends 90 per cent of his energy, while the second expends 60 per cent. As an example of varying sacrifice, let us take the ditch digger, and the driver who sits all day on the dump wagon. The former expends more painful exertion than the latter. This would seem to make a difference in their moral desert. Justice would seem to require that in each case compensation should be proportionate to exertion rather than to needs. At any rate, the claims of needs should be modified to some extent in favor of the claims of exertion. It is upon the principle of efforts and sacrifices that we expect our eternal rewards to be based by the infinitely just Rewarder. The principle of needs is likewise in conflict with the principle of comparative productivity. Men generally demand rewards in proportion to their products and assume that the demand is just.

Like the rule of arithmetical equality, the rule of proportional needs is not only incomplete ethically but impossible socially. Men's needs vary so widely and so imperceptibly that no human authority could use them as the basis of even an approximately accurate distribution. Moreover, any attempt to distribute rewards on this basis alone would be injurious to social welfare. It would lead to a great diminution in the productivity of the more honest, the more energetic, and the more efficient among the agents of production.

THE CANON OF EFFORTS AND SACRIFICES

The third canon of distribution, that of efforts and sacrifices, would be ideally just if we could ignore the questions of needs and productivity. But we cannot think it just to reward equally two men who have expended the same quantity of painful exertion, but who differ in their needs and in their capacities of self-development. To do so would be to treat them unequally in the matter of welfare, which is the end and reason of all distribution. Consequently the principle of efforts and sacrifices must be modified by the principle of needs. Apparently it must also give way in some degree to the principle of comparative productivity. When two men of unequal powers make equal efforts, they turn out unequal amounts of product. Almost invariably the more productive man believes that he should receive a greater share.

It is evident that the rule of efforts and sacrifices, like those of equality and needs, could not be universally enforced in practice. With the exception of cases in which the worker is called upon regularly to make greater sacrifices owing to the disagreeable nature of the task, attempts to measure the amounts of effort and painful exertion put forth by the different agents of production would on the whole be little more than rough guesses. These would probably prove unsatisfactory to the majority. Moreover, the possessors of superior productive power would in most instances reject the principle of efforts and sacrifices and refuse to do their best work under its operation. The principle is incompatible with social welfare.

The three rules already considered are formally ethical, inasmuch as they are directly based upon the dignity and claims of personality. The two following are primarily physical and social; for they measure economic value rather than ethical worth. Nevertheless, they must have a large place in any system which includes competition.

THE CANON OF PRODUCTIVITY

According to this rule, men should be rewarded in proportion to their contributions to the product. It is open to the obvious objection that it ignores the moral claims of needs and efforts. The needs and use-capacities of men do, indeed, bear some relation to their productive capacities: the man who can produce more usually needs more; but the differences between the two elements are so great that distribution based solely upon productivity would fall far short of satisfying the demands of needs. Between productivity on the one hand and efforts and sacrifices on the other, there are likewise important differences. When men of equal productive power are performing the same kind of labor, superior amounts of product do represent superior amounts of effort; when the tasks differ in irksomeness or disagreeableness, the larger product may be brought into being with a smaller expenditure of painful exertion. If men are unequal in productive power their products are obviously not in proportion to their efforts. Consider two men whose natural physical abilities are so unequal that they can handle with equal effort shovels differing in capacity by fifty per cent. Instances of this kind are innumerable in industry. If these two men are rewarded according to productivity, one will get fifty per cent more compensation than the other. Yet the surplus received by the more fortunate man does not represent any action or quality for which he is personally responsible. It corresponds to no larger output of personal effort, no superior exercise of will, no greater personal desert. It is based solely upon a richer physical endowment.

It is clear, then, that the canon of productivity cannot be accepted to the exclusion of the principles of needs and efforts. It is not the only ethical rule of distribution. Is it a valid partial rule? Superior productivity is frequently due to larger effort and expense put forth in study and in other forms of industrial preparation. In such cases it demands superior rewards by the title of efforts and sacrifices. Where, however, the greater productivity is due merely to higher native qualities, physical or mental, the greater reward is not so easily justified. For it represents no personal responsibility, will-effort, or creativeness. Nevertheless, the great majority of the more fortunately endowed think that they are unfairly treated unless they are recompensed in proportion to their products. Sometimes this conviction is due to the fact that such men wrongly attribute their larger product to greater efforts. In most cases, however, the possessors of superior productive power believe that they should be rewarded in proportion to their products, regardless of any other principle or factor.

Like the rules of equality, needs, and efforts, that of productivity cannot be universally enforced in practice. It is susceptible of accurate application among producers who perform the same kind of work with the same kind of instruments and equipment; for example, between two shovelers, two machine operators, two bookkeepers, two lawyers, two physicians. As a rule, it cannot be adequately applied to a product which is brought into existence through a combination of different processes. The engine driver and the track repairer contribute to the common product, railway transportation; the bookkeeper and the machine tender cooperate in the production of hats; but we cannot tell in either case whether the first contributes more or less than the second, for the simple reason that we have no common measure of their contributions.

Sometimes, however, we can compare the productivity of *individuals* engaged in different processes; that is, when both can be removed from the industry without causing it to come to a stop. Thus, it can be shown that a single engine driver produces more railway transportation than a single track repairer, because the labor of the latter is not indispensable to the hauling of a given load of cars. But no such comparison can be made as between the whole body of engine drivers and the whole body of track repairers, since both groups are indispensable to the production of railway transportation. Again, a man can be shown to exert superior productivity because he affects the productive process at more points and in a more intimate way than another who contributes to the product in a wholly different manner. While the surgeon and the attendant nurse are both necessary to a surgical operation, the former is clearly more productive than the latter. When due allowance is made for all such cases, the fact remains that in a large part of the industrial field it is simply impossible to determine remuneration by the rule of comparative productivity.

THE CANON OF SCARCITY

It frequently happens that men attribute their larger rewards to larger productivity, when the true determining element is scarcity. The immediate reason why the engine driver receives more than the track repairer, the general manager more than the section foreman, the floorwalker more than the salesgirl, lies in the fact that the former kinds of labor are not so plentiful as the latter. Were general managers relatively as abundant as section foremen their remuneration would be quite as low; and the same principle holds good of every pair of men whose occupations and products are different in kind. Yet the productivity of the general managers would remain as great as before. On the other hand, no matter how plentiful the more productive men may become, they can always command higher rewards than the less productive men in the same occupation, for the simple reason that their products are superior either in quantity or in quality.

Men engaged upon the more skilled tasks are likewise mistaken when they attribute their greater compensation to the intrinsic excellence of their occupation. The fact is that the community cares nothing about the relative nobility, or ingenuity, or other inherent quality of industrial tasks or functions. It is concerned solely with products and results. As between two men performing the same task, superior efficiency receives a superior reward because it issues in a larger or better product. As between two men performing different tasks, superior skill receives superior compensation simply because it can command the greater compensation; and it commands larger compensation because it is scarce.

In most cases where scarcity is the immediate determinant of rewards, the ultimate determinant is, partly at least, some kind of sacrifice. One reason why chemists and civil engineers are rarer than common laborers is to be found in the greater cost of preparation. The scarcity of workers in occupations that require no special degree of skill is due to unusual hazards and unpleasantness. In so far as scarcity is caused by the uncommon sacrifices preceding or involved in an occupation, the resulting higher rewards obviously rest upon most solid ethical grounds. However, some part of the differences in scarcity is the result of unequal opportunities. If all young persons had equal facilities for obtaining college and technical training, the supply of the higher kinds of labor would be considerably larger than it now is, and the compensation would be considerably smaller. Scarcity would then be determined by only three factors; namely, varying costs of training, varying degrees of danger and unattractiveness among occupations, and inequalities in the distribution of native ability. Competition would tend to apportion rewards according to efforts, sacrifices, and efficiency.

How can we justify the superior rewards of that scarcity which is not due to unusual costs of any sort, but merely to restricted opportunity? So far as society is concerned, the answer is simple: the practice pays. As to the possessors of the rarer kinds of ability, they are in about the same ethical position as those persons whose superior productivity is derived entirely from superior native endowment. In both cases the unusual rewards are due to factors outside the control of the recipients; to advantages which they themselves have not brought into existence. In the former case the decisive factor and advantage is opportunity; in the latter it is a gift of the Creator. In neither case can the demand for and the receipt of superior rewards be proved immoral.[1]

THE CANON OF HUMAN WELFARE

Human welfare means the well-being of all persons, considered individually as well as collectively. It includes but is not identical with public welfare or even social welfare. Not infrequently the latter phrase is synonymous with the welfare of the dominant social group. Nothing of that sort is implied here. Hence we use the word "human" rather than "social."

The canon of human welfare includes and summarizes all that is implied in the five other canons. This is its individual aspect. It requires that all human beings be treated as persons, as possessed of natural rights: this is equality. It demands that all industrial persons receive at least that amount of income which is necessary for decent living and reasonable self-development: this is a recognition of needs. The canon of human welfare declares that some consideration must be accorded to manifestations of good will by those who take part in the processes of industry: this is a recognition of efforts and sacrifices. And it gives reasonable recognition to the canons of productivity and scarcity.

Under its social aspect, the canon of human welfare authorizes the payment to every producer of that amount which is necessary to evoke his maximum *net* product. This is not necessarily the *absolute* maximum. The latter is not always worth the price demanded. In such a case human welfare may dictate an amount of compensation which is insufficient to call forth the absolute maximum. For example, a salary of $4,500 might induce a man to turn out a product which sells for $5,000, while a salary of $5,000 would evoke only the equivalent of $5,300. The latter is the absolute maximum; the former is the net maximum. Obviously it would be uneconomic and socially wasteful to give this man more than $4,500.[2] That is the amount which would be assigned to him by the canon of human welfare. When the natural rights and the essential needs of the individual have been safeguarded, all additional compensation should be determined by the rule of maximum net results.

Since the foregoing paragraphs first appeared, Pope Pius XI gave much attention and wide currency to the concept and the phrase, *social justice*.[3] It is a better and more accurate expression than "human welfare." Here is a statement of its functions: Social justice impels both individuals and public officials to promote the common good; that is, the common welfare, taken distributively as well as collectively; the good of the community, not only as a unified entity, but as composed of social groups and individuals.

CHAPTER 10

Just Profits in Conditions of Competition

We have seen that profits are that share of the product of industry which goes to the business man. They comprise that residual portion which he finds in his hands after he has made all expenditures and allowances for wages, salaries, interest at the prevailing rate on both his own and the borrowed capital, and all other proper charges. They constitute his compensation for his labor of direction, and for the risks of his enterprise and capital.

In the opinion of many, if not most, Socialists, profits are immoral because they are an essential element of an unjust industrial system, and because they are not entirely based upon labor. Under Socialism the organizing and directing functions that are now performed by the business man, would be allotted to salaried superintendents and managers. Their compensation would include no payment for the risks of capital, and it would be fixed instead of indeterminate. Hence it would differ considerably from profits.

To the assertion that profits are immoral, a sufficient reply at this time is that Socialism has already been shown to be impracticable and inequitable. Consequently the system of private industry is essentially just, and profits, being a necessary element of the system, are essentially legitimate. The question of their morality is one of degree; not of kind. It will be considered under two principal heads: The right of the business man to obtain indefinitely large profits; and his right to a certain minimum of profits.

This chapter is reprinted from *Distributive Justice: The Right and Wrong of Our Present Distribution of Wealth,* 3d ed., rev. (New York: Macmillan Co., 1942), 189–96.

THE QUESTION
OF INDEFINITELY LARGE PROFITS

As a general rule, business men who face conditions of active competition have a right to all the profits that they can get, so long as they use fair business methods. This means not merely fair and honest conduct toward competitors, and buyers and sellers, but also just and humane treatment of labor in all the conditions of employment, especially in the matter of wages. When these conditions are fulfilled, the freedom to take indefinitely large profits is justified by the canon of human welfare. The great majority of business men in competitive industries do not receive incomes in excess of their reasonable needs. Their profits do not notably exceed the salaries that they could command as hired managers, and generally are not more than sufficient to reimburse them for the cost of education and business training, and to enable them to live in reasonable conformity with the standard of living to which they have become accustomed.

Efforts and sacrifices are reflected to some extent in the different amounts of profits received by different business men. When all due allowance is made for chance, productivity, and scarcity, a considerable proportion of profits is attributable to harder labor, greater risk and worry, and larger sacrifices. Like the principle of needs, that of efforts and sacrifices is a partial justification of the business man's remuneration.

Those profits which cannot be justified by either of the titles just mentioned are ethically warranted by the principles of productivity and scarcity. This is particularly true of those exceptionally large profits which can be traced specifically to that unusual ability which is exemplified in the invention and adoption of new methods and processes in progressive industries. The receivers of these large rewards have produced them in competition with less efficient business men. While the title of productivity may not entirely satisfy the seeker for decisive ethical sanctions, it is stronger morally than any opposing considerations.

Nevertheless, it would seem that those business men who obtain exceptionally large profits could be reasonably required to transfer part of their gains to their employees in the form of higher wages, or to the consumers in the form of lower prices. While these practices are not required by strict justice, they have a solid basis in the principle of general equity or fairness;[1] indeed, they seem to be demanded by social justice. General equity is less definite than, and stands midway between, strict justice and charity. Notwithstanding its vagueness, it is sufficiently strong to make the average conscientious man feel uncomfortable if he neglects its prescriptions entirely. It seems to have sufficient application to the problem before us to justify the statement that the receivers of exceptionally large profits are bound in equity to share them with those persons who have cooperated in producing and providing them, namely, wage earners and consumers.

In the field of profits the canon of human welfare is not only sound ethically but expedient socially. It permits the great majority of business men to obtain, if they can, sufficient remuneration to meet their reasonable needs. Whether it requires society to *guarantee* at least this amount of profit-income is a question that we shall examine presently. It encourages efforts, and makes for the maximum social product by permitting business men to retain all the profits that they can get in conditions of fair competition. Does it forbid any attempt by society to limit exceptionally large profit-incomes? If the limit were placed very high, say at $50,000 per year, it would not apparently check the productive efforts of the great majority of business men, since they never hope to pass that figure. Whether it would have a seriously discouraging effect upon the activity and ambition of those who do hope to reach, and of those who have already reached that level, is uncertain. Among business men who are approaching or who have passed the $50,000 annual profit-income mark, the desire to possess more money is frequently weaker as a motive to business activity than the longing for power and the driving force of habit. At any rate, the question is not very practical. Any sustained attempt to limit competitive profits by law would require such extensive and minute supervision of business that the policy would prove to be socially intolerable and unprofitable. The espionage involved in the policy would provoke general resentment, and the amount of profits that could be diverted either to the State or to private persons would be relatively insignificant.

Thus far we have been considering the independent business man and business firm, not the joint-stock company or corporation. In the latter form of organization the labor of direction is remunerated by fixed salaries to the executive officers, while the risks of enterprise and capital are covered by the regular dividends received by the whole body of stockholders. Consequently the only revenues comparable to profits are the surplus gains that remain after wages, salaries, interest, dividends, rent, and all other expenses and charges have been met. These are apportioned through one process or another among the stockholders. On what ethical principle can they be thus distributed? The general principle of productivity, or superior productivity, is the only one available.

A corporation which, with fair methods of competition, obtains surplus gains is evidently more efficient than its competitors. Instead of awarding the fruits of this superior efficiency to the stockholders, it would be more economic and more scientific to distribute them among the active workers, from the president of the concern down to the humblest day laborer. This arrangement would return the surplus to those who had created it and would prove a powerful stimulus to sustained and increased efficiency. The stockholders, as such, do not produce the surplus. If they receive guaranteed and cumulative dividends, they have sufficient incentive to place and keep their money in the business. To pay them more than is necessary to attain these ends, is unprofitable and socially wasteful. It is contrary to the canon of human welfare. Of course, those stockholders who are also workers, whether they be officers of the corporation or ordinary employees, would and should share in the surplus; but in their capacity as workers, not as owners. Special rewards should be related to special efforts and productivity, not to mere proprietorship which is already sufficiently compensated. Until this obviously sensible plan is adopted, however, the division of surplus gains among the stockholders cannot be pronounced unjust.

THE QUESTION OF MINIMUM PROFITS

Has the business man a strict right to a minimum living profit? In other words, have all business men a right to a sufficient volume of sales at sufficiently high prices to provide them with living profits or a decent livelihood? Such a right would imply a corresponding obligation upon the consumers, or upon society, to furnish the requisite amount of demand at the required prices. Is there such a right, and such an obligation?

No industrial right is absolute. They are all conditioned by the possibilities of the industrial system, and by the desires, capacities, and actions of the persons who enter into industrial relations with one another. As we shall see later, this statement is true even of the right to a living wage. When the industrial resources are adequate, all persons of average ability who contribute a reasonable amount of labor to the productive process have a right to a decent livelihood on two conditions: First, that such labor is their only means of sustenance; and, second, that their labor is economically indispensable to those who utilize it or its product. "Economically indispensable" means that the beneficiary of the labor would rather give the equivalent of a decent livelihood for it than go without it. While both these conditions are apparently fulfilled in the case of the great majority of wage earners, they are only rarely realized with regard to business men. In most instances the business man who is unable to making living profits could become an employee, and thus convert his right to a decent livelihood into a right to a living wage.

Even when no such alternative is open to him, he cannot claim a strict right to living profits, for the second condition stated above remains unfulfilled. The consuming public does not regard the business function of such men as economically indispensable. Rather than pay the higher prices necessary to provide living profits for the inefficient business men, consumers will transfer their patronage to the efficient competitors. Should the retail grocer, for example, raise his prices in the effort to get living profits, his sales would fall off to such an extent as to reduce his profits still lower. While the consumers may be willing to fulfil their obligation of furnishing living profits for all necessary grocers, they are not willing, nor are they morally bound, to do so in the case of grocers whose inability to command sufficient patronage at remunerative prices shows that they are not necessary to the community. The consuming public does not want to employ such business men at such a cost.

Nor is the State under obligation to insure living profits for all business men. To carry out such a policy, either by enforcing a sufficiently high level of prices, or by subsidizing those who fail to obtain living profits, would be to compel the public to support inefficiency.[2]

In the foregoing paragraphs we have assumed that the inability of the business men under consideration to get living profits is due to their own lack of capacity as compared with their more efficient competitors. When, however, their competitors are not more efficient, but are enabled to undersell through the use of unfair methods, such as adulteration of goods and oppression of labor, a different moral situation is presented. Honest and humane business men undoubtedly have a claim upon society to protection against such unfair competition. And the consumers are under obligation to make reasonable efforts to withhold their patronage from those business men who practice dishonesty and extortion.

THE QUESTION
OF SUPERFLUOUS BUSINESS MEN

Although we have rejected as impractical the proposal to set a legal limit to profit-incomes, we have to admit that many of the abler business men would continue to do their best work even if the profits that they could hope to obtain were considerably smaller in volume. These men hold a strategic position in industry, inasmuch as they are not subject to the same degree of constant competition as the other agents of production.[3] Were the supply of superior business capacity more plentiful, their rewards would be automatically reduced, and the burden of profits resting upon society would be to that extent diminished. On the other hand, the number of mediocre business men, especially in the distributive industries, is much larger than is necessary to supply the wants of the community. This constitutes a second unnecessary volume of payments under the head of profits. Is there no way by which these wastes can be reduced?

The volume of exceptionally large profits could be diminished by an extension of the facilities of technical and industrial educational. Thus the number of persons qualifying as superior business men would be gradually increased, competition among this class of men would be intensified, and their rewards correspondingly diminished.

The profits that go to superfluous business men, especially in the class known as middlemen, can be largely eliminated through combination and cooperation. The tendency to unite into a single concern a large number of small and inefficient enterprises should be encouraged up to the point at which the combination threatens to become a monopoly. That this process is capable of effecting a considerable saving in business profits as well as in capital, has been amply demonstrated in several different lines of enterprise. As we have seen in a preceding chapter,* the cooperative movement, whether in banking, agriculture, or stores, has been distinctly successful in reducing profits. Millions of dollars are thus diverted every year from unnecessary profit-receivers to laborers, consumers, and to the man of small resources generally. Yet the cooperative movement is only in its infancy. It contains the possibility of eliminating entirely the superfluous business man, and even of diminishing considerably the excessive profits of the exceptionally able business man.†

---

*Editor's Note: The chapter on cooperatives, to which Ryan is referring in this paragraph, has been omitted in this edition.

†Editor's Note: Ryan's subsequent chapter on monopolies is understandably dated and has therefore been omitted.

CHAPTER 11

The Legal Limitation of Fortunes

If the measures of reform suggested in Section 1 were fully applied to our land system; if cooperative enterprise were extended to its utmost practicable limits for the correction of capitalism; if the wide extension of educational opportunities and the elimination of the surplus gains of monopolies restricted the profits of the business man to an amount strictly commensurate with his ability and risks—if all these results were accomplished the number of men who could become millionaires through their own efforts would be so small that their success would arouse popular applause rather than popular envy. Their claim to whatever wealth they might accumulate would be generally looked upon as entirely valid and reasonable. Their pecuniary eminence would be as willingly accepted as the literary eminence of a Lowell, the scientific eminence of a Pasteur, or the political eminence of a Lincoln.

In the meantime, these reforms are not realized, nor are they likely to be within the present generation. For some time to come it will be possible for the exceptionally able, the exceptionally cunning, and the exceptionally lucky to accumulate great riches through clever and fortuitous utilization of special advantages, natural and otherwise. Moreover, a great proportion of the large fortunes already in existence will persist, and will be transmitted to heirs who will in many cases cause them to increase. Can nothing be done to reduce these great accumulations? If so, is such a proceeding socially and morally desirable?

THE METHOD OF DIRECT LIMITATION

The law might directly limit the amount of property to be held by any individual. If the limit were placed fairly high, say at one hundred thousand dollars,

This chapter is reprinted from *Distributive Justice: The Right and Wrong of Our Present Distribution of Wealth,* 3d ed., rev. (New York: Macmillan Co., 1942), 223–32.

it could scarcely be regarded as an infringement on the right of property. In the case of a family numbering ten members, this would mean one million dollars. All the essential objects of private ownership could be abundantly met out of a sum of one hundred thousand dollars for each person. Moreover, a restriction of this sort need not prevent a man from bestowing unlimited amounts upon charitable, religious, educational, or other benevolent causes. It would, indeed, hinder some persons from satisfying certain unessential wants, such as the desire to enjoy gross or refined luxuries, great financial power, and the control of immense industrial enterprises; but none of these objects is necessary for any individual's genuine welfare.

Such a restriction would no more constitute a direct attack upon private ownership than limitations upon the use and kinds of property. At present a man may not do what he pleases with his gun, his horse, or his automobile, nor may he invest his money in the business of carrying the mails. The limitation of fortunes is just what the word expresses, a *limitation* of the right of property. It is not a denial nor *destruction* of that right. It does not differ in principle from a restriction upon the kinds of goods that may become the subject of private ownership. There is nothing in the nature of things nor in the purpose of property to indicate that the right of ownership is unlimited in quantity any more than it is in quality. The final end and justification of individual rights of property is human welfare; that is, the welfare of all individuals severally and collectively. Now it is quite within the bounds of physical possibility that the limitation under discussion might be conducive to the welfare of human beings both as individuals and as constituting society.

Nevertheless the dangers and obstacles confronting any legal restriction of fortunes are so real as to render the proposal socially inexpedient. It would easily lend itself to grave abuse. Once the community had habituated itself to a direct limitation of any sort, the temptation to lower it in the interest of better distribution and simpler living would become exceedingly powerful. Eventually the right of property might take such an attenuated and uncertain form in the public mind as to discourage labor and initiative, and thus seriously to endanger human welfare. In the second place, the manifold evasions to which the measure would lend itself would make it of very doubtful efficacy. To be sure, neither of these objections is absolutely conclusive, but taken together they are sufficiently weighty to dictate that such a proposal should not be entertained so long as other and less dangerous methods are available to meet the problem of excessive fortunes.

Four of the nine members of the Federal Commission on Industrial Relations suggested that the amount of property capable of being received by the heirs of any person be limited to one million dollars.[1] If we assume that by heirs the Commission meant the natural persons to whom property might come by bequest or succession, this limitation would permit a family of ten persons to inherit one hundred thousand dollars each, and a family of five persons to obtain two hundred thousand dollars apiece. Would such a restriction be a violation of the right of private ownership? The answer depends upon the effects of the measure on human welfare. The rights of bequest and succession are integral elements of the right of ownership; hence they are based upon human needs, and designed for the promotion of human life and development. A person needs private property not only to provide for his personal wants and those of his family during his lifetime, but also to safeguard the welfare of his dependents and to assist other worthy purposes, after he has passed away. Owing to the uncertainty of death, the latter objects cannot be adequately realized without the institutions of bequest and succession.

All the necessary and rational ends of bequest and succession could be attained in a society in which no man's heirs could inherit more than one million dollars. Under such an arrangement very few of the children of millionaires would be prevented from getting at least one hundred thousand dollars. That much would be amply sufficient for the essential and reasonable needs of any human being. Indeed, we may go further, and lay down the proposition that the overwhelming majority of persons can lead a more virtuous and reasonable life on the basis of a fortune of one hundred thousand dollars than when burdened with any larger amount. The persons who have the desire and the ability to use a greater sum than this in a rational way are so few that a limitation law need not take them into account. Corporate persons, such as hospitals, churches, schools, and other helpful institutions, should not, as a rule, be restricted as to the amount that they might inherit; for many of them could make a good use of more than the amount that suffices for a natural person.

So much for the welfare and rights of the beneficiaries of inheritance. The owners of estates would not be injured in their rights of property by the limitation that we are here considering. In the first place, the number of persons practically affected by the limitation would be extremely small. Only an insignificant fraction of property owners ever transmit or expect to be wealthy enough to transmit to their families more than one million dollars. Of these few a considerable proportion would not be deterred by the million dollar limitation from putting forth their best and greatest efforts in a productive way. They would continue to work either from force of habit and love of their accustomed tasks, or from a desire to make large gifts to their heirs during life, or because they wished to assist some benevolent enterprise. The infinitesimally small number whose energies would be diminished by the limitation could be treated as a socially negligible element. The community would be better off without them.

The limitation of inheritance would, indeed, be liable to abuse. Circumstances would undoubtedly arise in which the community would be strongly tempted to make the maximum inheritable amount so low as to discourage the desire of acquisition, and to deprive heirs of reasonable protection. While the bad effects of such a limitation would not be as great as those following a similar abuse with regard to possessions, they are sufficiently grave and sufficiently probable to suggest that the legal restriction of bequest and succession should not be considered except as a last resort, and when the transmission of great fortunes had become a great and certain public evil.

It seems reasonable to conclude, then, that neither the limitation of possessions nor the limitation of inheritance is necessarily a direct violation of the right of property, but that the possible and even probable evil consequences of both are so grave as to make these measures of very doubtful benefit. Whether the dangers in question are sufficiently great to render the adoption of either proposal morally wrong, is a question that cannot be answered with any degree of confidence. What seems to be fairly certain is that in our present conditions legislation of this sort would be an unnecessary and unwise experiment.

LIMITATION THROUGH PROGRESSIVE TAXATION

Is it legitimate and feasible to reduce great fortunes indirectly, through taxation? There is certainly no objection to the method on moral or social principles. As we have seen in an earlier chapter, taxes are not levied exclusively for the purpose of raising revenue. Some kinds of them are designed to promote social rather than fiscal ends. Now, to prevent and diminish dangerous accumulations of wealth is a social end which is at least as important as most of the objects sought in license taxes. The propriety of attempting to attain this end by taxation is to be determined entirely by reference to its probable effectiveness.

The method of taxation available is a progressive tax on incomes, inheritances, and excess profits. By a progressive tax is meant one whose rate advances in some definite proportion to the increases in the amount taxed. For example, a bequest of $100,000 might pay five per cent; $200,000, ten per cent; $300,000, fifteen per cent, and so forth. The reasonableness of the principle of progression in taxation has been well stated by Professor Seligman: "All individual wants vary in intensity, from the absolutely necessary wants of mere subsistence to the less pressing wants which can be satisfied by pure luxuries. Taxes, in so far as they rob us of the means of satisfying our wants, impose a sacrifice upon us. But the sacrifice involved in giving up a portion of what enables us to satisfy our necessary wants is very different from the sacrifice involved in giving up what is necessary to satisfy our less urgent wants. If two men have incomes of one thousand dollars and one hundred thousand dollars respectively, we impose upon them not equal but very unequal sacrifices if we take away from each the same proportion, say ten per cent. For the one thousand dollar individual now has only nine hundred dollars, and must deprive himself and his family of necessaries of life; the one hundred thousand dollar individual has ninety thousand dollars, and if he retrenches at all, which is very doubtful, he will give up only great luxuries, which do not satisfy any pressing wants. The sacrifice imposed on the two individuals is not equal. We are laying on the one thousand dollar man a far heavier sacrifice than on the one hundred thousand dollar man. In order to impose equal sacrifices we must tax the richer man not only absolutely, but relatively, more than the poor man. The taxes must be not proportional, but progressive; the rate must be lower in the one case than in the other."[2]

The principle of equality of sacrifices which underlies the progressive theory does not justify the leveling and communistic inferences that have sometimes been drawn from it. Equality of sacrifice does not mean equality of satisfied, or unsatisfied, wants after the tax has been collected. If Brown pays a tax of one per cent on his income of two thousand dollars, it does not follow that Jones with an income of ten thousand dollars should pay a sufficiently high rate to leave him with only the net amount remaining to Brown; namely, $1,980. Equality of sacrifice means proportional equality of burden, not equality of net resources after the tax has been deducted. The object of the progressive rate is to make relatively equal the sacrifices *caused by the tax itself*, not to equalize burdens or unsatisfied wants.

Another objection to progressive taxation is that it readily lends itself to confiscation of the largest incomes. All that is necessary to produce this result is to increase the rate with sufficient rapidity. This could be accomplished either by large steps in the rate itself or by small steps in the income increases which formed the basis of the advances in the rate. If a surtax of one per cent on incomes above $10,000 were increased geometrically with every increase of income specified in the schedules, it would be 256 per cent on incomes above $20,000! Should the rate increase arithmetically with every additional $1,000 of income it would reach 100 per cent on incomes above $60,000!

To this objection there are two valid answers. Even if the rate should ultimately reach one hundred per cent it need not, and on progressive principles it should not, effect confiscation of an entire income. The progressive theory is satisfied when the successive rates of the tax apply to successive increments of income, instead of to the entire income. For example, the rate might begin at one per cent on incomes of one thousand dollars, and increase by one per cent with every additional thousand, and yet leave a very large part of the income in the hands of the receiver. Each one thousand dollars would be taxed at a different rate, the first at one per cent, the fiftieth at fifty per cent, and the last at one hundred per cent. If the hundred per cent rate were applied to the whole of the higher incomes, it would be a direct violation of the principle of equality of sacrifice. In the second place, the progressive theory forbids rather than requires the rate to go as high as one hundred per cent. While the sacrifices imposed by a given rate are greater in the case of small than of large properties, they become approximately equal as between all properties above a certain high level. After this level is reached, additional increments of wealth will all be expended either for extreme luxuries, or converted into new investments. Consequently they will supply wants of approximately equal intensity. For example, the wants dependent upon a surplus of $25,000 in excess of an income of $100,000, and the wants dependent upon a surplus of $75,000 above the same level do not differ materially in strength. To diminish these surpluses by the same per cent, say, ten, would impose equal burdens.

In the years immediately following the Great War, progressive Federal taxes in the United States attained very high levels. On incomes, the maximum normal tax was twelve per cent and the maximum surtax, sixty-five per cent. Incomes above $1,000,000 paid seventy-seven per cent of the amount by which they exceeded that figure. In 1919 the *average* rate on the *whole* of such incomes was 64.87 per cent. The highest rate in a Federal inheritance tax was fifty per cent, applying to the amounts by which estates exceeded $5,000,000.

The tax law to provide revenue for the national defense program, enacted in late September, 1941, and known as the "Revenue Act of 1941," reduces the exemptions to $750 for single persons and $1500 for married persons. The normal rate on personal incomes is four per cent. The surtax rates are applicable to the first dollar of net income and progress from six per cent to seventy-seven per cent.

Following are some significant rates and amounts from the surtax table:

Net Income	*Surtax*
Not over $2,000	6% of the surtax net income.
Over $18,000 but not over $20,000	$3,740, plus 38% of excess over $18,000.
Over $44,000 but not over $50,000	$16,080, plus 55% of excess over $44,000.
Over $90,000 but not over $100,000	$43,380, plus 64% of excess over $90,000.
Over $750,000 but not over $1,000,000	$508,780, plus 74% of excess over $750,000.
Over $5,000,000	$3,723,780, plus 77% of excess over $5,000,000.

The Estate (Inheritance) Tax rates have a universal application, beginning at three per cent and ending at seventy-seven per cent. Following are some significant rates and amounts:

Net Estate	*Tax*
Not over $5,000	3% of the net estate.
Over $50,000 but not over $60,000	$7,000, plus 25% of excess over $50,000.
Over $100,000 but not over $250,000	$20,700, plus 30% of excess over $100,000.

Over $1,000,000 but not over
$1,250,000

$325,700, plus 39% of excess over
$1,000,000.

Over $2,500,000 but not over
$3,000,000

$998,200, plus 53% of excess over
$2,500,000.

Over $10,000,000

$6,088,200, plus 77% of excess over
$10,000,000.

The Excess Profits Tax applies to all profits on invested capital in excess of eight per cent. The tax rate begins at thirty-five per cent and reaches sixty per cent. Following are all the rates and amounts which are found in the law:

Excess Profits Net Income	*Tax*
Not over $20,000	35% of the adjusted excess profits net income.
Over $20,000 but not over $50,000	$7,000, plus 40% of excess over $20,000.
Over $50,000 but not over $100,000	$19,000, plus 45% of excess over $50,000.
Over $100,000 but not over $250,000	$41,500, plus 50% of excess over $100,000.
Over $250,000 but not over $500,000	$116,500, plus 55% of excess over $250,000.
Over $500,000	$254,000, plus 60% of excess over $500,000.[3]

On all three of the subjects of taxation described above, the rates are considerably higher than in the law enacted during the World War. In all probability, the rates exhibit some inequities as between incomes and estates of different magnitude, but it would be difficult to prove that the rates, as a whole, are unjust or excessive. Their power to prevent and reduce great fortunes indirectly is obvious.

CHAPTER 12

The Duty of Distributing
Superfluous Wealth

The correctives of the present distribution that were proposed before the beginning of the last chapter related mainly to the apportionment of the product
among the agents of production. They would affect that distribution which takes
place as an integral element of the productive process, not the shares that they
had acquired therefrom. Such were many of the proposals regarding land tenure,
and all of those concerning cooperative enterprises and monopoly. In the last
chapter we considered the possibility of neutralizing to some extent the abuses of
the primary distribution by the action of government through the taxation of
large fortunes. These were proposals directly affecting the secondary distribution.
And they involved the method of compulsion. In the present chapter we shall in-
quire whether desirable changes in the secondary distribution may not be effected
by voluntary action. The specific questions confronting us here are, whether and
how far proprietors are morally bound to distribute their superfluous wealth
among their less fortunate fellows.

THE QUESTION OF DISTRIBUTING SOME

The authority of revealed religion returns to the first of these questions a clear
and emphatic answer in the affirmative. The Old and the New Testaments
abound in declarations that possessors are under very strict obligation to give of
their surplus to the indigent. Perhaps the most striking expression of this teaching is that found in the Gospel according to St. Matthew, ch. 25, verses 32–46,
where eternal happiness is awarded to those who have fed the hungry, given drink

This chapter is reprinted from *Distributive Justice: The Right and Wrong of Our Present Distribution of
Wealth,* 3d ed., rev. (New York: Macmillan Co., 1942), 233–45.

to the thirsty, received the stranger, covered the naked, visited the sick, and called upon the imprisoned; and eternal damnation is meted out to those who have failed in these respects. The principle that ownership is stewardship, that the man who possesses superfluous goods must regard himself as a trustee for the needy, is fundamental and all-pervasive in the teaching of Christianity. No more clear or concise statement of it has ever been given than that of St. Thomas Aquinas: "As regards the power of acquiring and dispensing material goods, man may lawfully possess them as his own; as regards their use, however, a man ought not to look upon them as his own, but as common, so that he may readily minister to the needs of others."[1]

Reason likewise enjoins the benevolent distribution of surplus wealth. It reminds the proprietor that his needy neighbors have the same nature, the same faculties, capacities, wants, and destiny as himself. They are his equals and his brothers. Reason, therefore, requires that he should esteem them as such, love them as such, and treat them as such; that he should love them not merely by well wishing, but by well doing. Since the goods of the earth were intended by the Creator for the common benefit of all mankind, the possessor of a surplus is reasonably required to use it in such a way that this original purpose of all created goods shall be fulfilled. To refuse is to treat one's less fortunate neighbor as something different from and less than oneself, as a creature whose claim upon the common bounty of nature is something less than one's own. Multiplying words will not make these truths plainer. The man who does not admit that the welfare of his neighbor is of equal moral worth and importance with his own welfare, will logically refuse to admit that he is under any obligation of distributing his superfluous goods. The man who does acknowledge this essential equality will be unable to find any logical basis for such refusal.

Is this obligation one of charity or one of justice? At the outset a distinction must be made between wealth that has been honestly acquired and wealth that has come into one's possession through some violation of rights. The latter kind must, of course, be restored to those persons who have been wronged. If they cannot be found or identified the ill-gotten gains must be turned over to charitable or other worthy objects. Since the goods do not belong to the present holder by any valid moral title, they should be given to those persons who are qualified by the claim and title of needs.

Some of the Fathers of the Church maintained that all superfluous wealth, whether well or ill gotten, ought to be distributed to those in want. St. Basil of Cæsarea: "Will not the man who robs another of his clothing be called a thief? Is the man who is able and refuses to clothe the naked deserving of any other appellation? The bread that you withhold belongs to the hungry; the cloak that you retain in your chest belongs to the naked; the shoes that are decaying in your possession belong to the shoeless; the gold that you have hidden in the ground belongs to the indigent. Wherefore, as often as you were able to help men and refused, so often you did them wrong."[2] St. Augustine of Hippo: "The superfluities of the rich are the necessities of the poor. They who possess superfluities possess the goods of others."[3] St. Ambrose of Milan: "The earth belongs to all; not to the rich; but those who possess their shares are fewer than those who do not. Therefore, you are paying a debt, not bestowing a gift."[4] Pope Gregory the Great: "When we give necessaries to the needy, we do not bestow upon them our goods; we return to them their own; we pay a debt of justice rather than of mercy."[5]

The great systematizer of theology in the thirteenth century, St. Thomas Aquinas, who is universally recognized as the most authoritative private teacher in the Church, stated the obligation of distribution in less extreme and more scientific terms: "According to the order of nature instituted by Divine Providence, · the goods of the earth are designed to supply the needs of men. The division of goods and their appropriation through human law do not thwart this purpose. Therefore, the goods which a man has in superfluity are due by the natural law to the sustenance of the poor."[6]

That this is the official teaching of the Church to-day is evident from the words of Pope Leo XIII: "When one has provided sufficiently for one's necessities and the demands of one's state of life, there is a duty to give to the indigent out of what remains. It is a duty not of strict justice, save in case of extreme necessity, but of Christian charity."[7] Nearly thirteen year earlier, the same Pope had written: "The Church lays the rich under strict command to give their superfluity to the poor."[8]

In 1931, Pope Pius XI said:

> At the same time a man's superfluous income is not left entirely to his own discretion. We speak of that portion of his income which he does not need in order to live as becomes his station. On the contrary, the grave obligations of charity, beneficence and liberality which rest upon the wealthy are constantly insisted upon in telling words by Holy Scriptures and the Fathers of the Church.[9]

The only difference between the Fathers and the three authorities just quoted on this question, has reference to the precise nature of the obligation. According to the Fathers, the duty of distribution would seem to be a duty of justice. In the passage quoted above from St. Thomas, superfluities are said to "belong," or to be "due" (*debetur*) to the needy; but the particular moral precept that applies is not specified. In another place, however, the Angelic Doctor declares that almsgiving is an act of charity.[10] When Pope Leo XIII says "except in extreme cases," he is referring to the traditional doctrine that a person in extreme need, that is, in immediate danger of losing life, limb, or some equivalent personal good, is justified in the absence of any other means of succor in taking from his neighbor what is absolutely necessary. Such appropriation, says St. Thomas, is not, properly speaking, theft; for the goods seized belong to the needy person, "inasmuch as he must sustain life."[11] In a word, the medieval and the modern Catholic teaching would make the distribution of superfluous goods a duty of justice only in extreme situations, while the Fathers laid down no such specific limitation.

Nevertheless, the difference is less important than it appears to be on the surface. When the Fathers lived, theology had not been systematized nor given a precise terminology; consequently, they did not always make exact distinctions between the different classes of virtues and obligations. In the second place, the Patristic passages that we have quoted, and others of like import, were mostly contained in sermons addressed to the rich, and consequently were expressed in hortatory rather than scientific terms. Moreover, the needs of the time which the rich were exhorted to relieve were probably so urgent that they could correctly be classed as extreme, and therefore would give rise to an obligation of justice on the part of those who possessed superfluous wealth, at least, in the great majority of instances.

The important fact of the whole situation is that both the Fathers and the later authorities of the Church regard the task of distributing superfluous goods as one of strict moral obligation, which in serious cases is binding under pain of grievous sin. Whether it falls under the head of justice or of charity, is of no great practical consequence.

THE QUESTION OF DISTRIBUTING ALL

Is a man obliged to distribute *all* of his superfluous wealth? As regards the support of human life, Catholic moral theologians distinguish three classes of goods: First, the necessaries of life, those utilities which are essential to a healthy and humane existence for a man and his family, regardless of the social position that he may occupy, or the standard of life to which he may have been accustomed; second, the conventional necessities and comforts, which correspond to the social plane upon which the individual or family moves; third, those goods which are not required to support either existence or social position. Goods of the second class are said to be necessary as regards conventional purposes, but superfluous as regards the maintenance of life, while those of the third class are superfluous without qualification.

No obligation exists to distribute the first class of goods; for the possessor is justified in preferring his own primary and fundamental needs to the equal or less important needs of his neighbors. The owner of goods of the second class is under obligation to contribute something to persons who are in extreme need, since the preservation of the neighbor's life is more important morally than the full maintenance of the owner's conventional standard of living. On the other hand, there is no obligation of giving any of these goods to meet those needs of the neighbor which are social or conventional. Here, again, it is reasonable that the possessor should prefer his own interests to the equal interests of his fellows. Still less is he obliged to expend any of the second class of goods for the relief of ordinary or common distress. As regards the third class of goods, those which are absolutely superfluous, the proportion to be distributed is indefinite, depending upon the volume of need. The doctrine of the moral theologians on the subject is summed up in the following paragraph.

When the needs to be supplied are "ordinary," or "common;" that is, when they merely expose a person to considerable and constant inconvenience, without inflicting serious physical, mental, or moral injury, they do not impose upon any man the obligation of giving up all his superfluous goods. According to some moral theologians, the possessor fulfils his duty in such cases if he contributes that proportion of his surplus which would suffice for the removal of all such distress, provided that all other possessors were equally generous; according to others, if he gives two per cent of his superfluity; according to others, if he contributes two per cent of his annual income. These estimates are intended not so much to define the exact measure of obligation as to emphasize the fact that there exists some degree of obligation; for all the moral theologians agree that some portion of a man's superfluous goods ought to be given for the relief of ordinary or common needs. When, however, the distress is grave; that is, when it is seriously detrimental to welfare; for example, when a man or a family is in danger of falling to a lower social plane; when health, morality, or the intellectual or religious life is menaced,—possessors are required to contribute as much of their superfluous goods as is necessary to meet all such cases of distress. If all is needed all must be given. In other words, the entire mass of superfluous wealth is morally subject to the call of grave need. This seems to be the unanimous teaching of the moral theologians.[12] It is also in harmony with the general principle of the moral law that the goods of the earth should be enjoyed by the inhabitants of the earth in proportion to their essential needs. In any rational distribution of a common heritage, the claims of health, mind, and morals are surely superior to the demands of luxurious living, or investment, or mere accumulation.

SOME OBJECTIONS

Against such a thoroughgoing distribution of superfluous incomes it may be urged that a considerable part of the capital and organizing ability in industry are dependent upon the possession of superfluous goods by the richer classes. That surplus of the larger incomes which is not consumed or given away by its receivers, constitutes a very large portion of the whole supply of savings annually converted into capital. Were all of it to be withdrawn from industry and distributed among the needy, the process might involve more harm than good. Moreover, the very large industrial enterprises are initiated and carried on by men who have themselves provided a considerable share of the necessary funds. Without these large masses of personal capital, they would have much more difficulty in organizing these great enterprises, and would be unable to exercise their present dominating control.

To the first part of this objection we may reply that the distribution of superfluous goods need not involve any considerable withdrawal of existing capital from industry. The giving of large amounts to institutions and organizations, as distinguished from needy individuals, might mean merely a transfer of capital from one holder to another; for example, the stocks and bonds of corporations. The capital would be left intact, the only change being in the persons that would thenceforth receive the interest. Small donations could come out of the possessor's income. Moreover, there is no reason why the whole of the distribution could not be made out of income rather than out of capital. While the givers would still remain possessed of superfluous wealth, they would have handed over to needy objects, persons, and causes the thing that in modern times constitutes the soul and essence of wealth; namely, its annual revenues.

The second difficulty noted above, that such a thorough distribution of superfluous goods would lessen considerably the power of the captains of industry to organize and operate great enterprises, can be disposed of very briefly. Those who made the distribution from income rather than from invested wealth would still retain control of large masses of capital. All, however, would have deprived themselves of the power to enlarge their business ventures by turning great quantities of their own income back into industry. But if their ability and character were such as to command the confidence of investors, they would be able to find sufficient capital elsewhere to equip and carry on any sound and necessary enterprise. In this case the process of accumulating the required funds would, indeed, be slower than when they used their own, but that would not be an unmixed disadvantage. When the business was finally established, it would probably be more stable, would respond to a more definite and considerable need, and would be more beneficial socially, inasmuch as it would include a larger proportion of the population among its proprietors. And the diminished authority and control exercised by the great capitalist, on account of his diminished ownership of the stock, would in the long run be a good thing for society. It would mean the curtailment of a species of power that is easily liable to abuse, wider opportunities of industrial leadership, and a more democratic and stable industrial system.[13]

Only a comparatively small portion of the superfluous goods of the country could with advantage be immediately and directly distributed among needy individuals. The greater part would do more good if it were given to religious and benevolent institutions and enterprises. Churches, schools, scholarships, hospitals, asylums, housing projects, insurance against unemployment, sickness and old age, and benevolent and scientific purposes generally, constitute the best objects of effective distribution. By these means social and individual efficiency would be so improved within a few years that the distress due to economic causes would for the most part have disappeared.

The proposition that men are under moral obligation to give away the greater portion of their superfluous goods or income is, indeed, a "hard saying." Not improbably it will strike the majority of persons who read these pages as extreme and fantastic. No Catholic, however, who knows the traditional teaching of the Church on the right use of wealth, and who considers patiently and seriously the magnitude and the meaning of human distress, will be able to refute the proposition by reasoned arguments. Indeed, no one can logically deny it who admits that men are intrinsically sacred, and essentially equal by nature and in their claims to a reasonable livelihood from the common heritage of the earth. The wants that a man supplies out of his superfluous goods are not necessary for rational existence. For the most part they bring him merely irrational enjoyment, greater social prestige, or increased domination over his fellows. Judged by any reasonable standard, these are surely less important than those needs of the neighbor which are connected with humane living. If any considerable part of the community rejects these propositions the explanation will be found not in a reasoned theory, but in the conventional assumption that a man may do what he likes with his own. This assumption is adopted without examination, without criticism, without any serious advertence to the great moral facts that ownership is stewardship, and that the Creator intended the goods of the earth for the reasonable support of all the children of men.

A FALSE CONCEPTION OF WELFARE

If all the present owners of superfluous goods were to carry out their own conception of the obligation, the amount distributed would be only a fraction of the real superabundance. Let us recall the definition of absolute superfluity as that portion of individual or family income which is not required for the reasonable maintenance of life and social position. It allows, of course, a reasonable provision for the future. But the great majority of possessors, as well as perhaps the majority of others, do not interpret their needs, whether of life or social position, in any such strict fashion. Those who acquire a surplus over their present absolute and conventional needs, generally devote it to an expansion of social position. They move into larger and more expensive houses, thereby increasing their assumed requirements, not merely in the matter of housing, but as regards food, clothing, amusements, and the conventions of the social group with which they become affiliated. In this way the surplus which ought to have been distributed is all absorbed in the acquisition and maintenance of more expensive standards.

All classes of possessors adopt and act upon an exaggerated conception of both the strict and the conventional necessities. In taking this course, they are merely subscribing to the current theory of life and welfare. It is commonly assumed that to be worthwhile life must include the continuous and indefinite increase of the number and variety of wants, and a corresponding growth and variation in the means of satisfying them. Very little endeavor is made to distinguish between kinds of wants, or to arrange them in any definite scale of moral importance. Desires for purely physical goods, such as, food, drink, adornment, and sense gratifications generally, are put on the same level with the demands of the spiritual, moral, and intellectual faculties. The value and importance of any and all wants are determined mainly by the criterion of enjoyment. In the great majority of cases this means a preference for the goods and experiences that minister to the senses. Since these satisfactions are susceptible of indefinite increase, variety, and cost, the believer in this theory of life-values readily assumes that no practical limit can be set to the amount of goods or income that will be required to make life continuously and progressively worth living. Hence the question whether he has superfluous goods, how much of a surplus he has, or how much he is obliged to distribute, scarcely occurs to him at all. Everything that he possesses is included among the necessaries of life and social position. He adopts as his working theory of life those propositions which were condemned as "scandalous and pernicious" by Pope Innocent XI in 1679: "It is scarcely possible to find among people engaged in worldly pursuits, even among kings, goods that are superfluous to social position. Therefore, hardly any one is bound to give alms from this source."[14]

The practical consequences of this false conception of welfare are naturally most conspicuous among the rich, especially the very rich, but they are also manifest among the comfortable and middle classes. In every social group above the limit of very moderate circumstances, too much money is spent for material goods and enjoyments, and too little for intellectual, religious, and altruistic things.

THE TRUE CONCEPTION OF WELFARE

This working creed of materialism is condemned by right reason, as well as by Christianity. The teaching of Christ on the worth of material goods is expressed substantially in the following texts: "Woe to you rich." "Blessed are you poor." "Lay not up for yourselves treasures on earth." "For a man's life consisteth not in the abundance of things that he possesseth." "Be not solicitous as to what you shall eat, or what you shall drink, or what you shall put on." "Seek ye first the kingdom of God and His justice, and all these things shall be added unto you." "You cannot serve God and Mammon." "If thou wouldst be perfect, go, sell what thou hast and give to the poor, and come follow Me." Reason informs us that neither our faculties nor the goods that satisfy them are of equal moral worth or importance. The intellectual and spiritual faculties are essentially and intrinsically higher than the sense faculties. Only in so far as they promote, either negatively or positively, the development of the mind and soul have the senses any reasonable claim to satisfaction. They have no value in themselves; they are merely instruments to the welfare of the spirit, the intellect, and the distinterested will. Right life consists, not in the indefinite satisfaction of material wants, but in the progressive endeavor to know the best that is to be known, and to love the best that is to be loved; that is, God and His creatures in the order of their importance. The man who denies the intrinsic superiority of the soul to the senses, who puts sense gratifications on the same level of importance as the activities of mind and spirit and disinterested will, logically holds that the most degrading actions are equally good and commendable with those which mankind approves as the noblest.

Those who accept the view of life and welfare taught by Christianity and reason cannot, if they take the trouble to consider the matter, avoid the conclusion that the amount of material goods which can be expended in the rational and justifiable satisfaction of the senses, is very much smaller than is to-day assumed by the great majority of persons. Somewhere between ten and twenty thousand dollars a year lies the maximum expenditure that any family can reasonably devote to its material wants. This is independent of the outlay for education, religion, and charity, and the things of the mind generally. In the overwhelming majority of cases in which more than ten to twenty thousand dollars are expended for the satisfaction of material needs, some injury is done to the higher life. The interests of health, intellect, spirit, or morals would be better promoted if the outlay for material things were kept below the specified limit.

The distribution advocated in this chapter is obviously no substitute for justice or the deeds of justice. Inasmuch, however, as complete justice is a long way from realization, a serious attempt by the possessors of true superfluous goods to fulfill their obligations of distribution would greatly counteract and soften existing injustice, inequality, and suffering. Hence, benevolent giving deserves a place in any complete statement of proposals for a better distribution of wealth. Moreover, we are not likely to make great advances on the road of strict justice until we acquire saner conceptions of welfare, and a more effective notion of brotherly love. So long as men put the senses above the soul, they will be unable to see clearly what is justice, and unwilling to practice the little that they are able to see. Those who exaggerate the value of sense gratifications cannot be truly charitable, and those who are not truly charitable cannot perform adequate justice. The achievement of social justice requires not merely changes in the social mechanism, but a change in the social spirit, a reformation in men's hearts. To this end nothing could be more immediately helpful than a comprehensive recognition of the stewardship of wealth, and the duty of distributing superfluous goods.

The Moral Aspect of Wages

CHAPTER 13

Some Erroneous Theories
of Wage Justice

"It may be that we are not merely chasing a will-o'-the-wisp when we are hunting for a reasonable wage, but we are at any rate seeking the unattainable."

Thus wrote Professor Frank Haight Dixon in a paper read at the twenty-seventh annual meeting of the American Economic Association, December, 1914. Whether he reflected the opinion of the majority of the economists, he at least gave expression to a thought that has frequently suggested itself to everyone who has gone into the wage question free from prejudices and preconceived theories. One of the most palpable indications of the difficulty to which Professor Dixon refers is the number of doctrines concerning wage justice that have been laboriously built up during the Christian era, and that have failed to approve themselves to the majority of students and thinkers. In the present chapter the attempt is made to set forth some of the most important of these doctrines, and to show wherein they are defective. They can all be grouped under these heads: The Prevailing-Rate Theory; Exchange-Equivalence Theories; and Productivity Theories.

I. THE PREVAILING-RATE THEORY

This is not so much a systematic doctrine as a rule of expediency devised to meet concrete situations in the absence of any better guiding principle. Both its basis and its nature are well exemplified in the following extract from the Report of the Board of Arbitration in the Matter of the Controversy Between the Eastern Railroads and the Brotherhood of Locomotive Engineers:[1] "Possibly there should be some theoretical relation for a given branch of industry between the

This chapter is reprinted from *Distributive Justice: The Right and Wrong of Our Present Distribution of Wealth*, 3d ed., rev. (New York: Macmillan Co., 1942), 249–68.

amount of the income that should go to labor and the amount that should go to capital; and if this question were decided, a scale of wages might be devised for the different classes of employees which would determine the amount rightly absorbed by labor. . . . Thus far, however, political economy is unable to furnish such a principle as that suggested. There is no generally accepted theory of the division between capital and labor. . . .

"What, then, is the basis upon which a judgment may be passed as to whether the existing wage scale of the engineers in the Eastern District is fair and reasonable? It seems to the Board that the only practicable basis is to compare the rates and earnings of engineers in the Eastern District with those of engineers in the Western and Southern Districts, and with those of other classes of railway employees."

Six of the seven men composing this board of arbitration subscribed to this statement. Of the six one is the president of a great state university, another is a successful and large-minded merchant, the third is a great building contractor, the fourth is a distinguished lawyer, the fifth is a prominent magazine editor, and the sixth is a railway president. The dissenting member represented the employees. Since the majority could not find in any generally accepted theory a principle to determine the proper division of the product between capital and labor, they were perhaps justified in falling back upon the practical rule that they adopted.

Not in Harmony with Justice

From the viewpoint of justice, however, this rule or standard is utterly inadequate. It is susceptible of two interpretations. "Wages prevailing elsewhere," may mean either the highest rates or those most frequently occurring. According to the latter understanding, only those wages which were below the majority rates should be raised, while all those above that level ought to be lowered. In almost all cases this would mean a reduction of the highest wages, as these are usually paid only to a minority of the workers of any grade. The adoption of the highest existing rates as a standard would involve no positive losses, but it would set a rigid limit to all possible gains in the future. According to either interpretation of the prevailing rate, the increases in wages which a powerful labor union seeks to obtain are unjust until they have been established as the prevailing rates. Thus, the attorney for the street railways of Chicago dissented from the increases in wages awarded to the employees by the majority of the board of arbitration in the summer of 1915 because, "these men are already paid not only a fair wage but a liberal wage, when the wages in the same employment and the living conditions in other large cities are taken into consideration, or when comparison is made of these men's annual earnings with the earnings in any comparable line of work in the city of Chicago."[2] In other words, the dominant thing is always the right thing. Justice is determined by the preponderance of economic force. Now, a rule such as this, which condemns improvement until improvement has somehow become general, which puts a premium upon physical and intellectual strength, and which disregards entirely the moral claims of human needs, efforts, and sacrifices, is obviously not an adequate measure of either reason or justice. And we may well doubt that it would be formally accepted as such by any competent and disinterested student of industrial relations.

II. EXCHANGE-EQUIVALENCE THEORIES

According to these theories, the determining factor of wage justice is to be found in the wage contract. The basic idea is the idea of equality, inasmuch as equality is the fundamental element in the concept of justice. The principle of justice requires that equality should be maintained between what is owed to a person and what is returned to him, between the kinds of treatment accorded to different persons in the same circumstances. Similarly it requires that equality should obtain between the things that are exchanged in onerous contracts. An onerous contract is one in which both parties undergo some privation, and neither intends to confer a gratuity upon the other. Each exchanger desires to obtain the full equivalent of the thing that he transfers. Since each is equal in personal dignity and intrinsic worth to the other, each has a strict right to this full equivalent. Owing to the essential moral equality of all men, no man has a right to make of another a mere instrument to his own interests through physical force or through an onerous contract. Men have equal rights not only to subsist upon the earth, but to receive benefits from the exchange of goods.

The Rule of Equal Gains

The agreement between employer and employee is an onerous contract; hence it ought to be made in such terms that the things exchanged will be equal, that the remuneration will be equal to the labor. How can this equivalence be determined and ascertained? Not by a direct comparison of the two objects, work and pay, for their differences render them incommensurable. Some third term or standard of comparison is required in which both objects can find expression. One such standard is individual net advantage. Inasmuch as the aim of the labor contract is reciprocal gain, it is natural to infer that the gains ought to be equal for the two parties. Net gain is ascertained by deducting in each case the utility transferred from the utility received; in other words, by deducting the privation from the gross return. The good received by the employer when diminished by or weighed against the amount that he pays in wages should be equal to the good received by the laborer when diminished by or weighed against the inconvenience that he undergoes through the expenditure of his time and energy. Hence the contract should bring to employer and employee equal amounts of net advantage or satisfaction.

Plausible as this rule may appear, it is impracticable, inequitable, and unjust. In the vast majority of labor contracts it is impossible to know whether both parties obtain the same quantity of net advantage. The gains of the employer can, indeed, be frequently measured in terms of money, being the difference between the wages paid to and the specific product turned out by the laborer. In the case of the laborer no such process of deduction is possible; for advantage and expenditure are incommensurable. We cannot subtract the laborer's privation, that is, his expenditure of time and energy, from his gross advantage, that is, his wages. How can we know or measure the net benefit obtained by a man who shovels sand ten hours for a wage of two dollars? How can we deduct his pain-cost from or weigh it against his compensation?

So far as the two sets of advantages are comparable at all, those of the employee would seem to be always greater than those of the employer. A wage of one dollar a day enables the laborer to satisfy the most important wants of life. Weighed against this gross advantage, his pain-cost of toil is relatively insignificant. His net advantage is the continuation of his existence. The net advantage received by the employer from such a wage contract is but a few cents, the equivalent of a cigar or two. Moreover, the sum total of an employer's gains from all his labor contracts is less quantitatively than the sum total of the gains obtained by all his employees. The latter gains provide for many livelihoods, the former for only one. Again, no general rate of wages could be devised which would enable all the members of a labor group to gain equally. Differences in health, strength, and intelligence would cause differences in the pain-cost involved in a given amount of labor; while differences in desires, standards of living, and skill in spending would bring about differences in the satisfactions derived from the same compensation. Finally, various employers would obtain various money gains from the same wage outlay, and various advantages from the same money gains. Hence if the rule of equality of net advantages were practicable it would be inequitable. At best, it would mean equal treatment of unequals.

It is also fundamentally unjust because it ignores the moral claims of needs, efforts, and sacrifices as regards the laborer. As we have seen in the chapter on profits in competitive conditions, and as we shall have occasion to recognize again in a later chapter, no canon or scheme of distributive justice is acceptable that does not give adequate consideration to these attributes of human personality.

The Rule of Free Contract

Another form of the exchange-equivalence theory would disregard the problem of *equality* of gains, and assume that justice is realized whenever the contract is free from force or fraud. In such circumstances both parties gain something, and presumably are satisfied; otherwise, they would not enter the contract. Probably the majority of employers regard this rule as the only available measure of practicable justice. The majority of economists likewise subscribed to it during the first half of the nineteenth century. In the words of Henry Sidgwick, "the teaching of the political economists pointed to the conclusion that a free exchange, without fraud or coercion, is also a fair exchange."[3] Apparently the economists based this teaching on the assumption that competition was free and general among both laborers and employers. In other words, the rule as understood by them was probably identical with the rule of the market rate, which we shall examine presently. It is not at all likely that the economists here referred to would have given their moral approval to those "free" contracts in which the employer pays starvation wages because he takes advantage of the ignorance of the laborer, or because he exercises the power of monopoly.

No matter by whom it is or has been held, the rule of free contract is unjust. In the first place, many labor contracts are not free in any genuine sense. When a laborer is compelled by dire necessity to accept a wage that is insufficient for a decent livelihood, his consent to the contract is free only in a limited and relative way. It is what the moralists call *voluntarium imperfectum*. It is vitiated to a substantial extent by the element of fear, by the apprehension of a cruelly evil alternative. The laborer does not agree to this wage because he prefers it to any other, but merely because he prefers it to unemployment, hunger, and starvation. The agreement to which he submits in these circumstances is no more free than the contract by which the helpless wayfarer gives up his purse to escape the pistol of the robber. While the latter action is free in the sense that it is chosen in preference to a violent death, it does not mean that the wayfarer gives, or intends to give, the robber the right of ownership in the purse. Neither should the laborer who from fear of a worse evil enters a contract to work for starvation wages, be regarded as transferring to the employer the full moral right to the services which he agrees to render. Like the wayfarer, he merely submits to superior force. The fact that the force imposed upon him is economic does not affect the morality of the transaction.

To put the matter in another way, the equality which justice requires is wanting in an oppressive labor contract because of the inequality existing between the contracting parties. In the words of Professor Ely: "Free contract supposes equals behind the contract in order that it may produce equality."[4]

Again, the rule of free contract is unjust because it takes no account of the moral claims of needs. A man whose only source of livelihood is his labor does wrong if he accepts a starvation wage willingly. Such a contract, however free, is not according to justice because it disregards the requirements of reasonable life. No man has a right to do this, any more than he has a right to perpetrate self-mutilation or suicide.

The Rule of Market Value

A third method of interpreting exchange-equivalence is based upon the concept of value. Labor and compensation are thought to be equal when the value of one is equal to the value of the other. Then the contract is just and the compensation is just. The only objection to these propositions is that they are mere truisms. What does value mean, and how is it to be determined? If it is to receive an ethical signification; if the value of labor is to be understood as denoting not merely the value that labor will command in a market, but the value that labor ought to have, the statement that wages should equal the value of labor is an identical proposition. It tells us that wages ought to be what they ought to be.

The doctrine that the social value or market price of labor is also the ethical value or just price, is sometimes called the classical theory, inasmuch as it was held, at least implicitly, by the majority of the early economists of both France and England.[5] Under competitive conditions, said the physiocrats, the price of labor as of all other things corresponds to the cost of production; that is, to the cost of subsistence for the laborer and his family. This is the natural law of wages, and being natural it is also just. Adam Smith likewise declared that competitive wages were natural wages, but he refrained from the explicit assertion that they were just wages. Nevertheless, it was implied in his theory that men's powers were substantially equal. Although the great majority of his followers denied that economics had moral aspects, their teaching tended to convey the thought that competitively fixed wages were more or less in accordance with justice. As noted above, their belief in the efficacy of competition led them to the inference that a free contract is also a fair contract. By a free contract they meant for the most part one that is made in the open market, that is governed by the forces of supply and demand, and that expresses the social economic value of the things exchanged.

All the objections that have been brought against the rule of the prevailing rate apply even more strongly to the doctrine of the market rate. The former takes as a standard the scale of wages most frequently paid in the market, while the latter approves any scale that obtains in any group of laborers or section of the market. Both accept as the ultimate determinant of wage justice the preponderance of economic force. Neither gives any consideration to the moral claims of needs, efforts, or sacrifices. Unless we are to identify justice with power, might with right, we must regard these objections as irrefutable, and the market value doctrine as untenable.

The Mediaeval Theory

Another exchange-equivalence theory which turns upon the concept of value is that found in the pages of the mediaeval canonists and theologians. But it interprets value in a different sense from that which we have just considered. As the measure of exchange-equivalence the mediaeval theory takes objective value, or true value. However, the proponents of this view did not formally apply it to wage contracts, nor did they discuss systematically the question of just wages. They were not called upon to do this, for they were not confronted by any considerable class of wage earners. In rural areas the number of persons who got their living exclusively as employees was extremely small, while in the towns the working class was composed of independent producers who sold their wares instead of their labor.[6] The question of fair compensation for the town workers was, therefore, the question of a fair price for their products. The latter question was discussed by the mediaeval writers formally and in great detail. Things exchanged should have equal values, and commodities should always sell for the equivalent of their values. By what rule was equality to be measured and value determined? Not by the subjective appreciations of the exchangers, for these would sometimes sanction the most flagrant extortion. Were no other help available, the starving man would give all he possessed for a loaf of bread. The unscrupulous speculator could monopolize the supply of foodstuffs and give them an exorbitantly high price which purchasers would accept and pay rather than go hungry. Hence we find the mediaeval writers seeking a standard of *objective* value which should attach to the commodity itself, not to the varying opinions of buyers and sellers.

In the thirteenth century Albertus Magnus[7] and Thomas Aquinas[8] declared that the proper standard was to be found in labor. A house is worth as many shoes as the labor embodied in the latter is contained in the labor embodied in the former. It is worthy of note that the diagram which Albertus Magnus presents to illustrate this formula of value and exchange had been used centuries before by Aristotle. It is likewise noteworthy that this conception of ethical value bears a striking resemblance to the theory of economic value upheld by Marxian Socialists. However, neither Aristotle nor the Schoolmen asserted that all kinds of labor had equal value.

Now this mediaeval labor-measure of value could be readily applied only to cases of barter, and even then only when the value of different kinds of labor had already been determined by some other standard. Accordingly we find the mediaeval writers expounding and defending a more general interpretation of objective or true value.

This was the concept of normal value; that is, the average or medium amount of utility attributed to goods in the average conditions of life and exchange. On the one hand, it avoided the excesses and the arbitrariness of individual estimates; on the other hand, it did not attribute to value the characters of immutability and rigidity. Contrary to the assumptions of some modern writers, the Schoolmen never said that value was something as fixedly inherent in goods as physical and chemical qualities. When they spoke of "intrinsic" value, they had in mind merely the constant capacity of certain commodities to satisfy human wants. Even to-day bread has always the intrinsic potency of alleviating hunger, regardless of the fluctuations of human appraisement. The objectivity that the mediaeval writers ascribed to value was relative. It assumed normal conditions as against exceptional conditions. To say that value was objective merely meant that it was not wholly determined by the interplay of supply and demand, but was based upon the stable and universally recognized use-qualities of commodities in a society where desires, needs, and tastes were simple and fairly constant from one generation to another.

How or where was this relatively objective value of goods to find concrete expression? In the *communis aestimatio,* or social estimate, declared the canonists. Objective value and just price would be ascertained practically through the judgment of upright and competent men, or preferably through legally fixed prices. But neither the social estimate nor the ordinances of lawmakers were authorized to determine values and prices arbitrarily. They were obliged to take into account certain objective factors. In the thirteenth and fourteenth centuries, the factors universally recognized as determinative were the utility or use-qualities of goods, but especially their cost of production. Later on, in the sixteenth and seventeenth centuries, risk and scarcity were given considerable prominence as value determinants. Cost of production in the Middle Ages was mainly labor costs; hence the standard of value was chiefly a labor standard.

How was labor cost to be measured, and the different kinds of labor evaluated? By the necessary and customary expenditures of the class to which the laborer belonged. Mediaeval society was composed of a few definite, easily recognized, and relatively fixed orders or grades, each of which had its own function in the social hierarchy, its own standard of living, and its moral right to a livelihood in accordance with that standard. Like the members of the other orders, the laborers were conceived as entitled to live in conformity with their customary class-requirements. From this it followed that the needs of the laborer became the main determinant of the cost of production, and of the value and just price of goods. Inasmuch as the standards of living of the various divisions of the workers were fixed by custom, and limited by the restricted possibilities of the time, they afforded a fairly definite measure of value and price—much more definite than the standard of general utility. To Langenstein, vice chancellor of the University of Paris in the latter half of the fourteenth century, the matter seemed quite simple; for he declared that everyone could determine for himself the just price of his wares by referring to the customary needs of his rank of life.

Class needs are not, indeed, a direct criterion of equality, a common denominator, a third term of comparison, between labor and wages. When we say that a given amount of wages is equal to a given content of livelihood, we express a purely economic, positive, and mathematical relation. When we say that a given amount of labor is equal to a given content of livelihood, we are either talking nonsense or expressing a purely ethical relation; that is, declaring that this labor *ought* to equal this livelihood. In other words, we are introducing a fourth term of comparison; namely, the moral worth or personal dignity of the laborer. Thus, we have not a single and common standard to measure both labor and wages, and to indicate a relation of equality between them. While class needs directly measure wages, they do not measure labor, either quantitatively, or qualitatively, or under any other aspect or category.[9]

The canonist doctrine of wage justice was fairly satisfactory as applied to the conditions of the Middle Ages. It assured to the laborer of that day a certain rude comfort, and probably as large a proportion of the product of industry as was practically attainable. Nevertheless it is not a universally valid criterion of justice in the matter of wages; for it makes no provision for those laborers who deserve a wage in excess of the cost of living of their class; nor does it furnish a principle by which a whole class of workers can justify their advance to a higher standard of living. It is not sufficiently elastic and dynamic.

To sum up the entire discussion of exchange-equivalence theories: Their underlying concept is fundamentally unsound and impracticable. All but one of them involve an attempt to compare two entities which are utterly incommensurate. There exists no third term, or standard, or objective fact, which will inform men whether any rate of wages is the equivalent of any quantity of labor.

III. PRODUCTIVITY THEORIES

The productivity concept of wage justice appears in a great variety of forms. One of them is advocated mainly by the Socialists, and is usually referred to as the theory of the "right to the whole product of labor."[10]

Labor's Right to the Whole Product

We have seen that Adam Smith's belief in the normality and beneficence of free competition would have logically led him to the conclusion that competitive wages were just; and we know that this doctrine is implicit in his writings. On the other hand, his theory that all value is determined by labor would seem to involve the inference that all the value of the product belongs to the laborer. As a matter of fact, Smith restricted this conclusion to primitive and precapitalist societies. Apparently he, and his disciples in an even larger degree, was more interested in describing the supposed beneficence of competition than in justifying the distribution that resulted from the competitive process.

The early English Socialists were more consistent. In 1793 William Godwin, whom Anton Menger calls "the first scientific Socialist of modern times," laid down in substance the doctrine that the laborer has a right to the whole product.[11] In 1805 Charles Hall formulated and defended the doctrine with greater precision and consistency.[12] In 1824 the doctrine was stated more fundamentally, systematically, and completely by William Thompson.[13] He accepted the labor theory of value laid down by Adam Smith, and formally derived therefrom the ethical conclusion that the laborer has a right to the whole product. "Thompson and his followers are only original in so far as they consider rent and interest to be *unjust* deductions, which violate the right of the laborer to the whole product of his labor."[14] He denounced the laws which empowered the land owner and the capitalist to appropriate value not created by them, and gave to the value thus appropriated the name, "surplus value." In the use of this term he anticipated Karl Marx by several years. His doctrines were adopted and defended by many other English Socialist writers, and were introduced into France by the followers of Saint-Simon. "From his works," says Menger, "the later Socialists, the Saint-Simonians, Proudhon, and above all, Marx and Rodbertus, have directly or indirectly drawn their opinions."[15]

Although Saint-Simon never accepted the doctrine of the laborer's right to the whole product, his disciples, particularly Enfantin and Bazard, taught it implicitly. In a just social state, they maintained, every one would be expected to labor according to his capacity, and would be rewarded according to his product.[16]

Perhaps the most theoretical and extreme statement of the theory that we are considering is found in the writings of P. J. Proudhon.[17] He maintained that the real value of products was determined by labor time, and that all kinds of labor should be regarded as equally effective in the value-creating process, and he advocated therefore equality of wages and salaries. For the realization of this ideal he drew the outlines of a semi-anarchic social order, of which the main feature was gratuitous public credit. Neither his theories nor his proposals ever obtained any considerable number of adherents.

A milder and better reasoned form of the theory was set forth by Karl J. Rodbertus.[18] Professor Wagner calls him, "the first, the most original, and the boldest representative of scientific Socialism in Germany." Yet, as Menger points out, Rodbertus derived many of his doctrines from Proudhon and the Saint-Simonians. He admitted that in a capitalist society the value of commodities does not always correspond to the labor embodied in them, and that different kinds of labor are productive in different degrees. Therefore, he had recourse to the concept of a normal, or average, day's labor in any group, and would have the various members of the group remunerated with reference to this standard. This was to be brought about by a centralized organization of industry in which the whole product would ultimately go to labor, and the share of the individual worker be determined by his contribution of socially necessary labor.

As we have seen in chapter viii,* many, if not most, followers of Karl Marx have drawn from his labor theory of value the inference that all the value of the product belongs by a moral right to the laborer. So deeply fixed in the human conscience is the conception of justice, and so general is the conviction of the laborer's right to his product, that most Socialists have not been able to maintain a position of consistent economic materialism. Indeed, Marx himself did not always succeed in evading the influence and the terminology of idealistic conceptions. He frequently thought and spoke of the Socialist régime as not only inevitable but as morally right, and of the capitalist system as morally wrong. Despite his rigid, materialistic theorizing, his writings abound in passionate denunciation of existing industrial evils, and in many sorts of "unscientific" ethical judgments.[19]

---

*Editor's Note: The chapters to which Ryan refers here and on the following page are omitted from this edition. Ryan's positive arguments for the right of owners to interest appear in chapter 7 of this edition.

In so far as the right to the whole product of labor has been based upon the labor theory of value, it may be summarily dismissed from consideration. The value of products is neither created nor adequately measured by labor; it is determined by utility and scarcity. Labor does, indeed, affect value, inasmuch as it increases utility and diminishes scarcity, but it is not the only factor that influences these categories. Natural resources, the desires, and the purchasing power of consumers determine value quite as fundamentally as does labor, and cause it to vary out of proportion to the labor expended.

Upon whatever grounds it may be based, the doctrine that labor has a right to the whole product is false. As we have seen in chapters viii and xi, some part of the product belongs of right to the owner of capital, by the titles of the common good and social justice.

Moreover, the doctrine is radically incomplete. It attempts to describe the requirements of justice as between the landowners and capitalists on the one side, and the wage earners on the other; but it provides no rule for determining distributive justice as between different classes of labor. In none of its forms does it provide any comprehensive rule or principle to ascertain the difference between the products of different laborers, and to decide how the product belonging to any group of men as a whole should be divided among the individual members. Does the locomotive engineer produce more than the section hand, the bookkeeper more than the salesman, the ditch digger more than the teamster? These and countless similar questions are, from the nature of the productive process, unanswerable. Even if it were ethically acceptable, the doctrine of the right to the whole product is hopelessly inadequate.

A Modified Version of Productivity

The only other productivity theory that we shall consider is that defended by Dr. Thomas N. Carver, who was for many years professor of political economy at Harvard University. Refraining from the futile attempt to ascertain the exact physical productivity of labor as compared with that of capital, he confines his attention to what he calls the "economic" productivity of a given unit of labor in a given productive process.[20] "Find out accurately how much the community produces with his [the laborer's] help, over and above what it produces without his help, and you have an exact measure of his productivity."[21] By this rule we can determine a man's productivity not only as compared with his inactivity in relation to a given industry or establishment, but as compared with the productivity of some other man who might be substituted for him. Thus understood, productivity expresses the value of a man to the industrial process in which he participates. It "determines how much a man is worth, and consequently, according to our criterion of justice, how much a man ought to have as a reward for his work."[22]

While this conception of productivity is relatively simple, and the canon of justice somewhat plausible, neither is adequate. To many situations the productivity test is substantially inapplicable. The removal from industry of the man who works alone; for example, the independent shoemaker, blacksmith, tailor, or farmer would result not in a certain diminution, but in the entire non-appearance of the product, and the same effect would follow the removal of the capital or tools. In the one case, the laborer is to be credited with the whole product, and capital with nothing; in the other case capital produces everything, and labor nothing.

Even when several laborers are employed, the test is inapplicable to those who are engaged upon indispensable tasks; for example, the engineer in the boiler room of a small factory, and the bookkeeper in a small store. Remove them, and you have no product at all; hence a rigid enforcement of Professor Carver's test would award them the whole product. To be sure, we can get some measure of the productivity of these men by observing the effect on the product when inferior men are put in their places; but this merely enables us to tell how much more they are worth than other men, not their total worth.

Even the substitution test is not always practicable. The attempt to ascertain the productivity of a workman of high technical skill by putting in his place an utterly unskilled laborer, would not yield very satisfactory results, either to the inquiry or to the industry. In the majority of such cases the difference in the resulting product would probably far exceed the difference in the existing wage rates of the two men, thus showing that the skilled worker is getting considerably less than he is "economically worth."

In the field to which it is applicable; namely, that of more or less unspecialized labor in large establishments, Professor Carver's theory violates some of the most fundamental conceptions of justice and humanity. He admits that it takes no account of the laborer's efforts, sacrifices, or needs, and that when unskilled labor becomes too plentiful, the value of the product may fall below the cost of supporting a decent standard of living. While he looks with some sympathy upon the demand for a minimum wage of two dollars per day, he contends that unless the laborer really *earns* that amount, some other man will be paid less than he earns, "which would be unjust." To "earn" two dollars a day means, in Professor Carver's terminology, to add that much value to the product of the establishment in which the laborer is employed; for this is the measure of the laborer's productivity. If all the men who are now getting less than two dollars a day are receiving the full value of their product, and if all the other workers are likewise given the full value of their product, an increase in the remuneration of the former will mean a deduction from the compensation of the latter.

These conclusions of ethical pessimism are extremely vulnerable. As we have shown in chapter xiv [Editor's note: chapter 9 in this edition], efforts, sacrifices, and needs are superior to productivity as claims to reward, and must be given due consideration in any just scheme of distribution. Professor Carver would leave them out of account entirely. In the second place, it is not always nor necessarily ever true that to raise the wages of the poorest paid laborers will mean to lower the remuneration of those who are better paid. Many workers, particularly women, are now receiving less than the measure of their "productivity," less than they "earn," less than their worth to the employer, less than he would be willing to pay rather than go without their services. Professor Carver would, of course, not deny that the wages of all such laborers could be raised without affecting the remuneration of other workers. Even when the poorest paid class is receiving all that its members are at present worth to the employer, an increase in their compensation would not necessarily come out of the fund available for the better paid. It could be deducted from excessive profits and interest. In many industries competition does not automatically keep down these shares to the minimum necessary to retain the services of business ability and capital. It could be provided to some extent out of the enlarged product that would result from improvements in the productive process, and from the increased efficiency of those workers whose wages had been raised.

Finally, the increased remuneration could be derived from increased prices. When we speak of the unskilled laborer as getting all that he produces, or all that he earns, we refer not to his concrete product, but to the value of that product, to the selling price of the product. Neither this price, nor any other existing price, has anything about it that is either economically or ethically sacred. In a competitive market current prices are fixed by the forces of supply and demand, which often involve the exploitation of the weak; in a monopoly market they are set by the desires of the monopolist, which are likewise destitute of moral validity. Hence a minimum wage law which would raise the price and value of the product sufficiently to provide living wages for the unskilled workers, thus increasing their "productivity" and enabling them to "earn" the legal wage, would neither violate the principles of justice, nor necessarily diminish the compensation of any other laboring group. To be sure, the increased prices might be followed by such a lessening of demand for the product as to diminish employment; but this is another matter which has no direct bearing on either the economic or the ethical phases of productivity and earning power. And the disadvantages involved in the supposition of a reduced volume of employment may possibly be not so formidable socially as those which accompany a large volume of insufficiently paid occupations.

We conclude that Professor Carver's rule is inapplicable to a large part of the industrial field, and that where it does apply it frequently runs counter to some of the principles of distributive justice.

CHAPTER 14

The Minimum of Justice: A Living Wage

Many of the early French Socialists of the Utopian school advanced this formula of distribution: "From each according to his powers; to each according to his needs." It was also put forward by the German Socialists in the Gotha Program in 1875.[1] To adopt needs as the sole rule of distribution would mean, of course, that each person should be rewarded in proportion to his wants and desires, regardless of his efforts or of the amount that he had produced. The mere statement of the proposal is sufficient to refute it as regards the men and women of whom we have any knowledge. In addition to this objection, there is the insuperable difficulty of measuring fairly or accurately the relative needs of any group composed of men, women, and children. Were the members' own estimates of their needs accepted by the distributing authority, the social product would no doubt fall far short of supplying all. If the measurement were made by some official person or persons, "the prospect of jobbery and tyranny opened up must give the most fanatical pause." Indeed, the standard of needs should be regarded as a canon of Communism rather than of Socialism; for it implies a large measure of common life as well as of common ownership, and paternalistic supervision of consumption as well as collectivist management of production.

While the formula of needs must be flatly rejected as a complete rule of distributive justice, or of wage justice, it is valid and indispensable as a partial standard. It is a partial measure of justice in two senses: First, inasmuch as it is consistent with the admission and operation of other principles, such as productivity and sacrifice; second, inasmuch as it can be restricted to certain fundamental requisites of life, instead of being applied to all possible human needs. It can be made

This chapter is reprinted from *Distributive Justice: The Right and Wrong of Our Present Distribution of Wealth*, 3d ed., rev. (New York: Macmillan Co., 1942), 269–88.

to safeguard the minimum demands of reasonable life, and therefore to function as a minimum standard of wage justice.

Human needs constitute the primary ethical title or claim to material goods. None of the other recognized titles, such as productivity, effort, sacrifice, purchase, gift, inheritance, or first occupancy, is a fundamental reason or justification of either rewards or possessions. They all assume the existence of needs as a prerequisite to their validity. If men did not need goods they could not reasonably lay claim to them by any of the specific titles just enumerated. First comes the general claim or fact of needs; then the particular title or method by which the needs may be conveniently supplied. While these statements may seem elementary and platitudinous, their practical value will be quite evident when we come to consider the conflicting claims that sometimes arise out of the clash between needs and some of the other titles. We shall see that needs are not merely a physical reason or impulse toward acquisition and possession, but a moral title which rationalizes the claim to a certain amount of goods.

THREE FUNDAMENTAL PRINCIPLES

The validity of needs as a partial rule of wage justice rests ultimately upon three fundamental principles regarding man's position in the universe. The first is that God created the earth for the sustenance of *all* His children; therefore, that all persons are equal in their inherent claims upon the bounty of nature. As it is impossible to demonstrate that any class of persons is less important than another in the eyes of God, so it is impossible for any believer in Divine Providence to reject this proposition. The man who denies God or Providence can refuse assent to the second part of the proposition only be refusing to acknowledge the personal dignity of the human individual, and the equal dignity of all persons. Inasmuch as the human person is intrinsically sacred and morally independent, he is endowed with those inherent prerogatives, immunities, and claims that we call rights. Every person is an end in himself; none is a mere instrument to the convenience or welfare of any other human being. The worth of a person is something intrinsic, derived from within, not determined or measurable by reference to any earthly object or purpose without. In this respect the human being differs infinitely from, is infinitely superior to, a stone, a rose, or a horse. While these statements help to illustrate what is meant by the dignity of personality, by the intrinsic worth, importance, sacredness of the human being, they do not prove the existence of this inherent juridical quality. Proof in the strict sense is irrelevant and impossible. If the intrinsic and equal moral worth of all persons be not self-evident to a man, it will not approve itself to him through any process of argumentation. Whosoever denies it can also logically deny men's equal claims of access to the bounty of the earth; but he cannot escape the alternative conclusion that brute force, exercised either by the State or by individuals, is the only proper determinant of possessions and of property. Against this contention it is not worthwhile to offer formal argument.

The second fundamental principle is that the inherent right of access to the earth is conditioned upon, and becomes actually valid through, the expenditure of useful labor. Generally speaking, the fruits and potentialities of the earth do not become available to men without exertion. "In the sweat of thy brow thou shalt eat thy bread," is a physical no less than a moral commandment. There are, indeed, exceptions: The very young, the infirm, and the possessors of a sufficient amount of property. The two former classes have claims to a livelihood through piety and charity, while the third group has at least a presumptive claim of justice to rent and interest, and a certain claim of justice to the money value of their goods. Nevertheless, the general condition is that men must work in order to live. "If a man will not work neither shall he eat." For those who refuse to comply with this condition the inherent right of access to the earth remains suspended.

The two foregoing principles involve as a corollary a third principle: The men who are in present control of the opportunities of the earth are obliged to permit reasonable access to these opportunities by persons who are willing to work. In other words, possessors must so administer the common bounty of nature that non-owners will not find it unreasonably difficult to get a livelihood. To put it still in other terms, the right to subsist from the earth implies the right of access thereto on reasonable terms. When any man who is willing to work is denied the exercise of this right, he is no longer treated as the moral and juridical equal of his fellows. He is regarded as inherently inferior to them, as a mere instrument to their convenience; and those who exclude him are virtually taking the position that their rights to the common gifts of the Creator are inherently superior to his birthright. Obviously this position cannot be defended on grounds of reason. Possessors are no more justified in excluding a man from reasonable access to the goods of the earth than they would be in depriving him of the liberty to move from place to place. The community that should arbitrarily shut a man up in prison would not violate his rights more fundamentally than the community or the proprietors who should shut him out from the opportunity of getting a livelihood from the bounty of the earth. In both cases the man demands and has a right to a common gift of God. His moral claim is as valid to the one good as to the other, and it is as valid to both as is the claim of his fellows.

THE RIGHT
TO A DECENT LIVELIHOOD

Every man who is willing to work has, therefore, an inborn right to sustenance from the earth on reasonable terms or conditions. This cannot mean that all persons have a right to equal *amounts* of sustenance or income; for we have seen on a preceding page that men's needs, the primary title to property, are not equal, and that other canons and factors of distribution have to be allowed some weight in determining the division of goods and opportunities. Nevertheless, there is a certain minimum of goods to which every worker is entitled by reason of his inherent right of access to the earth. He has a right to at least a *decent* livelihood; that is, he has a right to so much of the requisites of sustenance as will enable him to live in a manner worthy of a human being. The elements of a decent livelihood may be summarily described as: Food, clothing, and housing sufficient in quantity and quality to maintain the worker in normal health, in elementary comfort, and in an environment suitable to the protection of morality and religion; sufficient provision for the future to bring elementary contentment, and security against sickness, accident, and invalidity; and sufficient opportunities of recreation, social intercourse, education, and church-membership to conserve health and strength and to render possible the exercise of the higher faculties.

On what ground is it contended that a worker has a right to a decent livelihood, as thus defined, rather than to a bare subsistence? On the same ground that validates his right to life, marriage, or any of the other fundamental goods of human existence. On the dignity of personality. Why is it wrong and unjust to kill or maim an innocent man? Because human life and the human person possess intrinsic worth; because personality is sacred. But the intrinsic worth and sacredness of personality imply something more than security of life and limb and the material means of bare existence. The man who is not provided with the requisites of normal health, efficiency, and contentment lives a maimed life, not a reasonable life. His physical condition is not worthy of a human being. Furthermore, man's personal dignity demands not merely the conditions of reasonable physical existence, but the opportunity of pursuing self-perfection through the harmonious development of all his faculties. Unlike the brutes, he is endowed with a rational soul, and the capacity of indefinite self-improvement. A due regard to these endowments requires that man shall have the opportunity of becoming not only physically stronger, but intellectually wiser, morally better, and spiritually nearer to God. If he is deprived of these opportunities he cannot realize the potentialities of his nature nor attain its divinely appointed end. He remains on the plane of the lower animals. His personality is violated quite as fundamentally as when his body is injured or his life destroyed.

While it is impossible to define with mathematical precision the degree of personal development that is necessary to satisfy the claims of personal dignity, it is entirely practicable to state with sufficient definiteness the *minimum conditions* of such development. They are that quantity of goods and opportunities which fair-minded men would regard as indispensable to humane, efficient, and reasonable life. The summary description of a decent livelihood at the end of the second last paragraph, would probably be accepted by all men who really believe in the intrinsic worth of personality.

THE LABORER'S RIGHT
TO A LIVING WAGE

The wage earner's right to a decent livelihood in the abstract means in the concrete a right to a living wage. To present the matter in its simplest terms, let us consider first the adult male laborer of average physical and mental ability who is charged with the support of no one but himself, and let us assume that the industrial resources are adequate to such a wage for all the members of his class. Those who are in control of the resources of the community are morally bound to give such a laborer a living wage. If they fail to do so they are unreasonably hindering his access to a livelihood on reasonable terms, and his right to a livelihood on reasonable terms is violated. The central consideration here is evidently the *reasonableness* of the process. Unlike the business man, the rent receiver, and the interest receiver, the laborer has ordinarily no other means of livelihood than his wages. If these do not furnish him with a decent subsistence he is deprived of a decent subsistence. When he has performed an average day's work, he has done all that is within his power to make good his claim to a decent livelihood.

On the other hand, the community is the beneficiary of his labor, and desires his services. If, indeed, the community would rather do without the services of an individual laborer than pay him a living wage, it is morally free to choose the former alternative, precisely as it is justified in refusing to pay a price for groceries that will enable an inefficient grocer to obtain living profits. Whatever concrete form the right of such persons to a decent livelihood may take, it is not the right to living wages or living profits from their present occupations. Here, however, we are discussing the laborer to whom the community would rather pay a living wage than not employ him at all. To refuse such a one a living wage merely because he can be constrained by economic pressure to work for less, is to treat him unreasonably, is to deprive him of access to a livelihood on reasonable terms. Such treatment regards the laborer as inferior to his fellows in personal worth, as a mere instrument to their convenience. It is an unreasonable distribution of the goods and opportunities of the earth.

No man who accepts the three fundamental principles stated some pages back, can deny the right of the laborer to a living wage. The man who does not accept them must hold that all property rights are the arbitrary creation of the State, or that there is no such thing as a moral right to material goods. In either supposition the distribution and possession of the earth's bounty are subject entirely to the decisions of might.

What persons, or group, or authority is charged with the obligation which corresponds to the right to a living wage? We have referred to "the community," but we do not mean the community in its corporate capacity, i.e., the State. As regards private employment, the State is not obliged to pay a living wage, nor any other kind of wage, since it has not assumed the wage-paying function in this field. As protector of natural rights, the State is obliged to enact laws which will enable the laborer to obtain a living wage; but the duty of actually providing this measure of remuneration rests upon the class which has assumed the wage-paying function. In our present industrial system, the employer is society's pay-master. He, not the State, receives the product out of which all the agents of production must be rewarded. Where the laborer is engaged in rendering personal services to his employer, the latter is the only beneficiary of the laborer's activity. In either case the employer is the only person upon whom the obligation of paying a living wage can primarily fall.

If the State were in receipt of the product of industry, the wage-paying fund, it would naturally be charged with the obligation that now rests immediately upon the employer. If any other class in the community were the owner of the product that class would be under this specific obligation. As things are, the employer is in possession of the product, and discharges the function of wage payer; consequently he is the person who is required to perform this function in a reasonable manner.

WHEN THE EMPLOYER IS UNABLE
TO PAY A LIVING WAGE

Evidently the employer who cannot pay a living wage is not obliged to so so, since moral duties suppose a corresponding physical capacity. In such circumstances the laborer's right to a living wage becomes suspended and hypothetical, as does the claim of a creditor when the debtor becomes insolvent. Let us see, however, precisely what meaning should reasonably be given to the phrase, "inability to pay a living wage."

An employer is not obliged to pay a full living wage to all his employees so long as that action would deprive himself and his family of a decent livelihood. As active director of a business, the employer has quite as good a right as the laborer to a decent livelihood from the product, and in case of conflict between the two rights, the employer may take advantage of that principle of charity which permits a man to prefer himself to his neighbor, when the choice refers to goods of the same order of importance. Moreover, the employer is justified in taking from the product sufficient to support a somewhat higher scale of living than generally prevails among his employees; for he has become accustomed to this higher standard, and would suffer a considerable hardship if compelled to fall notably below it. It is reasonable, therefore, that he should have the means of maintaining himself and family in moderate conformity with their customary standard of living; but it is unreasonable that they should indulge in anything like luxurious expenditure, so long as any of the employees fail to receive living wages.

Suppose that an employer cannot pay all his employees living wages and at the same time provide the normal rate of interest on the capital in the business. So far as the borrowed capital is concerned, the business man has no choice; he must pay the stipulated rate of interest, even though it prevents him from giving a living wage to all his employees. Nor can it be reasonably contended that the loan capitalist in that case is obliged to forego the interest due him. He cannot be certain that this interest payment, or any part of it, is really necessary to make up what is wanting to a complete scale of living wages. The employer would be under great temptation to defraud the loan capitalist on the pretext of doing justice to the laborer, or to conduct his business inefficiently at the expense of the loan capitalist. Anyhow, the latter is under no obligation to leave his money in a concern that is unable to pay him interest regularly. The general rule, then, is that the loan capitalist is not obliged to refrain from taking interest in order that the employees may have living wages.

Is the employer justified in withholding the full living wage from his employees to provide himself with the normal rate of interest on the capital that he has invested in the enterprise? Speaking generally, he is not. In the first place, the right to any interest at all, except as a return for genuine sacrifices in saving, has no such firm and definite basis as the right to a living wage.[2] In the second place, the right to interest, be it ever so definite and certain, is greatly inferior in force and urgency. It is an axiom of ethics that when two rights conflict, the less important must give way to the more important. Since all property rights are but means to the satisfaction of human needs, their relative importance is determined by the relative importance of the ends that they serve. Now the needs that are supplied through interest on the employer's capital are not essential to his welfare; the needs that are supplied through a living wage are essential to a reasonable life for the laborer. On the assumption that the employer has already taken from the product sufficient to provide a decent livelihood, interest on his capital will be expended for luxuries or converted into new investments; a living wage for the laborer will all be required for the fundamental goods of life, physical, mental, or moral. Evidently, then, the right to interest is inferior to the right to a living wage. To proceed on the contrary theory is to reverse the order of nature and reason, and to subordinate essential needs and welfare to unessential needs and welfare.[3]

Nor can it be maintained that the capitalist-employer's claim to interest is a claim upon the product prior to and independent of the claim of the laborer to a living wage. That would be begging the question. The product is in a fundamental sense the common property of employer and employees. Both parties have cooperated in turning it out, and they have equal claims upon it, in so far as it is necessary to yield them a decent livelihood. Having taken therefrom the requisites of a decent livelihood for himself, the employer who appropriates interest at the expense of a decent livelihood for his employees, in effect treats their claims upon the common and joint product as essentially inferior to his own. If this assumption were correct it would mean that the primary and essential needs of the employees are of less intrinsic importance than the superficial needs of the employer, and that the employees themselves are a lower order of being. The incontestable fact is that such an employer deprives the laborers of access to the goods of the earth on reasonable terms, and gives himself an access thereto that is unreasonable.

AN OBJECTION
AND SOME DIFFICULTIES

Against the foregoing argument it may be objected that the employer does his full duty when he pays the laborer the full value of the product or service. Labor is a commodity of which wages are the price; and the price is just if it is the fair equivalent of the labor. Like any other onerous contract, the sale of labor is governed by the requirements of commutative justice; and these are satisfied when labor is sold for its moral equivalent. What the employer is interested in and pays for, is the laborer's activity and product. There is no reason why he should take into account the laborer's livelihood.

Most of these assertions are correct, platitudinously correct, but they yield us no specific guidance because they use language vaguely and even ambiguously. The contention underlying them was adequately refuted in the last chapter, under the heads of theories of value and theories of exchange-equivalence. At present it will be sufficient to repeat summarily the following points: If the value of labor is to be understood in a purely economic sense it means market value, which is obviously not a universal measure of justice; if by the value of labor we mean its ethical value we cannot determine it in any particular case merely by comparing labor and compensation; we are compelled to have recourse to some extrinsic ethical principle; such an extrinsic principle is found in the proposition that the personal dignity of the laborer entitles him to a wage adequate to a decent livelihood; therefore, the ethical value of labor is always equivalent to at least a living wage, and the employer is morally bound to give this much remuneration.

Moreover, the conception of the wage contract as a matter of commutative justice only, is inadequate. The transaction between employee and employer involves other questions of justice than that which arises immediately out of the relation between the things exchanged. When a borrower repays a loan of ten dollars, he fulfills the obligation of justice because he returns the full equivalent of the article that he received. Nothing else is pertinent to the question of justice in this transaction. Neither the wealth nor the poverty, the goodness nor the badness, nor any other quality of either lender or borrower, has a bearing on the justice of the act of repayment. In the wage contract, and in every other contract that involves the distribution of the common bounty of nature, or of the social product, the juridical situation is vitally different from the transaction that we have just mentioned. The employer has obligations of justice, not merely as the receiver of a valuable thing through an onerous contract, but as the *distributor* of the common heritage of nature. His duty is not merely contractual, but social. He fulfills not only an individual contract, but a social function. Unless he performs this social and distributive function in accordance with justice, he does not adequately discharge the obligation of the wage contract. For the product out of which he pays wages is not his in the same sense as the personal income out of which he repays a loan. His claim upon the product is subject to the obligation of just distribution: The obligation of so distributing the product that the laborers who have contributed to the product shall not be denied their right to a decent livelihood on reasonable terms from the bounty of the earth.

This distributive function of the employer is governed by social justice. Said Pius XI:

> In reality, besides commutative justice, there is also social justice with its own set obligations, from which neither employers nor workingmen can escape.... But social justice cannot be said to have been satisfied as long as workingmen are denied a salary that will enable them to secure proper sustenance for themselves and their families; as long as they are denied the opportunity of acquiring a modest fortune and forestalling the plague of universal pauperism; as long as they cannot make suitable provision through public or private insurance for old age, for periods of illness and unemployment.[4]

When the economic situation is such that the employer really cannot pay living wages, social justice still applies and governs. It requires not only employers but the State to change the situation so that the payment of living wages will become economically feasible. As Pius XI said in *Quadragesimo Anno:*

> Every effort must therefore be made that fathers of families receive a wage sufficient to meet adequately ordinary domestic needs. If in the present state of society this is not always feasible, social justice demands that reforms be introduced without delay which will guarantee every adult workingman just such a wage.[5]

Some difficulties occur in connection with the wage rights of adult males whose ability is below the average, and female and child workers. Since the dignity and the needs of personality constitute the moral basis of the claim to a decent livelihood, it would seem that the inefficient worker who does his best is entitled to a living wage. Undoubtedly he has such a right if it can be effectuated in the existing industrial organization. As already noted, the right of the workman of average ability to a living wage does not become actual until he finds an employer who would rather give him that much than do without his services. Since the obligation of paying a living wage is not an obligation to employ any particular worker, an employer may refrain from hiring or may discharge any laborer who does not add to the product sufficient value to provide his wages. For the employer cannot reasonably be expected to employ any one at a positive loss to himself. Whence it follows that he may pay less than living wages to any worker whose services he would rather dispense with than remunerate at that figure.[6]

Women and young persons who regularly perform a full day's work, have a right to compensation adequate to a decent livelihood. In the case of minors, this means living at home, since this is the normal condition of all, and the actual condition of almost all. Adult females have a right to a wage sufficient to maintain them away from home, because a considerable proportion of them live in this condition. If employers were morally free to pay home-dwelling women less than those adrift, they would employ only the former. This would create a very undesirable situation. The number of women away from home who are forced to earn their own living is sufficiently large to make it reasonable that for their sakes the wage of all working women should be determined by the cost of living outside the parental precincts. This is one of the social obligations that reasonably falls upon the employer on account of his function in the present industrial system. In all the American minimum wage laws, the standard of payment is determined by the cost of living away from home. Besides, the difference between the living costs of women in the two conditions is not nearly as great as is commonly assumed. Probably it never amounts to more than a dollar a week.

THE FAMILY LIVING WAGE

Up to the present we have been considering the right of the laborer to a wage adequate to a decent livelihood for himself as an individual. In the case of an adult male, however, this is not sufficient for normal life, nor for the reasonable development of personality. The great majority of men cannot live well-balanced lives, cannot attain a reasonable degree of self-development outside the married state. Therefore, family life is among the essential needs of a normal and reasonable existence. It is not, indeed, so vitally necessary as the primary requisites of individual life, such as food, clothing, and shelter, but it is second only to these. Outside the family, men cannot, as a rule, command that degree of contentment, moral strength, and moral safety which are necessary for reasonable and efficient living. It is unnecessary to labor this point, as very few would assert that the average man can live a normal and complete human life without marriage.

Now, the support of the family falls properly upon the husband and father, not upon the wife and mother. The obligation of the father to provide a livelihood for the wife and young children is quite as definite as his obligation to maintain himself. If he has not the means to discharge this obligation he is not justified in getting married. Yet marriage is essential to normal life for the great majority of men. Therefore, the material requisites of normal life for the average adult male include provision for his family. In other words, his decent livelihood means a family livelihood. Consequently, he has a right to obtain such a livelihood on reasonable terms from the bounty of the earth. In the case of the wage earner, this right can be effectuated only through wages; therefore, the adult male laborer has a right to a family living wage. If he does not get this measure of remuneration his personal dignity is violated, and he is deprived of access to the goods of the earth quite as certainly as when his wage is inadequate to personal maintenance. The difference between family needs and personal needs is a difference only of degree. The satisfaction of both is indispensable to his reasonable life.

Just as the woman worker who lives with her parents has a right to a wage sufficient to maintain her away from home, so the unmarried adult male has a right to a family living wage. If only married men get the latter wage they will be discriminated against in the matter of employment. To prevent this undesirable condition, it is necessary that a family living wage be recognized as the right of all adult male workers. No other arrangement is reasonable in our present industrial system. In a competitive régime the standard wage for both married and unmarried men is necessarily the same. It will be determined by the living costs of either the one class or the other. At present the wage of the unskilled is unfortunately adjusted to the subsistence cost of the man who is not married. Since two prevailing scales of wages are impossible, the remuneration of the unmarried must in the interests of justice to the married be raised to the living costs of the latter. Moreover, the unmarried laborer needs more than an individual wage in order to save sufficient money to enter upon the responsibilities of matrimony. He must have the opportunity to save.

Only two objections of any importance can be brought against the male laborer's claim to a family living wage. The first is that just wages are to be measured by the value of the labor performed, and not by such an extrinsic consideration as the needs of a family. It has already been answered in this and the preceding chapters. Not the economic but the ethical value of the service rendered, is the proper determinant of justice in the matter of wages; and this ethical value is always the equivalent of at least a decent livelihood for the laborer and his family. According to the second objection, the members of the laborer's family have no claim upon the employer, since they do not participate in the work that is remunerated. This contention is valid, but it is also irrelevant. The claim of the laborer's family to sustenance is directly upon him, not upon his employer; but the laborer has a just claim upon the employer for the means of meeting the claims of his family. His right to this amount of remuneration is directly based neither upon the needs nor the rights of his family, but upon his own needs, upon the fact that family conditions are indispensable to his own normal life. If the wife and young children were self-supporting, or were maintained by the State, the wage rights of the father would not include provision for the family. Since, however, family life involves support by the father, the laborer's right to such a life necessarily includes the right to a wage adequate to family support.

FAMILY ALLOWANCES

In recent years a new method of establishing, or at least approximating, the family living wage has been introduced in France, Belgium, Holland, Germany, and, to a smaller extent, in several other European countries. In France it received the name, *sur-salaire,* while its common designation in English is the "Family Allowance System." It is a voluntary arrangement by a group of employers and employees, according to which married male wage earners are remunerated in proportion to the number of their children. At the birth of each child, the wage of the father is increased and the total amount of extra compensation is determined by the number of children who are below the fixed maximum age. In order to make it a matter of indifference to the employer whether he has many or few married men on his pay roll, the allowances are derived from a general fund. To this fund each employer contributes in proportion either to the amount of his wage payments or the number of his employees. Hence, the individual employer is no more disturbed when new births occur in the families of his own employees than when they take place in other families.

An important question in the operation of the system relates to the basic wage upon which the extra compensation is built. Should it suffice for the support of a man and wife, or be merely adequate to that of the adult male? In the former case single men would obtain more than enough for their present maintenance. In the latter case, they would begin to share in the allowance fund as soon as they married. The wife, as well as each child, would be the occasion of an increase in the husband's wages. If this method included provision for saving in the single man's wages, it would probably be more conducive to matrimony than the other, and would call for a smaller total outlay for wages. On the other hand, it would involve considerably greater administrative costs and friction.

In view of the very large number of women wage earners who have to support dependents, they ought to be included in any family allowance system. The objections drawn from the integrity of the family, the normal place of the mother, and the responsibility of the father, seem insufficient to outweigh the actual human needs of so many thousands of working women and their children. At any rate, it is not probable that the number of husbands who desert or die would be materially increased through this arrangement.[7]

OTHER ARGUMENTS IN FAVOR
OF A LIVING WAGE

Thus far, the argument has been based upon individual natural rights. If we give up the doctrine of natural rights, and assume that all the rights of the individual come to him from the State, we must admit that the State has the power to withhold and withdraw all rights from any and all persons. Its grant of rights will be determined solely by considerations of social utility. In the concrete this means that some citizens may be regarded as essentially inferior to other citizens, that some may properly be treated as mere instruments to the convenience of others. Or it means that all citizens may be completely subordinated to the aggrandizement of the State. Neither of these positions is logically defensible. No group of persons has less intrinsic worth than another; and the State has no rational significance apart from its members.

Nevertheless, a valid argument for the living wage can be set up on grounds of social welfare. A careful and comprehensive examination of the evil consequences to society and the State from the underpayment of any group of laborers, would show that a universal living wage is the only sound social policy. Among competent social students, this proposition has become a commonplace. It will not be denied by an intelligent person who considers seriously the influence of low wages in diminishing the efficiency, physical, mental, and moral, of the workers; in increasing the volume of crime, and the social cost of meeting it; in the immense social outlay for the relief of unnecessary poverty, sickness, and other forms of distress; and in the formation of a large and discontented proletariat.[8]

The living wage doctrine also receives strong support from various kinds of authority. Of these the most important and best known is the famous Encyclical, *On the Condition of Labor,* May 15, 1891, by Pope Leo XIII. "Let it then be granted that workman and employer should, as a rule, make free agreements, and in particular should agree freely as to wages; nevertheless, there is a dictate of natural justice more imperious and ancient than any bargain between man and man; namely, that the remuneration should be sufficient to maintain the wage earner in reasonable and frugal comfort." Although the Pope refrained from specifying whether the living wage that he had in mind was one adequate merely to an individual livelihood, or sufficient to support a family, other passages in the Encyclical leave no room for doubt that he regarded the latter as the normal and equitable measure of remuneration. Within a dozen lines of the sentence quoted above, he made this statement: "If the workman's wages be sufficient to maintain himself, his wife, and his children in reasonable comfort, he will not find it difficult, if he be a sensible man, to practice thrift; and he will not fail, by cutting down expenses, to put by some little savings and thus secure a small income."[9]

When the representatives of the American Hierarchy asserted the priority of the right to a living wage over the right to profits, they added: "By the term living wage we understand a wage sufficient not merely for the decent support of the workingman himself but also of his family."[10]

In 1919 the Federal Council of the Churches of Christ in America, representing the principal Protestant denominations, declared that, "the living wage should be the first charge upon industry, before dividends are considered." All the important non-Catholic denominations, Protestant and Jewish, have made similar pronouncements since the beginning of the century. Indeed, it would be difficult to find any prominent person who to-day would have the temerity to deny that the laborer is entitled to a wage sufficient for decent family life. Employers rarely give public utterance to the opinion that the wage contract is

merely an economic transaction, or that the living wage principle is without rational and ethical force.

The money measure of a living wage in the United States is susceptible of definition sufficiently precise for all practical purposes. Between 1905 and 1923, no
less than thirty-seven studies and estimates were made in twenty different cities
and industrial regions, from Boston to San Francisco. Despite variations in details and viewpoints, they exhibit a considerable measure of agreement. In any
large city, the minimum cost of decent living for a single woman worker is between 14 and 17 dollars a week; for a single male worker, between 750 and 800
dollars a year; and for the "standard" family of five, between 1400 and 1600 dollars per annum.[11]

CHAPTER 15

The Problem
of Complete Wage Justice

A living wage for all workers is merely the *minimum* measure of just remuneration. It is not in every case complete justice. Possibly it is not the full measure of justice in any case? How much more than a living wage is due to any or all of the various classes of laborers? How much more may any group of workers demand without exposing themselves to the sin of extortion? By what principles shall these questions be answered?

The problem of complete wage justice can be conveniently and logically considered in four distinct relations, as regards: The respective claims of the different classes of laborers to a given amount of money available for wage payments; the claims of the whole body of laborers, or any group thereof, to higher wages at the expense of profits; at the expense of interest; and at the expense of the consumer.

COMPARATIVE CLAIMS
OF DIFFERENT LABOR GROUPS

In the division of a common wage fund, no section of the workers is entitled to anything in excess of living wages until all the other sections have received that amount of remuneration. The need of a decent livelihood constitutes a more urgent claim than any other that can be brought forward. Neither efforts, nor sacrifices, nor productivity, nor scarcity can justify the payment of more than living wages to any group, so long as any other group in the industry remains below that level; for the extra compensation will supply the non-essential needs of the

This chapter is reprinted from *Distributive Justice: The Right and Wrong of Our Present Distribution of Wealth*, 3d ed., rev. (New York: Macmillan Co., 1942), 289–302.

former by denying the essential needs of the latter. The two groups of men be treated unequally in respect of those qualities in which they are equal; nan their personal dignity and their claims to the minimum requisites of reasonable life and self-development. This is a violation of justice.

Let us suppose that all the workers among whom a given amount of compensation is to be distributed, have already received living wages, and that there remains a considerable surplus. On what principles should the surplus be apportioned? For answer we turn to the canons of distribution, as explained in chapter xiv [chapter 9 in this edition]. Proportional justice would seem to suggest that the surplus ought to be distributed in accordance with the varying needs and capacities of men to develop their faculties beyond the minimum reasonable degree. As we have already pointed out, this would undoubtedly be the proper rule if it were susceptible of anything like exact application, and if the sum to be distributed were not produced by and dependent upon those who were to participate in the distribution. However, we know that the first condition is impracticable, while the second is nonexistent. Inasmuch as the sharers in the distribution have produced and constantly determine the amount to be apportioned, the distributive process must disregard nonessential needs, and govern itself by other canons of justice.

The most urgent of these is the canon of efforts and sacrifices. Superior effort, as measured by unusual will-exertion, is a fundamental rule of justice, and a valid title to exceptional reward. Men who strive harder than the majority of their fellows are ethically deserving of extra compensation. At least, this is the pure theory of the matter. In practice, the situation is complicated by the fact that unusual effort cannot always be distinguished, and by the further fact that some exceptional efforts do not fructify in correspondingly useful results. Among men engaged at the same kind of work, superior effort is to a great extent discernible in the unusually large product. As such it actually receives an extra reward in accordance with the canon of productivity. When men are employed at different tasks, unusual efforts cannot generally be distinguished and compensated. Hence the general principle is that superior efforts put forth in the production of utilities, entitle men to something more than living wages, but that the enforcement of this principle is considerably hindered by the difficulty of discerning such efforts.

The unusual sacrifices that deserve extra compensation are connected with the costs of industrial functions and the disagreeable character of occupations. Under the first head are included the expense of industrial training and the debilitating effects of the work. Not only justice to the worker but a farsighted view of social welfare dictates that all unusual costs of preparation for an industrial craft or profession should be repaid in the form of unusual compensation. This means something more than a living wage. For the same reasons the unusual hazards and disability resulting from industrial accidents and diseases should be compensated by higher remuneration. In the absence of such provision, these costs will have to be borne by parents, by society in the form of charitable relief, or by the worker himself through unnecessary suffering and incapacity. The industry that does not provide for all these costs is a social parasite, the workers in it are deprived of just compensation for their unusual sacrifices, and society suffers a considerable loss through industrial friction and diminished productive efficiency. In so far, however, as any of the foregoing costs are borne by society, as in the matter of industrial education, or by the employer, as by accident compensation or sickness insurance, they do not demand provision in the form of extra wages.

Other unusual sacrifices that entitle the worker to more than living wages, are inherent in disagreeable or despised occupations. The scavenger and the bootblack ought to get more than the performers of most other unskilled tasks. On the principle of comparative individual desert, they should receive larger remuneration than many persons who are engaged upon skilled but relatively pleasant kinds of work. For if they were given the choice of expending the time and money required to fit them for the latter tasks, or of taking up immediately their present disagreeable labor, they would select the more pleasant occupations, for the same or even a smaller remuneration. And the majority of those who are now in the more skilled occupations would make the same choice. Hence the sacrifices inherent in disagreeable kinds of work are in many cases as great as or greater than the sacrifices of preparation for the more pleasant tasks; consequently the doers of the former are relatively underpaid. If all wages were regulated by some supreme authority according to the principles of complete justice, the workers in disagreeable occupations would receive something more than living wages.

Nor would this determination of rewards be in any way contrary to social welfare or the principle of maximum net results; for the superior attractiveness of the other kinds of work would draw a sufficient supply of labor to offset the advantage conferred by higher wages upon the disagreeable occupations. The main reason why the latter kind of labor is so poorly paid now is the fact that it is very plentiful, a condition which is in turn due to the unequal division of industrial opportunity. Were the opportunities of technical education and of entrance to the higher crafts and professions more widely diffused, the laborers offering themselves for the disagreeable tasks would be scarcer and their remuneration correspondingly larger. This would be not only more conformable to the principles of justice, but more conducive to social efficiency.

To sum up the discussion concerning the canon of efforts and sacrifices: Laborers have a just claim to more than living wages whenever they put forth unusual efforts and whenever their occupations involve unusual sacrifices, either through costs of preparation, exceptional hazards, or inherent disagreeableness. The precise amount of extra compensation due under any of these heads can be determined, as a rule, only approximately.

The next canon to be considered as a reason for more than living wages is that of productivity. This offers little difficulty; for the unusual product is always visible among men who are performing the same kind of work, and the employer is always willing to give the producer extra compensation. While superior productive power which is based solely upon superior native ability has only presumptive validity as a canon of justice, it is ethically sufficient in our workaday world. Moreover, the canon of human welfare demands that superior productivity receive superior rewards, so long as these are necessary to evoke the maximum net product.

The canon of scarcity has the same value as that of productivity. Society and the employer are justified in giving extra compensation to scarce forms of labor when the product is regarded as worth the corresponding price. This remains true even when the scarcity is due to restricted opportunity of preparation, rather than to sacrifices of any sort. In that case the higher rewards are as fully justified as the superior remuneration of that superior productivity which is based upon exceptional native endowments. The amount of extra compensation which may properly be given on account of scarcity is determined either by the degree of sacrifice involved or by the ordinary operation of competition. When men are scarce because they have made exceptional sacrifices of preparation, they ought to be rewarded in full proportion to these sacrifices. When they are scarce merely because of exceptional opportunities, their extra compensation should not exceed the amount that comes to them through the interplay of supply and demand.

The canon of human welfare has already received implicit application. When due regard is given to efforts, sacrifices, productivity, and scarcity, the demands of human welfare, both in its individual and its social aspects, are sufficiently safeguarded.

In the foregoing pages the attempt has been made to describe the proportions in which a given wage fund ought to be distributed among the various classes of laborers who have claims upon the fund. The first requisite of justice is that all should receive living wages. It applies to all workers of average ability, even to those who have no special qualifications of any sort. When this general claim has been universally satisfied, those groups of workers who are in any wise special, whose qualifications for any reason differentiate them from and place them above the average, will have a right to something more than living wages. They will have the first claim upon the surplus that remains in the wage fund. Their claims will be based upon the various canons of distribution explained in detail above; and the proper amounts of extra remuneration will be determined by the extent to which their special qualifications differentiate them from the average and unspecialized workers. If the total available wage fund is merely sufficient to provide universal living wages and the extra compensation due to the specialized groups, no section of the labor force will be justified in exacting a larger share.

This does not mean that a powerful body of workers who are already receiving their due proportion as compared with other labor groups would not be justified in seeking any increase in remuneration. The increase might come out of profits, or interest, or the consumer, and thus be in no sense detrimental to the rights of the other sections.

Of course, the wage-fund hypothesis which underlies the foregoing discussion is not realized in actual life, any more than was the "wage fund" of the classical economists. Better than any other device, however, it enables us to describe and visualize the comparative claims of different groups of laborers who have a right to unequal amounts in excess of living wages.

WAGES VERSUS PROFITS

Let us suppose that the wage fund is properly apportioned among the different classes of laborers, according to the specified canons of distribution. May not one or all of the labor groups demand an increase in wages on the ground that the employer is retaining for himself an undue share of the product?

As we have seen, the right of the laborers to living wages is superior to the right of the employer or business man to anything in excess of that amount of profits which will insure him against risks, and afford him a decent livelihood in reasonable conformity with his accustomed plane of expenditure. It is also evident that those laborers who undergo more than average sacrifices have a claim to extra compensation which is quite as valid as the similarly based claim of the employer to more than living profits. In case the business does not provide a sufficient amount to remunerate both classes of sacrifices, the employer may prefer his own to those of his employees, on the same principle that he may prefer his own claim to a decent livelihood. The law of charity permits a man to satisfy himself rather than his neighbor, when the needs in question are of the same degree of urgency or importance. As to those laborers who turn out larger products than the average, or whose ability is unusually scarce, there is no practical difficulty; for the employer will find it profitable to give them the corresponding extra compensation. The precise question before us, then, is the claims of the laborers upon profits for remuneration above universal living wages and above the extra compensation due on account of unusual efforts, sacrifices, productivity, and scarcity. Let us call the wage that merely includes all these factors "the equitable minimum."

In competitive conditions this question becomes practical only with reference to the exceptionally efficient and productive business men. The great majority have no surplus available for wage payments in excess of the "equitable minimum." Indeed, the majority do not now pay the full "equitable minimum;" yet their profits seldom bring to them more than a decent livelihood. The relatively small number of establishments that show such a surplus as we are considering have been brought to that condition of prosperity by the exceptional ability of their directors, rather than by the unusual productivity of their employees. In so far as this exceptional directive ability is due to unusual efforts and sacrifices, the surplus returns which it produces may be claimed with justice by the employer. In so far as the surplus is the outcome of exceptional native endowments, it may still be justly retained by him in accordance with the canon of productivity. In other words, when the various groups of workers are already receiving the "equitable minimum," they have no strict right to any additional compensation out of those rare surplus profits which come into existence in conditions of competition.

This conclusion is confirmed by reference to the canon of human welfare. If exceptionally able business men were not permitted to retain the surplus in question they would not exert themselves sufficiently to produce it; labor would gain nothing; and the community would have a smaller product.

WAGES VERSUS INTEREST

Turning now to the claims of the laborers as against the capitalists, or interest receivers, we perceive that the right to any interest at all is morally inferior to the right of all the workers to the "equitable minimum." As heretofore pointed out more than once, interest is ordinarily utilized to meet less important needs than those supplied by wages. Through his labor power the interest receiver can supply all those fundamental needs which are satisfied by wages in the case of the laborer. Therefore, it seems clear that the capitalist has no right to interest until all laborers have received the "equitable minimum." It must be borne in mind, however, that any claim of the laborer against interest falls upon the owners of the productive capital in a business, upon the undertaker-capitalist, not upon the loan-capitalist.

When all the laborers in an industry are receiving the "equitable minimum," have they a right to exact anything more at the expense of interest? By interest we mean, of course, the prevailing or competitive rate that is received on productive capital. Any return to the owners of capital in excess of this rate is properly called profits rather than interest, and its relation to the claims of the laborers has received consideration in the immediately preceding section of this chapter. The question, then, is whether the laborers who are already getting the "equitable minimum" would act justly in demanding and using their economic power to obtain a part or all of the pure interest. No conclusive reason is available to justify a negative answer. The title of the capitalist is sufficient to justify him in retaining interest that comes to him through the ordinary processes of competition and bargaining; but it is not of such definite and compelling moral efficacy as to render the laborers guilty of injustice when they employ their economic power to divert further interest from the coffers of the capitalist to their own pockets.

The foregoing conclusion may seem to be a very unsatisfactory solution of a problem of justice. However, it is the only one that is practically defensible. If the capitalist's claim to interest were as definite and certain as the laborer's right to a living wage, or as the creditor's right to the money that he has loaned, the solution would be very simple: The laborers that we are discussing would have no right to strive for any of the interest.

If the economic forces which determine actual possession operate in such a way as to divert the interest-share to the laborers, they, not the capitalists, will have the valid moral title, just as Brown with his automobile rather than Jones with his spavined nag will enjoy the valid title of first occupancy to a piece of ownerless land which both have coveted.

This conclusion is confirmed by reference to the rationally and morally impossible situation that would follow from its rejection. If we deny to the laborers the moral freedom to strive for higher wages at the expense of the capitalist, we must also forbid them to follow this course at the expense of the consumer. For the great majority of consumers would stand to lose advantages to which they have as good a moral claim as the capitalists have to interest. Practically this would mean that the laborers have no right to seek remuneration in excess of the "equitable minimum;" for such excess must in substantially all cases come from either the consumer or the capitalist. On what principle can we defend the proposition that the great majority of laborers are forever restrained by the moral law from seeking more than bare living wages, and the specialized minority from demanding more than that extra compensation which corresponds to unusual efforts, sacrifices, productivity, and scarcity? Who has authorized us to shut against these classes the doors of a more liberal standard of living, and a more ample measure of self-development?

WAGES VERSUS PRICES

The right of the laborers to the "equitable minimum" implies obviously the right to impose adequate prices upon the consumers of the laborer's products. This is the ultimate source of the rewards of all the agents of production. Suppose that the laborers are already receiving the "equitable minimum." Are they justified in seeking any more at the cost of the consumer? If all the consumers were also laborers the answer would be simple, at least in principle: Rises in wages and prices ought to be so adjusted as to bring equal gains to all individuals. The "equitable minimum" is adjusted to the varying moral claims of the different classes of laborers; therefore, any rise in remuneration must be equally distributed in order to leave this adjustment undisturbed. It is a fact, however, that a large part of the consumers are not laborers; consequently they cannot look to rises in wages as an offset to their losses through rises in prices. Can they be justly required to undergo this inconvenience for laborers who are already getting the "equitable minimum"?

Let us consider first the case of higher wages versus lower prices. A few progressive and efficient manufacturers of shoes find themselves receiving large surplus profits which are likely to continue. So far as justice is concerned, they may, owing to their superior productivity, retain these profits for themselves. Seized, however, with a feeling of benevolence, or a scruple of conscience, they determine to divide future profits of this class among either the laborers or the consumers. If they reduce prices the laborers will gain something as users of shoes, but the other wearers of shoes will also be beneficiaries. If the surplus profits are all diverted to the laborers in the form of higher wages the other consumers of shoes will gain nothing. Now there does not seem to be any compelling reason, any certain moral basis, for requiring the shoe manufacturers to take one course rather than the other. Either will be correct morally. Possibly the most perfect plan would be to compromise by lowering prices somewhat and giving some rise in wages; but there is no strict obligation to follow this course.

Turning now to the question of higher wages at the cost of higher prices, we note that this would result in at least temporary hardship to four classes of persons: The weaker groups of wage earners; all self-employing persons, such as farmers, merchants, and manufacturers; the professional classes; and persons whose principal income was derived from rent or interest. All these groups would have to pay more for necessaries, comforts, and luxuries, without being immediately able to raise their own incomes correspondingly.

So far as the wage earners are concerned, all would have a right to whatever advance in the money measure of the "equitable minimum" was necessary to neutralize the higher cost of living resulting from the success of the more powerful groups in obtaining higher wages. The right of a group to the "equitable minimum" of remuneration is obviously superior to the right of another group to more than that amount. And a supreme wage-determining authority would act on this principle. It cannot be shown, however, that in the absence of any such authority empowered to protect the "equitable minimum" of the weaker laborers, the more powerful groups are obliged to refrain from demanding extra remuneration. The reason of this we shall see presently. In the meantime we call attention to the fact that, owing to the greater economic opportunity resulting from the universal prevalence of the "equitable minimum" and of industrial education, even the weaker groups of wage earners would be able to obtain some increases in wages. In the long run the more powerful groups would enjoy only those advantages which arise out of superior productivity and exceptional scarcity. These two factors could not in any system of industry be prevented from conferring advantages upon their possessors.

The other three classes would not always have an immediate recourse against the decrease in their purchasing power, brought about by the increase in wages. If the latter merely raised the remuneration of labor to the "equitable minimum," the receivers of "fixed" incomes would have no legitimate ground for complaint. If wage rates went above the "equitable minimum" in only a minority of instances, the consequent rise in prices would not be sufficient to inflict clear and certain injustice upon any of the three groups that we are considering. If the increase in wages and prices were general and considerable—in excess of the "equitable minimum"—the weaker and poorer members of the three groups would undoubtedly suffer some injustice. The situation would be very complex, and men of competence and principle who attempted to deal with it would have to take into account many considerations and circumstances in order to promote the common good and social justice.

Two objections come readily to mind against the foregoing paragraphs. The more skilled labor groups might organize themselves into a monopoly and raise their wages so high as to inflict the same degree of extortion upon consumers as that accomplished by a monopoly of capitalists. This is, indeed, possible. The remedy would be intervention by the State to fix maximum wages. Just where the maximum limit ought to be placed is a problem that could be solved only through study of the circumstances of the case, on the basis of the canons of efforts, sacrifices, productivity, scarcity, and human welfare. The second objection calls attention to the fact that we have already declared that the more powerful labor groups would not be justified in exacting more than the "equitable minimum"out of a common wage fund, so long as any weaker group was below that level; yet this is virtually what would happen when the former caused prices to rise to such an extent that the weaker workers would be forced below the "equitable minimum" through the increased cost of living. While this contingency is likewise possible, it is not a sufficient reason for preventing any group of laborers from raising their remuneration at the expense of prices. Not every rise in prices would affect the expenditures of the weaker sections of the wage earners. In some cases the burden would be substantially all borne by the better paid workers and the self-employing, professional, and propertied classes. When it did fall to any extent upon the weaker laborers, causing their real wages to fall below the "equitable minimum," it could be removed within a reasonable time by organization or by legislation. Even if these measures were found ineffective, if some of the weaker groups of workers should suffer through the higher prices, this arrangement would be preferable on the whole to one in which no class of laborers was permitted to raise its remuneration above the "equitable minimum" at the expense of prices. A restriction of this sort, whether by the moral law or by civil regulation, would tend to make wage labor a status with no hope of pecuniary progress.

CONCLUDING REMARKS

All the principles and conclusions defended in this chapter have been stated with reference to the present distributive system. Were all incomes and rewards fixed by some supreme authority, the same canons of justice would be applicable, and the application would have to be made in substantially the same way, if the authority were desirous of establishing the greatest possible measure of distributive justice. The main exception to this statement would occur in relation to the problem of raising wages above the "equitable minimum" at the expense of prices. In making any such increase, the wage-fixing authority would be obliged to take into account the effects upon the other classes of laborers, and upon all the non-wage-earning classes. Substantially the same difficulties would confront the government in a collectivist organization of industry. The effect that a rise in the remuneration of any class would produce, through a rise in the prices of commodities, upon the purchasing power of the incomes of other classes, would have to be considered and as nearly as possible ascertained. This would be no simple task. Simple or not, it would have to be faced; and the guiding ethical principles would always remain efforts, sacrifices, productivity, scarcity, and human welfare.

The greater part of the discussion carried on in this chapter has a highly theoretical aspect. From the nature of the subject matter this was inevitable. Nevertheless the principles that have been enunciated and applied seem to be incontestable. In so far as they are enforceable in actual life, they seem capable of bringing about a wider measure of justice than any other ethical rules that are available.

Possibly the applications and conclusions have been laid down with too much definiteness and the whole matter has been made too simple. On the other hand, neither honesty nor expediency is furthered by an attitude of intellectual helplessness, academic hyper-modesty, or practical agnosticism. If there exist moral rules and rational principles applicable to the problem of wage justice, it is our duty to state and apply them as fully as we can. Obviously we shall make mistakes in the process; but until the attempt is made, and a certain (and very large) number of mistakes are made, there will be no progress. We have no right to expect ready-made applications of the principles from Heaven.

For a long time to come, however, many of the questions discussed in this chapter will be devoid of large practical interest. The problem immediately confronting society is that of raising the remuneration and strengthening generally the economic position of those laborers who are now below the level, not merely of the "equitable minimum," but of a decent livelihood. This problem will be the subject of the next chapter.

CHAPTER 16

Methods of Increasing Wages

Proposals for the reform of social conditions are important in proportion to the magnitude of the evils which they are designed to remove, and are desirable in proportion to their probable efficacy. Applying these principles to the labor situation, we find that among the remedies proposed the primacy must be accorded to a minimum wage. It is the most important project for improving the condition of labor because it would increase the compensation of at least one-third of the wage earners, and because the needs of this group are greater and more urgent than the needs of the better-paid two-thirds. The former are below the level of reasonable living, while the latter are merely deprived of the opportunities of a more ample and liberal scale of living. Hence the degree of injustice suffered by the former is much greater than that of the latter. A legal minimum wage is the most desirable single measure of industrial reform because it promises a more rapid and comprehensive increase in the wages of the underpaid than any alternative device that is now available.

EARLY AMERICAN LEGISLATION

The first minimum wage law in the United States was passed by Massachusetts in 1912. The other states and jurisdictions that enacted such legislation are: Arizona, Arkansas, California, Colorado, District of Columbia, Kansas, Minnesota, Nebraska, North Dakota, Oregon, Puerto Rico, South Dakota, Texas, Utah, Washington, and Wisconsin. All these statutes were compulsory except that of Massachusetts, which imposed no penalty for violation of its provisions except the publication of the offenders' names in the newspapers. All of them,

This chapter is reprinted from *Distributive Justice: The Right and Wrong of Our Present Distribution of Wealth*, 3d ed., rev. (New York: Macmillan Co., 1942), 303–20.

except those of Arizona, Arkansas, South Dakota, and Utah, required the rates of wages to be determined by the official commissions, assisted by advisory boards or conferences representing employers, employees, and the general public. In the four states just specified the wage rates were established by the legislature in the statute itself. None of the statutes applied to adult males. The laws of Colorado, Nebraska, and Texas were never put into full operation. Steps toward the legislation were taken by Louisiana and Ohio in the form of amendments to their constitutions, but these actions were not followed by statutes. The effectiveness of this legislation is fairly described in the following excerpts:

"The minimum wage laws of certain of our states caused the wages of women to rise by as much as eighty per cent, without affecting the prices of their products or causing unemployment. That such a change as this could have occurred without being followed by one or both of these consequences can argue only that these workers were receiving less than their economic worth prior to the passing of the laws."[1]

"As to the results of minimum wage legislation, it can not be gainsaid that there have been general wage increases as the initial result of every order or piece of legislation. Orders have been outgrown and legislative rates left behind as a result of industrial changes, but this only indicates that a more efficient administration of the law with prompt adjustment methods was needed, as higher costs have regularly accompanied higher wage rates and even advanced beyond them. The fear that the minimum fixed by law would become the maximum in practice has been unrealized thus far, and some experience under a falling labor market is in the records; however, the experience of wider application and more varied conditions will be of interest, though there would seem to be no danger of such a development.

"The disinclination of employers to submit to public regulation in such matters as wage rates, hours of labor, and the number of days women may be employed per week is the survival of the individualistic attitude that has been compelled to give way to a large body of legislation affecting other fields throughout a number of years, though more recently coming into action in regard to these particulars. However, many employers have given hearty approval to both principle and results, following experience under minimum wage laws. They adopt the position that the regulation of competition is desirable and that the benefit is not to the workers alone, who are guaranteed by the law at least a minimum living cost and a sense of stability in their positions as against cheap, underbidding workers, but they are themselves likewise safeguarded against competitors who are disposed to make use of the least expensive types of woman labor or to underpay that employed."[2]

DECLARED UNCONSTITUTIONAL

When the first American laws were enacted, grave and numerous doubts were expressed of their constitutionality. The fifth and fourteenth amendments to the

Federal Constitution forbid, respectively, the Congress and the states to deprive any person of "life, liberty, or property without due process of law." It was clear that a legal requirement that women workers should be paid a certain fixed minimum wage would deprive both employers and employees of some liberty of contract and also might deprive the former of some property, in so far as it increased their wage bills. On the other hand, the legislation seemed to be in accord with due process of law as a valid exercise of the police power. Laws reducing the hours of labor of women (and in two states of certain groups of adult male workers) had been upheld by the courts, even though they lessened freedom of contract and possibly reduced employers' profits. The legislation was unsuccessfully attacked in the courts of Oregon, Minnesota, Arkansas, Washington, and Massachusetts. Only two of the twenty-nine state judges who passed upon the legislation saw in it a violation of the "due process" clause of the Constitution. On appeal to the Supreme Court of the United States, the Oregon law was upheld, April 9, 1917, by a vote of four to four.

In consequence of these decisions the friends of the legal minimum wage were fairly confident that its constitutionality was assured. For example, Lindley D. Clark wrote in 1921: "The foregoing cases may be said to establish the principle of the constitutionality of laws of this class, and to discount the probability of the success of any further efforts along this line of action. . . ."[3] Six years to the day after the Supreme Court had refused to nullify the Oregon statute, it affirmed the sentence of extinction pronounced by the Court of Appeals of the District of Columbia, upon the minimum wage law of that jurisdiction.[4] The decision was by a vote of five to three, with Justice Brandeis again refraining from participation. The verdict of unconstitutionality was based upon the fifth amendment, which forbids Congress to deprive any person of life, liberty, or property without due process of law. A year and a half later the Supreme Court invalidated the minimum wage law of Arizona, as contravening the fourteenth amendment, which puts the same restriction upon the states that the fifth amendment imposes upon Congress. In consequence of these two decisions all the compulsory minimum wage laws in the United States were swept away.

The majority of the Court in the Adkins case distinguished regulation of wages from regulation of hours, which had been sustained in several decisions. They seem to have based their distinction upon an argument which had been offered by opposing counsel in the first attack upon the legislation (before the Supreme Court of Oregon) and which had been repeated in the majority of subsequent judicial hearings. It is in substance this: A shorter-day law aims to protect the worker from some harmful effects arising out of the employment itself; for example, an injury to health through labor carried on for too many hours in one day; a minimum wage law endeavors to safeguard the workers against an evil, namely insufficient means of living, which does not arise out of the employment but rather out of the employee's own needs, which exist independently of any employment. In other words, the employment produces the evil conditions to be prevented by a shorter-day law, but not those affected by a minimum wage law. The needs of a livelihood, said the majority of the Court, have "no causal connection with the business or the contract or the work;" they are "an extraneous circumstance." Hence, the logic of the favorable decisions in the hours of labor cases was not accepted as applying to minimum wage legislation.

This sophistical and artificial argument had been fully answered more than eight years earlier by counsel for the Oregon law in these words: "Stettler is Simpson's employer, and no other person is, who alone has the use of her working energy, to maintain which a cost of not less than $8.64 per week is essential. This personal and exclusive relation," continued counsel, "differentiates the employer from any other citizen and justifies imposing upon him the minimum cost of his employee's livelihood, which is the minimum cost of her labor, given exclusively for the benefit of her employer, so that he alone should meet the essential cost. The State does not compel him to use it; all that it says to him is that if he chooses to take its benefit he must pay at least its cost."

The harm suffered by an employee whose wages do not suffice for a decent livelihood does not, indeed, originate formally in the employment or in the contract. The fact that a woman receives a wage inadequate to proper maintenance does not create the need of such maintenance; it does not always render her unable to supply that need, since she may have outside resources. Nevertheless, a contract for insufficient wages is the *indirect cause* of the evil condition experienced by a worker who has no other source of livelihood than labor. Inasmuch as the contract requires her to give all her reasonably available working time in return for a wage inadequate to a decent livelihood, it sets up a practical and economic obstacle to the attainment of that object. Contrary to the assertion of the majority of the Supreme Court, there *is* a "causal connection" between an unfair wage contract and the employee's subsistence. It is not quite as immediate as the causal relation between a labor contract imposing an excessively long working day and her health, but it is quite as real, as effective, and as injurious.

In his dissenting opinion, Chief Justice Taft flatly rejected the distinction drawn by the majority of the Court between a maximum hour law and a minimum wage law. "In absolute freedom of contract the one term is as important as the other, for both enter equally into the consideration given and received, a restriction as to one is not any greater in essence than the other, and is of the same kind. One is the multiplier and the other the multiplicand." His argument on this point is summed up thus: "I do not feel, therefore, that either on the basis of reason, experience, or authority, the boundary of the police power should be drawn to include maximum hours and exclude a minimum wage."

At any rate, the distinction has no basis in economic or practical considerations. The employer may suffer quite as great pecuniary hardship through legal reduction of the working day as through a legal increase of wages. The employee may suffer quite as much injury to health through an insufficient wage as through an excessively long working day. The exercise of the police power is as normal and legitimate in the one situation as in the other; and the artificial distinction between direct and indirect causality is entirely devoid of either rational or constitutional warrant.

Through the unjustified distinction between an hour-law and a wage-law, the majority of the Court got rid of the judicial precedents which called for a favorable decision. But this was no more than a negative achievement. Upon what positive ground did they find the minimum wage law in conflict with the Constitution? They pronounced it to be an arbitrary and unreasonable interference with that liberty which is protected by the "due process" clause of the fifth amendment. Their argument in support of this proposition will be noticed a little later. At present it will be helpful to consider how these general terms in the Constitution have been transmuted into the specific rule, "reasonable freedom of contract."

The fifth and fourteenth amendments to the Federal Constitution forbid the legislature (respectively, Congress and state law-making bodies) to "deprive any person of life, liberty, or property without due process of law." Through a series of decisions which began about half a century ago, the naked and general term, "liberty," acquired the meaning, "liberty of contract." Mr. Justice Holmes tersely and neatly characterized the development in his dissenting opinion: "The earlier decisions construing this clause began within our own memory and went no further than the unpretentious assertion of the liberty to follow the ordinary callings. Later that innocuous generality was expanded into the dogma, liberty of contract."

Nevertheless, the Supreme Court had frequently declared that constitutional freedom of contract is not unlimited. Even in the present case, the majority of the Court said: "There is, of course, no such thing as absolute freedom of contract. It is subject to a great variety of restraints." What are these restraints and how are they determined? The judicial doctrine and the judicial development concerning lawful restraints upon freedom of contract involve the words, "due process of law." The men who put that phrase into the fifth and fourteenth amendments, understood it as merely judicial process, a regular proceeding in court. Through a series of decisions, starting about the year 1890, the Supreme Court read into these words "reasonable legislation."[5]

Owing to these two courses of judicial construction and expansion, the entire "due process" clause had, at least in relation to industrial legislation, virtually assumed this form: "The legislature shall not deprive any person of liberty of contract except by a law which is reasonable."

Now we can return to the question suggested a few paragraphs back. Upon what basis did the majority of the Court conclude that the minimum wage law was arbitrary and unreasonable? Upon their general notions and theories about economics, ethics, and politics. The last six pages of the majority opinion make this fact abundantly clear. Replying to the economic objections set forth in the opinion, Chief Justice Taft made this somewhat sharp observation: "But it is not the function of this Court to hold congressional acts invalid simply because they are passed to carry out economic views which the Court believes to be unwise or unsound." The political theory set forth in the argument of the majority differs but little from eighteenth century individualism or the discredited doctrine of *laissez faire*. Their ethical theory is that wages should equal "the value of the service rendered," instead of being determined by such an "extraneous circumstance" as "the necessities of the employee." Passing over the question-begging phrase, "the value of the service," which the majority opinion carefully refrains from attempting to define, let us set over against this ethical opinion the principle laid down by Pope Leo XIII, that a wage is unjust which does not provide the worker with at least a decent livelihood. In the doctrine of the majority of the Court, the needs of the employee are an "extraneous circumstance," having no bearing upon the justice of the wage. In the doctrine of Leo XIII the worker's needs are so vital to the justice of the labor contract that if he is required by an employer to accept a wage inadequate to supply them, he is "a victim of force and injustice." All the ethical authorities of the Western world agree with the Pope and disagree with the Court.[6]

From the foregoing paragraphs it should be fairly clear just what is involved in the statement that minimum wage legislation is prohibited by the Constitution. A minimum wage law may or may not be in conflict with the theories of "freedom of contract" and "due process of law" which have been judicially construed from certain clauses in the fifth and fourteenth amendments. Whether it will be found to exhibit such a disagreement, depends upon the social and ethical philosophy of a majority of the Court. In the case, *Adkins* v. *Children's Hospital,* a bare majority were moved by an individualistic social and ethical philosophy.[7]

As we have seen in chapter xix [chapter 13 in this edition], Catholic authorities define the value of labor in terms of the worth and the needs of the laborer himself, not according to the market value, or any other value, of his work, considered independently. In the Adkins decision, the Court construed the value of labor as somehow expressed in the value of the service, taken by itself; however, the Court provided no formula by which this value could be determined. Between service and wage, said the Court, there should exist "some relation of just equivalence." If by value of service the Court meant existing market value, then competitive starvation wages are the "just equivalent" of the service. Probably the Court would have shrunk from this interpretation and inference. Obviously, its utterances on this point are merely words.

However, we should not be too hard on the men who subscribed to the majority opinion of the Supreme Court in the Adkins case, in 1923. For some years after the appearance of Pope Leo's Encyclical, in 1891, more than one Catholic theologian in Europe found difficulty in reconciling the doctrine of *Rerum Novarum* with what they conceived to be the traditional teaching on just price. Leo had declared that the wage and the value of labor were equal, at the least, to a decent livelihood. The doctrine of just price seemed to these writers to disregard considerations of livelihood and to require merely that the wage should be the

"moral equivalent" of the work. These writers were as erroneous in their understanding of the doctrine of just price as they were unsound in their conception of
industrial justice. As we saw in chapter xix [chapter 13 in this edition], the great medieval authorities on just price unanimously held that the value and just price of labor were always equivalent to the laborer's customary standard of living. These were
the two terms of the "just equivalence." That *Rerum Novarum* did not depart from
this, the traditional doctrine, was very soon shown in the famous *Responsum Ro-
manum,* issued under the direction of Pope Leo XIII, September, 1891, which declared that the equality required between work and pay was to be determined, at
the minimum, by the worker's cost of decent living; that a wage inadequate to this
purpose was not the equivalent of the work and therefore violated strict justice.[8]

A few years after the District of Columbia law was judicially nullified, certain
advocates of the legal minimum wage drew up a statute which, they hoped,
would pass the test of constitutionality. Mindful of the position taken by the
Supreme Court, that the essential vitiating provision of the D.C. law was its determination of the wage by the cost of the worker's living instead of by the value
of her labor, the authors of the law passed by the State of New York, in 1933, defined a fair wage as one that is "fairly and reasonably commensurate with the
value of the service, or class of service, rendered." The law forbade employers to
pay an "oppressive and unreasonable wage;" that is, a wage which is "*both* less
than the fair and reasonable value of the services rendered and less than sufficient
to meet the minimum cost of living necessary for health."

Notwithstanding these new definitions, an employer who was paying insufficient wages could easily escape conviction. If the wage was adequate to the "minimum cost of living," but lower than the "fair and reasonable value of the services," the employer could plead that, since he was not paying less than both, he
was not violating the law. If the wage was clearly inadequate to the cost of living,
he could, in most cases, successfully contend that it was commensurate with the
services, and, therefore, not below *both* standards.

At any rate, the New York law was attacked in the state courts. On a writ of
certiorari, the case reached the Supreme Court of the United States.[9] There, on
June 1, 1936, the law was pronounced unconstitutional by a vote of five to four,
on the ground that it exhibited the same defect which had moved the Court, thirteen years earlier, to nullify the law of the District of Columbia.

As definitely as the latter, the former forbade the employer to pay less than a
living wage; hence, it, too, violated freedom of contract and the constitutional
requirement of "due process."

BECOMES CONSTITUTIONAL

This decision was one of the most important factors in creating sentiment for
President Roosevelt's proposal to enlarge and reorganize the Supreme Court. Al-

though that project failed, it seems to have stimulated some of the justices to re-examine their conceptions of the meaning and scope of those clauses in the Constitution upon which they had previously relied when they placed the stamp of unconstitutionality upon minimum wage legislation and other measures of social and economic reform. Ten months after the decision in the New York case, the Supreme Court upheld the minimum wage law of the State of Washington.[10] The two laws were substantially the same, and the personnel of the Court remained unchanged, but the interpretation of the "due process" clause had undergone change in the mind of one of the justices. The vote had been five to four against the New York law; now it was five to four in favor of the Washington statute. In the course of his opinion in the latter case, Chief Justice Hughes made two utterances which ought to become historic. Replying to the contention that "minimum wage regulation for women is deprivation of freedom of contract," the Chief Justice said:

> What is this freedom? The Constitution does not speak of freedom of contract. It speaks of liberty and prohibits the deprivation of liberty without due process of law. In prohibiting that deprivation the Constitution does not recognize an absolute and uncontrollable liberty. Liberty in each of its phases has its history and connotation. But the liberty safeguarded is liberty in a social organization which requires the protection of law against the evils which menace the health, safety, morals, and welfare of the people. Liberty under the Constitution is thus necessarily subject to the restraints of due process, and regulation which is reasonable in relation to its subject and is adopted in the interests of the community is due process.[11]

The second last sentence of the opinion reads: "Our conclusion is that the case of *Adkins* v. *Children's Hospital, supra,* should be, and it is, overruled."[12]

Like almost all the other state laws, that of Washington applied only to women and minors. Would the Court uphold a law which also comprehended men? A favorable answer came when the Fair Labor Standards Act was sustained, February 3, 1941.[13] While the question received no explicit mention in either of the two decisions handed down that day, it was answered by clear implication in a single sentence. Justice Stone, who wrote the opinions in both cases, said tersely in *Darby:*

> Since our decision in *West Hotel Co.* v. *Parrish,* 300 U. S. 379, it is no longer open to question that the fixing of a minimum wage is within the legislative power and that the bare fact of its exercise is not a denial of due process under the fifth more than under the fourteenth Amendment. Nor is it any longer open to question that it is within the legislative power to fix maximum hours.[14]

In other words, since a wage law is constitutional for women, it is also constitutional for men.

The greater part of the argument in both opinions dealt with the authority of Congress over wages and hours in interstate commerce. The Court held that

Congress has constitutional power to regulate not only the actual transportation of goods in interstate commerce but their "production for interstate commerce," and also the power to regulate "intrastate activities where they have a substantial effect upon interstate commerce." Therefore, the Federal government has the authority to fix minimum wages and maximum hours in the fairly extensive field covered by these interpretations of interstate commerce.

In *Carter* v. *Carter,* decided less than six years before *Darby* and *Opp,* the Supreme Court had held that manufacture was *not* interstate commerce, and therefore was outside the regulatory power of Congress. The *Carter* opinion was rendered by a vote of six to three; yet the decision in the *Darby* and *Opp* cases was unanimous! What had happened in the meantime? Two of the six justices had forsaken their previous views, while the other four had been replaced by new members. It should be noted that in the *Darby* case, the Court explicitly rejected the narrow definition of interstate commerce given in the decision which held the Keating-Owen Child Labor Act unconstitutional.[15] "It should be and now is overruled," said the Court.

In 1905, it seemed to me that the legal minimum wage could not become juridically valid without an amendment to the Constitution, particularly as applied to men. Referring to "that perverse individualism which prefers irrational liberty and industrial anarchy to a legal régime of order and justice," I said:

> This spirit is still sufficiently potent to render exceedingly difficult those changes in the Federal constitution and in the constitutions of the several states which would be a preliminary requisite to any such legislation.[16]

This judgment seemed to be vindicated in 1908, when the Court upheld the Oregon ten hour law for women workers.[17] At one point in the opinion, the Court referred to its invalidation of the New York ten hour day for men in bakeries,[18] declaring that the citation of this decision against the constitutionality of the Oregon law "assumes that the difference between the sexes does not justify a different rule respecting a restriction of the hours of labor." Continuing, the Court pointed out that:

> Woman's physical structure and the performance of maternal functions place her at a disadvantage in the struggle for subsistence . . . continuance for a long time on her feet at work, repeating this from day to day, tends to injurious effects upon the body, and as healthy mothers are essential to vigorous offspring, the physical well-being of woman becomes an object of public interest and care in order to preserve the strength and vigor of the race . . . Differentiated by these matters from the other sex, she is properly placed in a class by herself, and legislation designed for her protection may be sustained, even when like legislation is not necessary for men and could not be sustained.[19]

In the thirty-four years that have since elapsed, we have come a long way from the judicial position taken in *Muller* v. *Oregon.* At that time, the legal short hour work day (10 hours) was unconstitutional as applied to men. No legal minimum wage had yet been enacted. In 1923, the legal minimum wage, applying only to women and minors, was pronounced unconstitutional. In 1937, it became constitutional. In 1941, both the minimum wage and the short work week (40 hours) for both women and men, were pronounced in accord with the Constitution.

It will be observed that by far the greater part of the journey forward has been accomplished within the last five years. It will also be observed that I was right in 1905, when I declared that changes in the Constitution to render valid minimum wage legislation would be "exceedingly difficult," but wrong in assuming that this was the only available method to attain that end. No pertinent constitutional change has been effected; but the Constitution has been reinterpreted in accordance with reason, justice, and the requirements of our industrial life. No violence has been done to either the letter or the spirit of the Constitution.[20]

THE DOCTRINAL FOUNDATION

Whether it be considered from the viewpoint of ethics, politics, or economics, the principle of the legal minimum wage is impregnable. The State has not only the moral right but the moral duty to enact legislation of this sort, whenever any important group of laborers are receiving less than living wages. One of the elementary functions and obligations of the State is to protect citizens in the enjoyment of their natural rights; and the claim to a living wage is, as we have seen, one of the natural rights of the person whose wages are his only means of livelihood. Therefore, the establishment of minimum living wages is not among the so-called "optional functions" of the State in our present industrial society. Whenever it can be successfully achieved, it is a primary and necessary function.

So far as political propriety is concerned, the State may as reasonably be expected to protect the citizen against the physical, mental, and moral injury resulting from an unjust wage contract, as to safeguard his money against the thief, his body against the bully, or his life against the assassin. In all four cases the essential welfare of the individual is injured or threatened through the abuse of superior force and cunning. Inasmuch as the legal minimum wage is ethically legitimate, the question of its enactment is entirely a question of expediency.

The question of expediency is mainly economic. A great deal of nonsense has been written and spoken about the alleged conflict between the legal minimum wage and "economic law." Economists have used no such language, indeed, for they know that economic laws are merely the expected uniformities of social action in given conditions. The economists know that economic laws are no more opposed to a legal minimum wage than to a legal eight-hour day, or legal regulations of safety and sanitation in work places. All three of these measures tend to increase the cost of production, and sometimes carry the tendency into reality. A minimum wage law is difficult to enforce, but not much more so than most other labor regulations. At any rate, the practical consideration is whether even a partial enforcement of it will not result in a marked benefit to great numbers of underpaid workers. It may throw some persons, the slower workers, out of employment; but there, again, the important question relates to the balance of good over evil for the majority of those who are below the level of decent living. At every point, therefore, the problem is one of concrete expediency, not of agreement or disagreement with a real or imaginary economic law.

Some of those who oppose the measure as inexpedient offer an elaborate argument which runs about as follows: The increase in wages caused by a minimum wage law will be shifted to the consumer in the form of higher prices; this result will in turn lead to a falling off in the demand for products; a lessened demand for goods means a reduced demand for labor; and this implies a diminished volume of employment, so that the last state of the workers becomes worse than the first. Not only is this conception too simple, but it proves too much. If it were correct every rise in wages, howsoever brought about, would be ill advised; for every rise would set in motion the same fatal chain of events. Voluntary increases of remuneration by employers would be quite as futile as the efforts of a labor union. This is little more than the old wages fund theory in a new dress.

The argument is too simple because it is based upon an insufficient analysis of the facts. There are no less than four sources from which the increased wages required by a minimum wage law might in whole or in part be obtained. In the first place, higher wages will often give the workers both the physical capacity and the spirit that make possible a larger output. Thus, they could themselves equivalently provide a part at least of their additional remuneration. When, secondly, the employer finds that labor is no longer so cheap that it can be profitably used as a substitute for intelligent management, better methods of production, and up to date machinery, he will be compelled to introduce one or more of these improvements, and to offset increased labor cost by increased managerial and mechanical efficiency. In the third place, a part of the increased wage cost can be defrayed out of profits, in two ways: Through a reduction in the profits of the majority of business concerns in an industry; but more frequently through the elimination of the less efficient, and the consequent increase in the volume of business done by the more efficient. In the latter establishments the additional outlay for wages might be fully neutralized by the diminished managerial expenses and fixed charges per unit of product. This elimination of unfit undertakers would not only be in the direction of greater social efficiency, but in the interest of better employment conditions generally; for it is the less competent employers who are mainly responsible for the evil of "sweating," when they strive to reduce the cost of production by the only method that they know; that is, the oppression of labor. Should the three foregoing factors fall short of providing or neutralizing the increased wages, the recourse would necessarily be to the fourth source; namely, a rise in the price of products. However, there is no definite reason for assuming that the rise will in any case be sufficient to cause a net decrease of demand. In the case of possibly the majority of products, the lessened demand on the part of the other classes might be entirely counterbalanced by the increased demand at the hands of the workers whose purchasing power had been raised through the minimum wage law. The effect upon sales, and hence upon business and production, which follows from an increase in the effective consuming power of the laboring classes is frequently ignored or underestimated. So far as consumers' goods are concerned, it seems certain that a given addition to the income of the wage-earning classes will lead to a greater increase in the demand for products than an equal addition to the income of any other section of the people.*

---

*Editor's Note: The last four sections of this chapter have been omitted. They treat the existing minimum wage laws in 1942, labor unions, the reasons that labor organizations are not a substitute for minimum wage legislation, and the trends and possibilities for a living wage in 1942.

CHAPTER 17

A New Status for Labor

Neither the minimum wage nor the labor unions, nor a better distribution, nor all of them together, are capable of giving the laborers satisfactory conditions, or society a stable industrial system. Even though all the workers were receiving living wages and a continuously increasing proportion of them something more; even though all were enrolled in effective labor unions; even though all were continuously employed, neither their status nor the condition of industrial society would be reassuring. The defects inherent in the system may be summed up thus: The worker is not interested in his work and he has not sufficient control over his economic life. Indeed, the former evil is ultimately reducible to the latter.

The worker is not interested in his work for very simple reasons. In the great majority of occupations and tasks his creative faculties are not sufficiently invoked to give him a technical or artistic interest. This is all but universally true of machine operations. In the second place, his directive faculties are not permitted to function sufficiently to arouse in him the interest which results from control over the processes of production. Finally, the fact that his income (except when he is paid by the piece) is not closely dependent upon the quantity or quality of his product, deprives him of adequate economic interest. His efficiency is only that which is necessary to retain his job; his interest is mainly that of getting the best working conditions.

The industrial population is to-day rather sharply divided into two groups. A small number of persons own and direct the instruments of production. The great majority neither own nor direct. They merely carry out orders. As a natural consequence of this unnatural division of functions, we have lack of interest and lack of efficiency.

This chapter is reprinted from *Distributive Justice: The Right and Wrong of Our Present Distribution of Wealth,* 3d ed., rev. (New York: Macmillan Co., 1942), 333–42.

It is obvious that neither the injury to the workers nor the limitation upon social efficiency which are inherent in this situation can be remedied by mere increases in the remuneration and the economic security of the employees. What they require is nothing less than a change of status.

TOWARD INDUSTRIAL DEMOCRACY

The most effective change in status would be achieved if the workers were owners of the instruments of production. Individual ownership of the tools with which a man works is the best means yet devised for making him interested in his work and its results. In our system of large industrial units this is no longer possible for more than a small proportion of the wage earners. The industrial units, concerns, businesses, are too few and they cost too much.

Nevertheless, it is entirely feasible to introduce the great majority of the workers to the functions and advantages of ownership by a gradual process. All the elements of ownership fall under management, profits, and relative independence. The methods by which these goods may be obtained are, respectively, labor sharing in management, profits, and ownership.

Labor sharing in management does not mean that labor should immediately take part in either the commercial or the financial operations of a business. Such activities as the purchase of materials, the marketing of the product, the borrowing of money, and many others of a commercial and financial character are at present beyond the competence of the great majority of wage earners. On the other hand, labor sharing in management means something more than helping to determine the labor contract. That is already a recognized function of labor unions.

In a general way, the phrase denotes participation by labor in the productive operations of industrial management. Men who spend their entire working time in a factory or shop or store or mine or railroad, naturally and necessarily come to know something about the processes upon which they are engaged. If they have ordinary intelligence they sometimes desire to exercise some control over these processes, to suggest improvements, to recommend ways of eliminating waste. After all, the vast majority of persons would like to determine their immediate environment. In every normal human being there exists some directive, initiative, creative capacity. Those who are engaged in industry are not sharply divided into two classes, the one possessing all the directive ability, the other unable to do anything but carry out orders. The wage earners have some directive ability, some capacity for becoming more than instruments of production.

A considerable number of industrial concerns have adopted under one form or another the principle of labor sharing in management. Some of them are frankly paternalistic, operated by the employer through a "company union" or some other kind of organization dominated by himself. Others exemplify equality of cooperation between employer and employee. Some have achieved considerable success; others have failed. In this place, only one such enterprise will receive specific notice. This is the plan in operation for many years in the shops of the Baltimore and Ohio Railroad. Three-fourths of a million railway employees have endorsed this form of employer and employee cooperation.

Some idea of the reality of labor's participation may be obtained from the fact that many thousands of suggestions relating to shop operations have been made at the bi-weekly meetings of the joint committees of workers and management. A very large proportion of these came from the employees. A fundamentally important feature of the arrangement is that it recognizes the established unions of the workers. The labor members of the joint committees are chosen by the regular shop unions. Among the matters and problems considered by the joint committees are: Employee grievances, employee training, better conditions of employment in respect to working facilities, sanitation, lighting and safety, conservation of materials, increased output, improved quality of workmanship, recruiting of employees, stabilizing employment, and employee sharing in the gains of cooperation.

The principles and methods of the B. & O. Plan can be applied to every variety of industry. Of course, modification of detail will be necessary to meet the needs of the particular industry into which the arrangement is introduced. In every case where sincere and sustained effort is made to give the plan a fair trial the following gains may reasonably be expected: The workers will have greater consciousness of their dignity, greater self-respect, greater interest in their work, and a feeling of responsibility for the results of their work; the merely business relation between employer and employee will be supplanted by a human relation which will cause the employee to look upon himself more as a partner than as a mere hired man, while both the employer and community will be benefited through a larger and better product.[1]

The second element of ownership which could be made available to the workers, is a share in the profits of the concern that employs them. In a sense this may be regarded as the most vital element in the system of private industry. It rests upon the theory that when men enter into competition with one another, attracted by the lure of indefinite gains, their energy and inventiveness will be aroused to such an extent that they will find and apply new methods of production and of labor organization, with the result that the cost of production will be constantly lowered. In this way the whole community will be benefited. Until competition became so widely supplanted by combination, this theory was verified in practice. To the extent that competition prevails in industry, the theory is still sound. Now the method of profit-sharing by the employees simply extends this general principle of indefinite gains to the wage-earning classes. If it is desirable to permit the directors of industry to obtain indefinitely large gains as a result of hard work and efficiency, why is it not equally desirable to hold out this hope to the rank and file of the workers?

Profit-sharing gives to the workers, in addition to their wages, a part of the *surplus* profits. So long as the régime of private capital obtains, the owners of capital will have to be assured the prevailing rate of interest. Therefore, it is not feasible to give any part of the profits of a concern to the workers until the owners of capital have obtained this prevailing rate. If five per cent, for example, is the rate of interest that can generally be obtained on investments of normal security, then the owners of the capital in a concern should be guaranteed that amount before profit-sharing is put into operation.

How much of the surplus which remains after the payment of normal and necessary interest and dividends should go to the workers? Various proportions have been allotted in various profit-sharing arrangements. Nevertheless, the most scientific method would be that which awarded the surplus profits to the *workers exclusively;* that is, to all persons who do any work in the concern in any capacity, whether subordinate or directive. Why should the nonworking stockholders receive any part of a surplus to the production of which they have contributed neither time nor thought nor labor? No one proposes that the bondholders of a corporation should share in the surplus profits. With the exception of the board of directors, executive officers, and a few others, the stockholders, so far as work is concerned, are in exactly the same position as the bondholders. If matters are so arranged that they are certain to receive the prevailing rate of interest each year, and if a sufficient reserve is set aside to protect them against losses, they are receiving all that seems to be fair and all that is necessary to induce men to invest their money in a concern of this sort. Therefore, the surplus profits should all be distributed among those who perform any function in the industry, from the president of the company down to the office boy. And the distribution should be in proportion to their respective salaries and wages.

The third advantage of ownership, relative independence, is obtainable only through ownership itself. Since only a few wage earners can hope to become individual, or dominant, owners of an entire business, the great majority will have to be content with partial ownership. At this point we must be on our guard against an insidious theory which has had the benefit of much propaganda in recent years. It is generally advanced under the designation, "employee ownership." Impressive totals are marshalled, describing the vast increase in the number of workers who own shares in the corporations that employ them, or in some other corporation. The climax of perfection is assumed to be reached when the majority of the employees of a concern are numbered among its stockholders.

As a method of providing the employees with those advantages of ownership which will at once make them interested in their work and give them an adequate status in the industrial system, mere proprietorship of securities, even though individually large, is inadequate. For it fails to give the workers *control.* It confers upon them no share in management, whether of the productive processes or of commercial and financial policies. Even in the most attractive descriptions of the most nearly complete participations in stock ownership, we find no statement of the *proportion of the total stock* which is held by the employees. As a matter of fact, it is always far less than a majority.[2]

Lacking this measure of ownership, the employees lack control. Lacking control, their share in the stock of the corporation which employs them has no more practical significance than an equal amount of property in some other corporation, or an equivalent quantity of deposits in savings banks.

The principle of industrial democracy underlying the foregoing paragraphs was endorsed by Pope Pius XI in the following paragraph:

> In the present state of human society, however, We deem it advisable that the wage-contract should, when possible, be modified somewhat by a contract of partnership, as is already being tried in various ways to the no small gain both of the wage earners and of the employers. In this way wage earners are made sharers in some sort in the ownership, or the management, or the profits.[3]

THE OCCUPATIONAL GROUP SYSTEM

Much more important than the statement just quoted is the plan outlined by Pope Pius for the reconstruction of the social order.[4] The plan is variously designated as, "the vocational group system," "the occupational group system," "the modern guild system," "the corporative organization of society." But never can it be properly called the "corporative state."[5]

In more than one place Pope Pius had declared that the root cause of all our economic evils is individualism. There is too much individual freedom for the strong, the cunning, and the unscrupulous. There is too much freedom for powerful individuals to combine and dominate the whole of society. There is too much antagonism between economic classes. The remedy can not be more freedom for individuals, or more power for combinations. The excesses of individualism, the tyranny of combinations, and the conflict between classes, can be adequately controlled only by the State. "When we speak of the reform of the social order," says Pope Pius, "it is principally the State we have in mind."

Many social reformers who applaud the Pope's analysis of evils and his proposal to seek a remedy in the State, will assume that he means, or ought to mean, some form of collectivism, some kind of Socialism. These persons are completely mistaken. The Holy Father does not want State ownership and operation of the means of production. He wants more, not less, rational freedom for all individuals. Class conflict he would eliminate not by a futile effort to abolish classes, but by bringing them into a practical scheme of cooperation. On the whole, he would decentralize the economic activities of the State. He would interpose a graded hierarchical order, a system of subsidiary organizations between the individual and the State.

"The aim of social legislation, therefore, must be," says the Pope, "the reestablishment of occupational groups." His choice of the word "reestablishment," instead of "establishment," shows that he is not proposing something new. He is taking as a model that organization of industry known as the Guild System. In that system, masters, journeymen, and apprentices, were all united in one association. Of course, that arrangement could not be set up without change in our machine system, where the place of the associated master workman is taken by the employing capitalist and that of the associated journeyman by the propertyless employee.

Nevertheless, the main principle and the spirit of the guilds could be adopted and adapted. Occupational groups could be organized, which, in the words of Pope Pius, "would bind men together, not according to the position which they occupy in the labor market but according to the diverse functions which they exercise in society." In the railroad industry, for example, the owners, managers and employees, would be united with reference to the common social function which all these classes perform, namely, that of carrying goods and passengers in cars over steel rails.

In other words, these organizations would comprise both employers and employees, both capitalists and laborers. The occupational group might be empowered by law to fix wages, interest, dividends, and prices, to determine working conditions, to adjust industrial disputes, and to carry on whatever economic planning was thought feasible. All the groups in the several concerns of an industry could be federated into a national council for the whole industry. There could also be a federation of all the industries of the nation. The occupational groups, whether local or national, would enjoy power and authority over industrial matters coming within their competence. This would be genuine self-government in industry.

Of course, the occupational groups would not be entirely independent of the government. No economic group, whether of capitalists or laborers, or of both in combination, can be trusted with unlimited power to fix their own profits and remuneration. While allowing to the occupational groups the largest measure of reasonable freedom in the management of their own affairs, the State, says Pius XI, should perform the tasks which belong to it and which it alone can effectively accomplish, namely, those of "directing, watching, stimulating, and restraining, as circumstances suggest or necessity demands. . . ."

It has been asserted that the occupational group system would involve the abolition of capitalism. Whether this is true depends upon our definition. If we take capitalism to mean merely the private ownership of capital, the system of occupational groups might still be called a capitalist system. If, however, we use the word capitalism in its historical sense, with its traditional philosophy, then it is automatically excluded by every important principle and proposal in *Quadragesimo Anno*.

For the underlying principles of capitalism are those of individualism and economic liberalism. In a dozen places, the Holy Father condemns individualism because it calls for unlimited competition and rejects state regulation. In a dozen places, he condemns liberalism because it authorizes men to seek unlimited profits and unlimited interest, and to pay the lowest wages which men can be coerced to accept under the guise of a "free" contract. In the words of J. L. and Barbara Hammond, liberalism asserted the "right to acquire and use property, subject to no qualifications . . . the right to take what interest and profit you could get; to buy and sell as you pleased . . . for the Divine Right of Kings it substituted the Divine Right of Capitalists." Capitalism in this sense would obviously be impossible under the Pope's system of occupational groups.

It should be noted that the association of employers and employees in the occupational group organizations does not exclude distinct organizations of either or both classes. The Holy Father points out that "those who are engaged in the same trade or profession will form free associations among themselves, for purposes connected with their occupations. . . . Not only is man free to institute those unions which are of a private character, but he has the right further to adopt such organization and such rules as may best conduce to the attainment of their respective objects."[6]

The new social order recommended by the Holy Father would exemplify neither individualism nor Socialism. Neither the individual nor the corporation would be permitted to make extortionate and anti-social "free" contracts. The profit motive would continue to function, but not to enjoy unlimited scope. It would be subjected to the restraints of reason and justice. On the other hand, the new social order would not be Socialism. It would not place the entire control and operation of industry in the hands of a supreme general staff. It would not abolish private property. It would not regiment labor or substantially restrict freedom of choice by the consumer.

In a word, the industrial system proposed by the Pope would occupy a middle ground between capitalism and Communism, between individualism and Socialism. It would provide all the freedom and opportunity which every individual needs to develop his personality; and it would avoid that concentration of power which would defeat itself and which free men would not long tolerate.

CHAPTER 18

Summary and Conclusion

Throughout this book we have been concerned with a twofold problem: To apply the principles of justice to the workings of the present distributive system, and to point out the modifications of the system that seem to promise a larger measure of justice. The mechanism of distribution was described in the introductory chapter as apportioning the national product among the four classes that contribute the necessary factors to the process of production, and the first part of the problem was stated as that of ascertaining the size of the share which ought to go to each of these classes.

THE LANDOWNER AND RENT

We began this inquiry with the landowner and his share of the product, i.e., rent. The arguments of Henry George against it are invalid because they do not prove that labor is the only title of property, nor that men's equal rights to the earth are incompatible with private landownership, nor that the so-called social production of land values confers upon the community a right to rent. Private ownership is not only socially preferable to the Socialist and the Single Tax systems of land tenure, but it is, as compared with Socialism certainly, and as compared with the Single Tax probably, among man's natural rights.

Nevertheless, the present system of land tenure is not perfect. Its principal defects are: The promotion of certain monopolies, as anthracite coal, steel, natural gas, petroleum, water power, and lumber; the diversion of excessive gains to landowners and the very large holdings by individuals and corporations; and the

This chapter is reprinted from *Distributive Justice: The Right and Wrong of Our Present Distribution of Wealth*, 3d ed., rev. (New York: Macmillan Co., 1942), 343–48.

exclusion of large masses of men from the land because the owners will not sell it at its present economic value. The remedies for these evils fall mainly under the heads of ownership and taxation. All mineral, timber, gas, oil, grazing, and water-power lands that are now publicly owned, should remain the property of the states and the nation, and be brought into use through a system of leases to private individuals and corporations. Cities should purchase land, and lease it for long periods to persons who wish to erect business buildings and dwellings. By means of taxation the State might appropriate a part of the future increases of land values; and it could transfer the taxes on improvements to land, provided that the process were sufficiently gradual to prevent any substantial decline in land values. In some cases a supertax might with advantage be applied to exceptionally large and valuable holdings and to farms in absentee ownership.

THE CAPITALIST AND INTEREST

The Socialist contention that the laborer has a right to the entire product of industry, and therefore that the capitalist has no right to interest, is invalid unless the former alleged right can be effectuated in a reasonable scheme of distribution; and we know that the contemplated Socialist scheme is impracticable. Nevertheless, the refutation of the Socialist position does not automatically prove that the capitalist has a right to take interest. Of the titles ordinarily alleged in support of such a right, productivity and service are inconclusive, while abstinence is valid only in the case of those capital owners to whom interest was a necessary inducement for saving. Since it is uncertain whether sufficient capital would be provided without interest, and since the legal suppression of interest is impracticable, the State is justified in permitting the practice of taking interest.

The only available methods of lessening the burden of interest are a reduction in the rate, and a wider diffusion of capital through cooperative enterprise. The second proposal contains great possibilities of betterment in the fields of banking, agriculture, stores, and manufacture. Through cooperation the weaker farmers, merchants, and consumers can do business and obtain goods at lower costs, and save money for investment with greater facility, while the laborers can slowly but surely become capitalists and interest-receivers, as well as employees and wage-receivers.

THE BUSINESS MAN
AND PROFITS

Just remuneration for the active agents of production, whether they be directors of industry or employees, depends fundamentally upon five canons of distribution; namely, needs, efforts and sacrifices, productivity, scarcity, and human welfare. In the light of these principles it is evident that business men who use fair methods in competitive conditions, have a right to all the profits that they can obtain. On the other hand, no business man has a strict right to a minimum living profit, since that would imply an obligation on the part of consumers to support superfluous and inefficient directors of industry. Those who possess a monopoly of their products or commodities have no right to more than the prevailing or competitive rate of interest on their capital, though they have the same right as competitive business men to any surplus gains that may be due to superior efficiency. The principal unfair methods of competition, that is, discriminative underselling, exclusive-selling contracts, and discrimination in transportation, are all unjust.

The remedies for unjust profits are to be found mainly in the action of government. The State should either own and operate all natural monopolies, or so regulate their charges that the owners would obtain only the competitive rate of interest on the actual investment, and only such surplus gains as are clearly due to superior efficiency. It should prevent artificial monopolies from practicing extortion toward either consumers or competitors. Inasmuch as overcapitalization has frequently enabled monopolist concerns to obtain unjust profits, and always presents a strong temptation in this direction, it should be legally prohibited. A considerable part of the excessive profits already accumulated can be subjected to a better distribution by progressive income, excess profits, and inheritance taxes. Finally, the possessors of large fortunes and incomes could help to bring about a more equitable distribution by voluntarily complying with the Christian duty of bestowing their superfluous goods upon needy persons and objects.

THE LABORER AND WAGES

None of the theories of fair wages that have been examined under the heads of "the prevailing rate," "exchange-equivalence," or "productivity" is in full harmony with the principles of justice. The minimum of wage justice can, however, be described with sufficient definiteness and certainty. The adult male laborer has a right to a wage sufficient to provide himself and family with a decent livelihood, and the adult female has a right to remuneration that will enable her to live decently as a self-supporting individual. At the basis of this right are three ethical principles: All persons are equal in their inherent claims upon the bounty of nature; this general right of access to the earth becomes concretely valid through the expenditure of useful labor; and those persons who are in control of the goods and opportunities of the earth are morally bound to permit access thereto on reasonable terms by all who are willing to work. In the case of the laborer, this right of reasonable access can be effectuated only through a living wage. The obligation of paying this wage falls upon the employer because of his function in the industrial organism. And the laborer's right to a living wage is morally superior to the employer's right to interest on his capital.

Laborers who put forth unusual efforts or make unusual sacrifices have a right to a proportionate excess over living wages, and those who are exceptionally productive or exceptionally scarce have a right to the extra compensation that goes to them under the operation of competition.

The methods of increasing wages are mainly four: A minimum wage by law, labor unions, profit-sharing, and ownership. The first has been fairly well approved by experience, and is in no wise contrary to the principles of either ethics, politics, or economics. The second has likewise been vindicated in practice, though it is of only small efficacy in the case of those workers who are receiving less than living wages. The third and fourth would enable laborers to supplement their wage incomes by profits and interest, and would render our industrial system more stable by giving the workers an influential voice in the conditions of employment, and by laying the foundation of that contentment and conservatism which arise naturally out of the possession of property.

CONCLUDING OBSERVATIONS

No doubt many of those who have taken up this volume with the expectation of finding therein a satisfactory formula of distributive justice, and who have patiently followed the discussion to the end, are disappointed and dissatisfied at the final conclusions. Both the particular applications of the rules of justice and the proposals for reform must have seemed complex and indefinite. They are not nearly so simple and definite as the principles of Socialism or the Single Tax. And yet, there is no escape from these limitations. Neither the principles of industrial justice nor the constitution of our socio-economic system is simple. Therefore, it is impossible to give our ethical conclusions anything like mathematical accuracy. They only claim that is made for the discussion is that the moral judgments are fairly reasonable, and the proposed remedies fairly efficacious. When both have been realized in practice, the next step in the direction of wider distributive justice will be much clearer than it is to-day.

Although the attainment of greater justice in distribution is the primary and most urgent need of our time, it is not the only one that is of great importance. Neither just distribution, nor increased production, nor both combined, will insure a stable and satisfactory social order without a considerable change in human hearts and ideals. The rich must cease to put their faith in material things, and rise to a simpler and saner plane of living; the middle classes and the poor must give up their envy and snobbish imitation of the false and degrading standards of the opulent classes; and all must learn the elementary lesson that the path to achievement worthwhile leads through the field of hard and honest labor, not of lucky "deals" or gouging of the neighbor, and that the only life worth living is that in which one's cherished wants are few, simple, and noble. For the adoption and pursuit of these ideals the most necessary requisite is a revival of genuine religion.[1]

A LIVING WAGE

CHAPTER 19

The Basis and Justification of Rights

The thesis to be maintained in this volume is that the laborer's claim to a Living Wage is of the nature of a *right*. This right is personal, not merely social: that is to say, it belongs to the individual as individual, and not as member of society; it is the laborer's personal prerogative, not his share of social good; and its primary end is the welfare of the laborer, not that of society. Again, it is a natural, not a positive right; for it is born with the individual, derived from his rational nature, not conferred upon him by a positive enactment. In brief, the right to a Living Wage is individual, natural and absolute.

A right in the moral sense of the term may be defined as an inviolable moral claim to some personal good. When this claim is created, as it sometimes is, by civil authority it is a positive or legal right; when it is derived from man's "rational nature" it is a natural right. All rights are means, moral means, whereby the possessor of them is enabled to reach some end. Natural rights are the moral means or opportunities by which the individual attains the end appointed to him by nature. For the present it is sufficient to say that this end is right and reasonable life. The exigencies of right and reasonable living, therefore, determine the existence, and number, and extent of man's natural rights. Just as his intellectual, volitional, sensitive, nutritive and motive faculties are the positive, or physical, agencies by which he lives and acts as a human being, so his natural rights are the *moral* faculties requisite to the same end. He cannot attain this end adequately unless he is regarded by his fellows as morally immune from arbitrary interference. They must hold themselves morally restrained from hindering him in the reasonable exercise of his faculties. His powers of intellect, will, sense, nutrition and motion will be of little use to him if his neighbors may licitly deprive him,

This chapter is reprinted from *A Living Wage: Its Ethical and Economic Aspects* (New York: Macmillan, 1906), 43–66.

whenever it may suit their convenience, of his external goods, or his liberty, or his members, or his life. In addition to his positive powers, he stands in need of those moral powers which give to his claim upon certain personal goods that character of sacredness which restrains or tends to restrain arbitrary interference by his fellows.

Man's natural rights are absolute, not in the sense that they are subject to no limitations—which would be absurd—but in the sense that their validity is not dependent on the will of anyone except the person in whom they inhere. They are absolute in existence but not in extent. Within reasonable limits their sacredness and binding force can never cease. Outside of these limits, they may in certain contingencies disappear. If they were not absolute to this extent, if there were no circumstances in which they were secure against *all* attacks, they would not deserve the name of rights. The matter may be made somewhat clearer by one or two examples. The right to life is said to be absolute because no human power may licitly kill an innocent man as a mere means to the realization of any end whatever. The life of the individual person is so sacred that, as long as the right thereto has not been forfeited by the perverse conduct of the subject himself, it may not be subordinated to the welfare of any other individual or any number of individuals. Not even to preserve its own existence may the State directly and deliberately put an unoffending man to death. When, however, the individual is not innocent, when by such actions as murder or attempted murder he has forfeited his right to live, he may, of course, be rightfully executed by civil authority, or killed in self-defense by his fellow man. He may also be compelled to risk his life on behalf of his country, for that is a part of his duty; and he may with entire justice be deprived of life indirectly and incidentally, as when noncombatants are unavoidably killed in a city that is besieged in time of war. Again, the right to liberty and property are not absolute in the sense that the individual may have as much of these goods as he pleases and do with them as he pleases, but inasmuch as within reasonable limits—which are always determined by the essential needs of personal development—these rights are sacred and inviolable.

With respect to their natural rights, all men are equal, because all are equal in the rational nature from which such rights are derived. By nature every man is a person, that is, a rational, self-active, independent being. Every man is rational because endowed with the faculties of reason and will. His will impels him to seek the good, the end, of his being, and his reason enables him to find and adjust means to this end. Every man is self-active, inasmuch as he is master of his own faculties and able in all the essentials of conduct to direct his own actions. Every man is independent in the sense that he is morally complete in himself, is not a part of any other man, nor inferior to any man, either in the essential qualities of his being or in the end toward which he is morally bound to move. In short, every individual is an "end in himself," and has a personality of his own to develop through the exercise of his own faculties. Because of this equality in the essentials of personality, men are of equal intrinsic worth, have ends to attain that are of equal intrinsic importance, and consequently have equal natural rights to the means without which these ends cannot be achieved.

Only in the abstract, however, are men's natural rights equal. In the concrete they are unequal, just as are the concrete natures from which they spring.[1] This is not to say that equality of rights is an empty abstraction, without any vital meaning or force or consequences in actual life. Men are equal as regards the *number* of their natural rights. The most important of these are the rights to life, to liberty, to property, to a livelihood, to marriage, to religious worship, to intellectual and moral education. These inhere in all men without distinction of person, but they have not necessarily the same *extension,* or content, in all. Indeed, proportional justice requires that individuals endowed with different powers should possess rights that vary in degree. For example, the right to a livelihood and the right to an education will include a greater amount of the means of living and greater opportunities of self-improvement in the cases of those who have greater needs and greater capacities. But in *every* case the natural rights of the individual will embrace a certain minimum of the goods to which these rights refer, which minimum is determined by the reasonable needs of personality. The rights that any person will possess in excess of this minimum will depend upon a variety of circumstances, individual and social. Hence, instead of saying that the natural rights of all men are equal in the abstract but not in the concrete, it would perhaps be more correct, or at least less misleading, to describe them as equal in kind, number and sacredness, and in extension relatively to their particular subjects; but not in quantity nor in *absolute* content.

Such in bare outline is the theory of the character, purpose, and extent of natural rights. Do they really exist? Is the individual really endowed with moral prerogatives, inviolable claims, in virtue of which it is wrong, for instance, to take from him, so long as he is innocent of crime, his life or his liberty? Whence comes the validity and sacredness of these claims? The answers to these questions have already been briefly indicated in the statement of the *end* for which the claims exist. Natural rights are necessary means of right and reasonable living. They are essential to the welfare of a human being, a person. They exist and are sacred and inviolable because the welfare of the person exists—as a fact of the ideal order—and is a sacred and inviolable thing. It was Cicero who wrote: "Fine in philosophia constituto, constituta sunt omnia." In problems of philosophy, when we have established the end we have established all things else. Let us look more deeply, then, into the scope and character of this end to which natural rights are but means.

Right and reasonable life, the welfare of the person, consist in the development of man's personality through the harmonious and properly ordered exercise of his facilities. He should subordinate his sense-faculties to his rational faculties; exercise his rational faculties consistently with the claims of his Creator and the reasonable demands of his fellows; and seek the goods that minister to the senses and the selfish promptings of the spirit in subordination to the higher goods, namely, those of the intellect and of the disinterested will. In a word, the supreme earthly goal of conduct is to know in the highest degree the best that is to be known, and to love in the highest degree the best that is to be loved. These highest objects of knowledge and love are God, and, in proportion to the degrees of excellence that they possess, His creatures. To prove that these moral and spiritual values are facts, we have only to appeal to the consciousness of any normally constituted human being. The average man has an abiding conviction that the rational faculties are higher, nobler, more excellent, of greater intrinsic worth than the sense-faculties; that consequently the goods of the mind are to be preferred to those of the senses; and that among the activities of the rational powers those dictated by disinterested love are intrinsically better than those which make for selfishness. These primary and general moral intuitions produce in the mind of the person who heeds them the conviction that it is not only reasonable but *obligatory* for him to pursue the path of conduct thus dimly outlined. The immediate objective basis of this obligation is the intrinsic superiority of the higher faculties, the infinite worth of God, and the essential sacredness of human personality. The ultimate source of the obligation is the Will of God; just as the ultimate source of the distinction between the higher and lower faculties, activities, and goods is the Divine Essence; and just as the ultimate source of the intuitions by which we perceive these distinctions is the Divine Reason.

Since, therefore, the individual is obliged to live a moral and reasonable life in the manner just described, the means to this end, i.e., natural rights, are so necessary and so sacred that all other persons than the one in whom they reside are morally restrained from interfering with or ignoring them. The dignity of personality imposes upon the individual the duty of self-perfection; he cannot fulfil this duty adequately unless he is endowed with natural rights. Such is the immediate basis of natural rights and the proximate source of their sacredness; their ultimate source is to be found in the Reason and Will of God, who has decreed that men shall pursue self-perfection and that they shall not arbitrarily deprive one another of the means essential to this purpose.

This method of basing the individual's natural rights upon his duties is perhaps the one most commonly employed by those writers who hold individual perfection to be the immediate end and rule of conduct. According to another mode of reasoning, they rest, not upon the duties of their possessor, but upon those duties of other men toward him which are called *juridical,* that is, the "other-regarding" duties that cover goods which in the strict sense *belong* to him as his own. Thus the fulfilment of lawful contracts is a juridicial duty, while assisting the needy is only a duty of charity. All juridical duties may be summed up in the command, "thou shalt not arbitrarily interfere with the external liberty of thy fellow man," for external liberty comprises all those opportunities of activity, acquisition and possession that are essential to the pursuit of reasonable self-perfection. Corresponding to and implied by these juridical duties in one man are those moral prerogatives in other men that we call natural rights. The foundation and source of these duties is that precept of the natural law (understanding by natural law that portion of God's eternal law which applies to human conduct and is written in the human reason) which enjoins men to respect the dignity of human personality in one another.[2]

This line of argument, however, suggests that not even the juridical duties of men are formally necessary as a basis and justification of natural rights. These duties are, indeed, imposed upon man by the natural law, but the reason why this particular precept of the law exists, as well as the reason that constrains us to believe that it does exist is to be found in the intrinsic and inviolable worth of the individual. That is the ultimate basis—on this side of God—of both juridical duties and natural rights. To prove the existence of the latter, it seems, therefore, logically sufficient to show that because of his intrinsic dignity a person is morally *privileged* to pursue self-perfection, and his fellows are morally restrained from hindering his exercise of the privilege. Natural rights may be likened to the legal right by which a man holds a piece of land that he has bought from the State. His claim thereto is founded neither upon his duty to support his family (to which end the produce of the land may be assumed to be the necessary means) nor upon the obligation which binds his neighbors to leave him in undisturbed possession. Similarly, the individual's natural rights may be regarded as independent both of his own duties and of the duties which these rights occasion in his fellows.[3]

Finally, natural rights can be logically defended on the principles of what may be called intuitive hedonism. There are men who maintain that the supreme end and rule of conduct is universal happiness. By this phrase they mean, not "the greatest happiness of the greatest number," nor the general happiness of the group or of society,—all of which are equivalent in the concrete to the happiness of the majority—but the happiness of each and every human being. They insist that, since human happiness is the good of a person, it has *intrinsic worth,* is in itself a sacred thing, and that all individuals have, therefore, essentially equal claims to the opportunity of pursuing it. This doctrine is hedonistic, inasmuch as it makes happiness the ultimate end, and intuitive, inasmuch as it postulates not merely the desirableness of personal happiness, but the intrinsic worth of all human happiness. The late Professor Sidgwick held substantially this view, although he admitted that it contains an inherent contradiction.[4] For if the intuition of "rational benevolence" be acknowledged as logically sufficient to compel me to forego my own happiness for the greater happiness of others, then the ultimate end, rule and determinant of right action is no longer *my* happiness— which is the only "desirable consciousness" that can have any meaning for me— but conformity to the dictates of reason. In other words, *reason* assures me that human happiness is valuable *per se,* while all my aspirations and experiences tell me happiness is a good only insofar as it provides *me* with agreeable states of consciousness. If, however, the general principle be admitted in spite of its inherent weakness, a system of natural rights can be logically deduced therefrom.

All of these methods, therefore, posit as the ultimate earthly basis of the individual's natural rights the inherent sacredness of his personality. This is true even of the argument which derives rights from the duty of perfecting one's self; for this duty is itself founded upon the intrinsic worth of the person, specifically of his higher faculties. Hence we find that those who reject the doctrine of natural rights, and who reason logically, reject likewise the principle of the essential and absolute dignity of every human being. They either deny that anything in the universe possesses intrinsic worth, or assert that social welfare is the highest good. To the former class belong the believers in egoistic hedonism; to the latter, the social utilitarians and the Hegelians.

For those who maintain that the supreme end of life and rule of conduct is one's own happiness, there can, of course, be no such thing as a right in the *moral* sense of the term. There is no sacredness, no intrinsic worth, no obligation-compelling force in either the concept or the fact of happiness unqualified and divorced from all consideration of the dignity of personality. The person who refuses to seek his own happiness can be condemned as unwise but not as immoral. And if he is not, in any true sense of the word, under moral obligation to procure happiness for himself, neither is he bound by any sort of duty to respect or refrain from hindering the happiness of others. As there is no sacredness in the end—happiness—and none in the persons pursuing it, so there can be no sacredness in the means—those opportunities of activity that we call rights—and no obligation to respect them. In such a system individual rights have neither logical foundation nor intelligible meaning. Again, if personal happiness be the ultimate aim and criterion of reasonable conduct it is altogether fitting and reasonable that each man should interpret happiness in his own way, and strive to obtain it by whatever means seem to him best, regardless of such unreasonable and unfounded restraints as rights and obligations.

This purely egoistic hedonism seems to be completely and consistently accepted by only a very small minority of the world's thinkers. Even with them it is a merely speculative belief. In practice they reject or at least modify it, in common with the overwhelming majority of the men and women who live outside of lunatic asylums. A formal refutation of it in the interest of the doctrine of natural rights is, therefore, unnecessary. Of much greater importance for our contention is the theory that all rights are positive, that is, derived from society, and conferred upon the individual primarily for the benefit of society and only secondarily for the sake of the individual.[5] Individual rights are valid insofar as they do not hinder the social weal. "By himself," says Mackenzie, "a man has no right to anything whatever. He is a part of the social whole; and he has a right only to that which it is for the good of the whole that he should have."[6] In this view the social organism becomes an end in itself; and its good becomes the final goal and rule of human conduct. Now society is, indeed, something more than an abstraction, something more than the sum of its component individuals. And its function is not simply to guarantee equal liberty to all its members, in the sense of Immanuel Kant and Herbert Spencer. It is a real entity, a moral body, an organism, whose purpose is to safeguard the rights and promote to a reasonable degree the welfare of every one of its members. It is an organism only by analogy, however; not literally or physically. It is an organism inasmuch as its members are mutually dependent, and have diverse functions; inasmuch as it persists amid continuous changes in its membership, and will retain its identity after all its present members shall have perished; and inasmuch as its health is determined by the health of its members, and in turn reacts upon the latter. When this much has been said the analogy between society and a biological organism is about exhausted. Society is not an organism in the sense that it is a finality. Its members do not exist and function for its welfare; they possess intrinsic worth and sacredness. Hence it is not an organism in which the individual's personality is merged and lost, like the branch in the tree, to use the illustration of Hegel. Society has, indeed, rights that are distinct from the rights of the individuals composing it, and its scope and aims reach beyond the welfare of the men and women that live in it at any given time. It has the right, for example, to make war, which the individual has not; and to prevent the ruthless destruction of forests, which prohibition may be contrary to the interests and wishes of its present members. Nevertheless, every right that society possesses, every act that it performs, every assertion that it makes of its legitimate power over individuals, is ultimately for the sake of individuals. It cannot otherwise be justified, for it is not an end in itself.

Let us concede for the moment that society exists for its own sake, is its own highest good. All its powers, prerogatives and activities will be naturally used as a means to this end. Whenever individuals, however innocent of wrong doing, impede society's progress they are to be relentlessly blotted out of existence. Let us suppose that as a result of this social selection the general level of the race is much higher than it would have been had regard been paid to the "superstition" of natural rights. Society has been treated as an end in itself, and the result is a more excellent society.

It must be evident that the individuals who have been removed to bring about this result could not reasonably have been expected to make the sacrifice willingly. They could not have been satisfied to efface themselves for the sake of society as distinct from its members, since this would be to die for an abstraction. Nor is it likely that any considerable number of them were willing to forego existence in order that the individuals who were left behind might enjoy a more complete existence in the improved society; for the real meaning of this situation is that the former have been used as mere instruments to the welfare of the latter. It is not reasonable to expect men to devote themselves completely to any other end than their own highest good, and a superior society cannot be the highest good for those who must be annihilated as a condition of its realization. They will very naturally prefer to run the risk of securing their own welfare in a less perfect social organization. There is no duty constraining one section of the community—not simply to risk their lives, as in a just war—but to submit to be killed by the social authority, in order that the surviving citizens may have the benefit of a more efficient State. The same statement may be made concerning any other of the individual's natural and essential rights. And if the individuals whose rights are treated as non-existent are neither willing nor bound by moral obligation to make the sacrifice, the State has certainly no right, no *moral* power, to treat them as a means pure and simple to the welfare of those of its members who are permitted to survive. For, juggle as we will with the terms "social utility" and "social welfare," talk as obscurely as we may about regarding the individual from the viewpoint of society, the true meaning of the assertion that the rights of the individual are derived from and wholly subordinate to society, is that the lives of those who are less useful to society are essentially inferior to the lives of those who are more useful. And not until those who reject natural rights have succeeded in proving that some human lives are less sacred, have less intrinsic worth, stand on a lower grade of being than others, can they indulge the hope of winning over any considerable number of thinkers to the contention that the individual—even the poorest and lowliest person that breathes—has no rights that are indestructible by society.

The positivist theory of rights becomes more formidable, at least at first sight, when it is stated in terms of Hegelianism. The question is no longer one between the relative interests and importance of the stronger, wiser and more virtuous citizens on the one hand, and of the weaker, less intelligent and more vicious on the other. Organized society, or the State, is in this system regarded as a good in itself, the highest manifestation of the Universal Reason, which is the only final reality. The all-important consideration, then, is to see that this highest embodiment of the Universal Reason or World-Spirit called the State, shall reach the fullest possible development. Compared with this purpose, the welfare of individuals, who are merely particular and imperfect realizations of the one great reality, is insignificant. Their importance is analogous to that of the individual trees in a beautiful grove: the totality called the grove is the supreme end, to which the existence and condition of any particular tree is entirely subordinate. The rights of the individual are, therefore, derived from the State and intended for the greater glory of the State. The late Professor Ritchie, one of the ablest of the Hegelians who wrote in English, describes the rights and dignity of the human person thus: "Every human being may claim a right to be considered as such, because he *potentially* shares in the consciousness of the Universal Reason,"[7] Each individual is, as it were, a receptacle of the Universal Reason, and derives therefrom all his worth and sacredness. When, consequently, the life or liberty of the individual begins to be an obstacle to the activity or unfolding of the Universal Reason, whenever the interests of the Universal Reason demand that any given individual should cease to embody it, he may lawfully be put to death, just as a diseased limb may be severed from the body, or a leaking pot be consigned to the scrap heap. If the Pantheistic basis of this deification of the State be accepted the theory of rights reared upon it is entirely logical. It may well be doubted, however, whether this blind, impersonal entity known as the Universal Reason seems to any considerable number of persons to have the moral authority requisite to oblige them to surrender their particular existence for Its aggrandizement. And of the few who may recognize the supreme rights of the Universal Reason, not all will acknowledge that Its loftiest manifestation is to be found in the very fallible and very imperfect State in which they happen to live. An attempt to refute the metaphysical assumptions underlying the Hegelian theory of rights is, consequently, not much needed at this time.

One of the most frequent of the popular arguments against natural rights runs thus: All rights come into existence, become necessary, and obtain adequate protection only in society; hence they are derived from society, exist for a social end, and should be exercised chiefly for the social welfare. This presentation is vitiated by an incorrect analysis and by unwarranted inferendes. Not all of man's rights require a social organization, or even social contact of any kind, in order that they should become existent. All that is necessary is that two men be alive at the same time. They may be thousands of miles apart, may not even know of each other's existence, yet each will possess in full validity such natural rights as those of life, liberty and property, and will be morally restrained from hindering his fellow in the reasonable exercise of these rights. As to the second contention, it is true that rights are not needed until men come into some form of social intercourse; for a right means the moral power of restraining others from interfering with one's personal goods, and if there is no one near enough to interfere the moral restraint is unnecessary and impracticable; but this does not prove that rights are created by society, any more than the fact that evening dress is worn only at certain "functions" proves that this form of apparel is created by or for the "functions." The clothes are intended for the individual wearers *on certain occasions*. In like manner, the individual's rights have for their primary purpose his own welfare *in society*. Finally, the fact that a man's rights can be sufficiently protected only in civil society is not a reason why they should be entirely subordinated to the ends of society, any more than the employer's dependence upon his employees puts him under obligation to turn over to them all his profits.

Academic opposition to the doctrine of natural rights is directed not so much against the moderate conception of them that has always prevailed in Catholic ethical teaching, as against the exaggerated and anti-social form in which they were proclaimed by the political philosophers of France, and even by some of those of England and America, in the latter half of the Eighteenth century. The Catholic view, which is the one defended in this chapter, is, as already noted, that the individual's natural rights are derived from and determined by his nature, that is to say, his essential constitution, relations and end. They are also said to proceed from the natural law, which is simply that portion of God's eternal law that applies to actions of human beings. The natural law is so expressed in man's nature that its general precepts may readily be known, partly by intuition and partly by analyzing man's faculties, tendencies and destiny. In the view of the

Revolutionary philosophers, however, "nature" and "natural" referred not to what is essential and permanent in man, but to that which is primitive and unconventional. Hence they laid more stress on the "state of nature" than on the "law of nature."[8] The natural law was merely that very simple and very primitive system of rules that would suffice for the state of nature, in which political restraints would be unknown, or at least reduced to a minimum. As the late Professor Ritchie has well said: "To the Thomist[9] the law of nature is an ideal *for* human law; to the Rousseauist it is an ideal to be reached by getting rid of human law altogether."[10] In the mind of the Revolutionist, therefore, to re-establish the law of nature meant to shake off the cumbersome and obstructive political regulations of the day, and get back to the simple state of nature, the semi-anarchical conditions of primitive times. This was, of course, a very inadequate interpretation of man's nature and of the natural law. No such "state of nature" ever existed or ever could exist compatibly with civilization. No valid conclusion regarding the individual's liberties, duties or rights could be deduced from his position and relations in this imaginary and irrational existence. Nevertheless, upon it were based and by it were measured men's natural rights in the Revolutionary system. As a consequence, the rights of the individual were exaggerated and the rights of society minimized. In practice this juristic liberalism has meant, and always will mean, that the State allows to the strong the legal right and power to oppress the weak. A good example of the evil is to be found in the results of the economic policy of *laissez-faire*. It is no wonder that there has been a reaction against this pernicious, anti-social and really *unnatural* theory of natural rights.

The doctrine of natural rights outlined in the foregoing pages holds, then, a middle ground between the Revolutionary and the positivistic theories of the origin and extent of the rights of the individual. It insists that the individual is endowed by nature, or rather, by God, with the rights that are requisite to a reasonable development of his personality, and that these rights are, within due limits, sacred against the power even of the State; but it insists that no individual's rights extend so far as to prevent the State from adjusting the conflicting claims of individuals and safeguarding the just welfare of all its citizens. In other words, man's natural rights must not be so widely interpreted that the strong, and the cunning, and the unscrupulous will be able, under the pretext of individual liberty, to exploit and overreach the weak, and simple, and honest majority. The formula that correctly describes the limits of individual rights is not the one enounced by Kant and Fichte, namely, that a person has a right to do everything that does not interfere with the equal liberty of others.[11] Interpreted in one way, this formula is utterly incapable of application, since the doing of an action by one man means the limitation to that degree of the liberty of all other men. Understood in a completely subjective sense, it would justify and legalize theft, adultery and murder; for I may claim the right to steal if I am willing that others should enjoy the same liberty. The true formula is that the individual has a right to all things that are essential to the reasonable development of his personality, consistently with the rights of others and the complete observance of the moral law. Where this rule is enforced the rights of *all* individuals, and of society as well, are amply and reasonably protected. On the other hand, if the individual's rights are given a narrower interpretation, if on any plea of public welfare they are treated by the State as non-existent, there is an end to the dignity of personality and the sacredness of human life. Man becomes merely an instrument of the State's aggrandizement, instead of the final end of its solicitude and the justification of its existence. If all rights are derived from the State, and determined by the needs of the State, the laborer has no such thing as a natural right to a Living Wage, nor any kind of right to any measure of wages, except in so far as the community would thereby be benefited. President Hadley tells us that some workers are more profitable at a low wage than at a high one, that the "economy of high wages" is not a universal law. "There are some men whose maximum efficiency per unit of food is obtained with small consumption and small output. These go into lines requiring neither exceptional strength nor exceptional skill, and remain poor because the best commercial economy in such lines is obtained by a combination of low output and low consumption."[12] Those who would measure the rights of the individual by the social weal must logically conclude that whenever "the best commercial economy" is secured by "low consumption," in other words, by low wages, the underpaid worker, let him be never so cruelly "sweated," is not treated unjustly and has no right to a larger remuneration. Hence the importance of the doctrine of rights to the subject of this volume: for it cannot be shown that every laborer has an ethical claim to a Living Wage unless the teaching of Christianity be accepted, to-wit: "That every individual by virtue of his eternal destination is at the core somewhat holy and indestructible; that the smallest part has a value of its own, and not merely because it is part of a whole: that every man is to be regarded by the community, never as a mere instrument, but also as an end."[13]

NOTES

NOTES TO EDITOR'S INTRODUCTION

1. John A. Ryan, *Social Doctrine in Action: A Personal History* (New York: Harper & Brothers, 1941), 8.

2. John A. Ryan, *Questions of the Day* (1931; reprint, Freeport: Books for Libraries Press, 1967), 223. Cited by Joseph M. McShane, S. J., *"Sufficiently Radical": Catholicism, Progressivism, and the Bishops' Program of 1919* (Washington, D.C.: The Catholic University Press of America, 1986), 32.

3. McShane develops this claim in the first chapter of *"Sufficiently Radical,"* 7–56, esp. 49.

4. Francis L. Broderick, *Right Reverend New Dealer: John A. Ryan* (New York: Macmillan Co., 1963), 21.

5. Ibid., 92.

6. See ibid., 105–9 and 156–59, for Broderick's fuller account of these revealing incidents regarding Ryan's role with the church.

7. Ryan, *Social Doctrine in Action*, 263.

8. In 1937, the Supreme Court reversed Adkins in *West Coast* v. *Parish*, and in 1938 Congress enacted a minimum wage of 25 cents per hour in the Fair Labor Standards Act.

9. *Social Doctrine*, 277–84.

10. For a more extensive treatment of these concepts, see my *Passion for Justice: Retrieving the Legacies of Walter Rauschenbusch, John A. Ryan, and Reinhold Niebuhr* (Louisville, Ky.: Westminster/John Knox Press, 1992), 110–88, 230–55. Readers may also want to examine other related writings by Ryan; I shall refer to some of these in the appropriate context.

11. Aquinas's understanding of justice was also informed by the supernatural telos of humans, but the ultimate end of humans in God did not influence Ryan's theory of rights and justice.

12. Immanuel Kant, *The Metaphysical Elements of Justice*, trans. John Ladd (Indianapolis: Bobbs-Merrill Co., 1965), 34.

13. Readers opposed to liberal concepts of dignity and rights may be tempted to conclude that Kantian ethics offers no way to justify limitations on individual property rights

and contractual agreements. Such precipitous conclusions are mistaken. The Kantian justification for such limitations would, however, have to be based on preserving individual autonomy rather than on providing the means to the end of human nature.

14. John A. Ryan, *A Living Wage: Its Ethical and Economic Aspects* (New York: Macmillan, 1906), 64–65 and 170–71 in the present volume. Readers interested in Ryan's teleological conception of human dignity and rational human nature will do well to read the second chapter of John A. Ryan, *The Norm of Morality: Defined and Applied to Particular Actions* (Washington, D.C.: National Catholic Welfare Conference [cited hereafter as NCWC], 1944), 7–18.

15. Ryan, *A Living Wage*, 44 and 161 in present volume.

16. The one exception might be the right to life, which Ryan calls "intrinsically valid," but even in this case Ryan appears to make this claim on the grounds that there are no "circumstances" in which the right is not an "immediate and direct" need for the good that it serves. See John A. Ryan, *Distributive Justice: The Right and Wrong of Our Present Distribution of Wealth*, 3d ed. (New York: Macmillan Co., 1942), 46 and 16 in present volume.

17. John A. Ryan, *The Church and Socialism and Other Essays* (Washington, D.C.: The University Press, 1919), 145.

18. Ryan, *Questions of the Day*, 305.

19. Ryan, *Distributive Justice*, 3d ed., 47 and n. 19, 11 in present volume.

20. For an explication of how this view of equality, liberty, and private property differs from other theories of rights in contemporary moral philosophy and in Catholic social teachings, see my *Passion for Justice*, 130–40, and especially "The Legacy of John A. Ryan's Theory of Justice," *The American Journal of Jurisprudence* 33 (1988): 61–98.

21. John A. Ryan and Morris Hillquit, *Socialism: Promise or Menace?* (New York: Macmillan, 1914), 58. Both Patrick W. Gearty, *The Economic Thought of Monsignor John A. Ryan* (Washington, D.C.: The Catholic University Press of America, 1953), 247–49, and Charles E. Curran, *American Catholic Social Ethics: Twentieth-Century Approaches* (Notre Dame, Ind.: Notre Dame University Press, 1982), 38–41, cite and comment on this exact quotation, indicating the extent to which it offers an entrée into Ryan's important thinking about the relationship between morality and economics.

22. Readers interested in Ryan's use of the economic thought of his day will want to consult Patrick Gearty, *The Economic Thought of Monsignor John A. Ryan*. Unfortunately, it is not readily available.

23. Ryan, *A Living Wage*, 79.

24. Ryan, *Distributive Justice*, 3d ed., 188 and 75 in present volume.

25. For Ryan's more developed treatment of commutative, distributive, and social justice, consult several of the brief essays in *Seven Troubled Years: 1930–1936: A Collection of Papers on the Depression and on the Problems of Recovery and Reform* (Ann Arbor, Mich.: Edwards Brothers, 1937), and especially "The Concept of Social Justice," 174–76.

26. Ryan, *A Living Wage*, 162. Not surprisingly, Ryan regarded this wage as a right for adult males because in his view they alone, as heads of the household, are responsible for the financial well-being of the other members of the family. See Ryan, *Distributive Justice*, 3d ed., 282–83 and 121–22 in present volume. I mentioned previously that Ryan's views on economic justice are illuminating in their errors as well as in their insights! Only a very small minority of the readers of this volume, I trust, will concur with Ryan's views on the roles of men and women in a family. The more challenging question for most of us is whether Ryan's justification of rights on the basis of a

conception of what is good for individuals inevitably leads to restrictions of personal freedoms that a just economic system should respect. To this question, I can offer no short and definite answer.

27. John A. Ryan, *Distributive Justice,* 1st ed. (1916; reprint, New York: Arno Press, 1978), 416–17. This bold claim for what appears from our standpoint to be a remarkably narrow remedy to injustice was not repeated in later editions of *Distributive Justice.*

28. John A. Ryan, *Social Reconstruction* (New York: Macmillan, 1920), 62–63. This volume offers Ryan's commentary on the Bishops' Program of 1919, the statement Ryan wrote for the Administrative Committee of the Catholic War Council. The Bishops' statement appears as an appendix to Social Reconstruction.

29. Ryan, *Distributive Justice,* 3d ed., 302, and 135 in the present volume.

30. For an accurate appreciation of the egalitarian reforms Ryan advocated in the '30s, readers will have to turn to short articles he wrote during that period, many of which are published in *Seven Troubled Years,* and to the published lectures on economics that Ryan gave at the University of Wisconsin in 1934. See John A. Ryan, *A Better Economic Order* (New York: Harper & Brothers, 1935), 1–115.

31. Ryan added his only new chapter to the third edition of *Distributive Justice,* "A New Status for Labor," in order to describe and give his moral reasons for advocating these new programs. Readers of this volume interested in Ryan's more complete treatment of these programs will want to examine scattered essays in *Seven Troubled Years,* especially "Organized Social Justice" (215–19) and "Two Programs of Social Reconstruction" (306–10), as well as the last two chapters in Ryan's *A Better Economic Order,* 148–89.

32. See John A. Ryan and Francis J. Boland, C.S.C., *Catholic Principles of Politics* (New York: Macmillan Co., 1940). The revisions in *Distributive Justice* are largely in the economics; there are minimal revisions in the ethics.

33. Ryan's method for advancing economic justice might also be instructively contrasted with Martin Luther King, Jr.'s, use of direct political action to redeem the collective conscience of white Americans. King viewed the collective conscience of white Americans as corrupted by years of racism embedded in the culture. Hence, political decision makers could not be expected to respond to moral argumentation until they and the people experienced a change of heart. King's hope was in exposing the collective white conscience, through dramatic public confrontations with the worst manifestations of racism, to its conflicting commitments to equality on the one hand and white racial superiority on the other. Only after being redeemed by the challenge of direct action could the collective conscience enact and enforce legislation. Therefore, King refused to limit his movement to the attempts by the NAACP to secure justice through moral and legal argument in the courts. Ryan's confidence in moral argument is incompatible with the similar views of King and Rauschenbusch regarding the need for redemptive movements in history to prepare the way for reform.

34. Ryan, *Distributive Justice,* 3d ed., 348, and 171 in present volume.

35. Ryan, *Social Doctrine in Action,* 280.

36. Ryan, *Social Reconstruction,* 121–40; idem, *The Church and Socialism and Other Essays* (Washington, D.C.: The University Press, 1919), 100–51; idem, *Declining Liberty and Other Papers* (New York: Macmillan, 1927), several essays in Part 2.

37. A complete bibliography of Ryan's publications is available through the theological librarian at the Archbishop Ireland Memorial Library at the University of St. Thomas in St. Paul, Minn.

NOTES TO CHAPTER 2

1. The marriage rights of criminals, degenerates, and other socially dangerous persons are passed over here as not pertinent to the present discussion. For the same reason nothing is said of the perfectly valid social argument in favor of the individual right of marriage.

2. Cf. Vermeersch, *Quaestiones de Justitia,* no. 204.

3. "The law, therefore, should favor ownership and its policy should be to induce as many as possible to become owners." (Pope Leo XIII in *Rerum novarum.*)

4. The argument in the text is obviously empirical, drawn from consequences. There is, however, a putatively intrinsic or metaphysical argument which is sometimes urged against the justice of the Single Tax system. It runs thus: Since the fruits of a thing belong to the owner of the thing, *res fructificat domino,* rent, which is the economically imputed fruit of land, necessarily and as a matter of natural right should go to the owner of the land. As will be shown in chapter vi (Editor's Note: Chapter 4 in this edition), the formula at the basis of this contention is not a metaphysical principle at all, but a conclusion from experience. Like every other formula or principle of property rights, it must find its ultimate basis in human welfare.

NOTES TO CHAPTER 3

1. *National Wealth and Income,* Report of the Federal Trade Commission, 1926, p. 71.

2. Cf. Hobson, *The Industrial System,* pp. 192–197.

3. Cf. *Progress and Poverty,* books iii and iv.

4. Cf. Walker, *Land and Its Rent,* pp. 168–182.

5. *The Wealth and Income of the People of the United States,* Macmillan, 1915, p. 160.

6. *National Income in the United States, 1929–35,* United States Department of Commerce, pp. 26, 27.

7. *Farm Tenancy,* Report of the President's Committee, February, 1937, p. 96.

8. Hobson, *The Evolution of Modern Capitalism,* London, 1907, p. 41.

9. *Harper's Monthly Magazine,* Jan., 1910.

10. Watkins, *The Growth of Large Fortunes,* N.Y., 1907, p. 75.

11. Idem., p. 93.

12. Youngman, *The Economic Causes of Great Fortunes,* N.Y., 1909, p. 45.

13. Howe, *Privilege and Democracy in America,* pp. 125, 126.

14. Cf. Commons, *The Distribution of Wealth,* N.Y., 1893, pp. 252, 257.

15. "In a growing city an advantageous site will command a price more than in proportion to its present rent because it is expected that the rent will increase still further as the years go on." Taussig, *Principles of Economics,* Macmillan, 1911, ii, 98.

NOTES TO CHAPTER 4

1. *Summary of Report of the Commissioner of Corporations on the Timber Industry in the United States,* p. 3.

2. *Report of the Commissioner of Corporations on Water Power Development in the United States,* pp. 193–195.

3. Cf. Marsh, *Land Value Taxation in American Cities,* p. 95.

4. Municipal purchase and ownership of land have been advocated by such a conservative authority as the Rev. Heinrich Pesch, S.J., in *Lehrbuch der Nationaloekonomie,* I, 203.

5. *Principles of Political Economy,* book v, ch. 2, sec. v.

6. *Progressive Taxation in Theory and Practice,* 1908, p. 130.

7. Cf. Taussig, *Principles of Economics,* ii, 516; Seligman, *The Shifting and Incidence of Taxation,* p. 223.

8. Cf. Fallon, *Les Plus-Values et l'Impôt,* Paris, 1914, pp. 455, sq.; Fillebrown, *A Single Tax Handbook for 1913,* Boston, 1912; Marsh, *Taxation of Land Values in American Cities,* New York, 1911, pp. 90–92; *The Quarterly Journal of Economics,* vols. 22, 24, 25; *The Single Tax Review,* March–April, 1912; *Stimmen aus Maria-Laach,* Oct., 1907.

9. Cf. Ely, *The Taxation of Land.* Reprinted from Proceedings of the National Tax Association, pp. 31, 32.

10. *New York Times,* March 26, 1941.

11. According to Alvin H. Hansen's *Fiscal Policy and Business Cycles,* Norton, 1941, pp. 129–31, the total amount of taxes collected in 1938 was: $14,832,000,000, divided as follows: federal, $6,029,000,000; state, $3,913,000,000; and local, $4,890,000,000.

12. *Encyclopaedia of the Social Sciences,* vol. xiv, p. 66, col. 2.

13. Probably the most concrete and satisfactory discussion of the increment tax and the project to transfer improvement taxes to land, is that presented in the *Final Report of the Committee on Taxation of the City of New York,* 1916. It contains brief, though complete, statements of all phases of the subject, together with concise arguments on both sides, majority and minority recommendations, a great variety of dissenting individual opinions, and considerable testimony by experts, authorities, and other interested persons. An interesting, if inconclusive, presentation of the effects of a total transfer of taxes from improvements to land was published in Portland, Oregon, in 1912. It shows the gains and losses that would have been experienced by all the thousands of real estate owners in Clakamas County.

14. Cf. Fallon, op. cit., pp. 442, sq.

15. Cf. Vermeersch, *Quaestiones de Justitia,* pp. 94–126; Seligman, *Progressive Taxation in Theory and Practice,* pp. 210, 211; Mill, *Principles of Political Economy,* book v, ch. ii, sec. 3. Also the able defense of the supertax by Professor Seligman in *Final Report of the Committee on Taxation of the City of New York,* pp. 112–116.

16. For example, Professor William G. Murray, of Iowa State College, submitted these observations: "Tractors and modern equipment are causing a steady expansion in the size of farm most profitable to operate. As a result, the 160-acre family-sized farm is growing into a 200- or 240-acre family-sized farm. Adjoining farms or parts of farms are being rented or bought by farmers in order to keep their tractors and equipment busy." (*Hearings,* August 19, 20, 21, 1940, Part 3, p. 998).

17. *Summary of Report of the Commissioner of Corporations on the Lumber Industry in the United States,* p. 8.

NOTES TO CHAPTER 5

1. Frank H. Knight in *Encyclopaedia of the Social Sciences,* vol. v, p. 138, col. 2.

2. Since 1930, interest rates in the United States have pretty generally fallen between one and two per cent.

NOTES TO CHAPTER 6

1. Hohoff, *Die Bedeutung der Marxschen Kapitalkritik,* Paderborn, 1908.
2. Pp. 64–67, 88, 89, 96.
3. Cf. Van Roey, *De Justo Auctario ex Contractu Crediti,* and Ashley, *English Economic History.*
4. Encyclical, *Vix Pervenit,* 1745.
5. Cf. St. Thomas, *Summa Theologica,* 2a.2ae, q. 78, a. 2 et 3.
6. *Summa, Secunda Secondae,* q. 77, a. 1, in corp.
7. *Theologia Moralis,* I, no. 1050.
8. *What Is Capital?* p. 27.
9. Cf. the excellent analysis of the various classes of savers in John A. Hobson's *Economics of Distribution,* pp. 257–265. Also B. W. Knight, *Economic Principles in Practice,* Farrar & Rinehart, Inc., 1940, pp. 490–492.
10. *Political Economy,* p. 507.

NOTES TO CHAPTER 7

1. *Growth of Capital,* p. 152.
2. *Principles of Economics,* II, 42. According to the Brookings Institution volume, *America's Capacity to Consume* (pp. 93–97), 86 per cent of all savings in 1929 were made by the richest ten per cent of the country's families, while two-thirds were provided by the richest 2.3 per cent of the families. Cf. National Resources Committee, *The Structure of the American Economy,* Washington, 1939, Part I, pp. 9, 90, 91.
3. The figures presented in *America's Capacity to Consume* (loc. cit.) seem to warrant the inference that if the incomes of all the families having less than 2000 dollars were raised to between 2000 and 5000, and if these families then saved at the same rate as the families actually within that income range in 1929, their savings would have increased from the meager sum of 250 million dollars to almost eight billion. That would substantially offset the savings of those families who enjoyed incomes in excess of 20,000 dollars. By far the greater part of those savings was evidently derived from interest rather than salaries. However, the families with income ranging from 5000 to 20,000 dollars saved $4,552,000,000, more than half of which probably originated in the receipt of interest. Would an amount equal to this portion of the savings of this group be forthcoming from their salaries and the salaries of other groups if interest were abolished?

"The problem is a highly speculative one, and no adequate data exist for attempting a solution, but the considerations above stated entitle us to question the generally accepted view that the marginal saving always requires the stimulus of objective interest." (Hobson, op. cit., p. 264.)
4. Cf. Fisher, *Elementary Principles of Economics,* pp. 396, 397. However, he does not discuss in this passage the possibility of suppressing interest on productive capital by a direct method.
5. Cf. Lehmkuhl, *Theologia Moralis,* I, nos. 917, 965, 1035.
6. Vol. 3, pp. 617–629; 2d ed.
7. *Contra Gentiles,* lib. 3, c. 123.

NOTES TO CHAPTER 8

1. The proportion of the national income that may be designated as profits ("Entrepreneurial Withdrawals") remained substantially uniform from 1929 to 1939, inclusive:

the low figure was 15.2 per cent, in 1936; the high was 16.6 per cent in 1932. Nathan, op. cit., p. 4.

NOTES TO CHAPTER 9

1. Cf. ch. xi. [Editor's Note: Chapter 7 in this edition.]
2. This is one illustration of diminishing returns.
3. See *Quadragesimo Anno* and *Atheistic Communism, passim.*

NOTES TO CHAPTER 10

1. Cf. pp. 212, 213 of Castelein's *Philosophia Moralis et Socialis.*
2. This principle is not violated by the action of the federal government in providing various kinds of subsidies, since 1933, to the farmers. The proportion of American farm operators who need and obtain these forms of governmental assistance is too great to deserve classification as "inefficient." The main cause of inadequate farm prices is excessive production, caused in turn by insufficient purchasing power in the hands of the industrial population. Until the public authorities are able to correct the latter evil, they are obliged by social justice to reduce the hardships suffered by the farmers. Besides, the theory that the way to make farm prices adequate is to eliminate one-third or one-half of the farm operators through the processes of unlimited competition, is not only inhumane but politically and socially impracticable.
3. Cf. Hobson, *The Industrial System,* chapter on "Ability."

NOTES TO CHAPTER 11

1. *Final Report,* p. 32.
2. *Progressive Taxation,* pp. 210, 211; cf. Vermeersch, *Quaestiones de Justitia,* pp. 94–126.
3. Figures are taken from Sections 101, 401, 201, respectively, of the "Revenue Act of 1941."

NOTES TO CHAPTER 12

1. *Summa Theologica,* 2a.2ae., q. 66, a. 3.
2. *Patrologia Graeca,* vol. 31, cols. 275, 278.
3. *Patrologia Latina,* vol. 37, col. 1922.
4. *Patrologia Latina,* vol. 14, col. 747.
5. *Patrologia Latina,* vol. 77, col. 87. These and several other extracts of like tenor may be found in Ryan's *Alleged Socialism of the Church Fathers,* ch. i; St. Louis, 1913.
6. Op. cit., 2a.2ae., q. 66, a. 7.
7. Encyclical, *On the Condition of Labor,* May 15, 1891.
8. Encyclical, *On Socialism, Communism, Nihilism,* Dec. 28, 1878.
9. Encyclical, *Quadragesimo Anno,* N.C.W.C. Edition, p. 18.
10. Op. cit., 2a.2ae., q. 32, a. 1.
11. *Idem.,* q. 66, a. 7.
12. A comprehensive, though brief, discussion of this question and numerous ref-

erences are contained in Bouquillon, *De Virtutibus Theologicis,* pp. 332–348. When Pope Leo XIII declared that the rich are obliged to distribute "out of" their superfluity, he did not mean that they are free to give only a portion thereof. The particle *"de"* in his statement, *"officium est de eo quod superat gratificari idigentibus,"* is not correctly translated by "some." It means rather "out of," "from," or "with;" so that the affluent are commanded to devote their superfluous goods indefinitely to the relief of the needy. In the Encyclical, *Quod Apostolici Muneris,* he used the expression, *"gravissimo divites urget praecepto ut quod superest pauperibus tribuant,"* which clearly declares the duty of distributing all.

13. See, however, [p. 56 supra] on the question of sufficient saving for the needs of society.

14. Denzinger, *Enchiridion,* prop. 12, p. 259.

NOTES TO CHAPTER 13

1. Page 47.
2. *The Chicago Daily Tribune,* July 17, 1915.
3. Article on "Political Economy and Ethics," in *Palgrave's Dictionary of Political Economy.*
4. *Property and Contract,* II, p. 603.
5. Cf. *L'Idée du Juste Salaire,* by Léon Polier, ch. iii. Paris; 1903.
6. Polier, op. cit., p. 33, sq.
7. *Ethica,* lib. v. tr. 2, cap. 5.
8. *Comment. ad Eth.,* XXI, 172.
9. Cf. Polier, op. cit., pp. 67–75, where the author reconciles the theory of equivalence with that of class needs in the mediaeval doctrine. Equivalence between labor and remuneration was determined by and ascertained from the "social estimate"; but the "social estimate" always demanded that the remuneration of labor be sufficient to maintain the laborer in conformity with his customary standard and cost of living.

Oswald von Nell-Breuning, S.J., interprets the principle of equivalence as holding, not between wages and work, or wages and product, but between wages and decent livelihood: "Surprise was once expressed that the Pope in his demands for the evaluation of human work did not mention *performance* and efficiency, and the question was raised regarding the Encyclical's attitude toward *wages according to efficient performance.* The surprise might be unjustified. It is impossible to determine the value of work performed by performance. This would mean to determine a quantity by itself." A few pages further on he says that according to the divine moral law labor has a right to demand at least the equivalent of a decent livelihood. "This is just another way of saying that the work is *worth so much."* (*Die Soziale Enzyklika,* pp. 116, 117, 120. English translation by B. W. Dempsey, S. J., entitled, *Reorganization of Social Economy,* pp. 169, 173. Cf. infra, p. 311.)

10. Polier, op. cit., pp. 219–359; Menger, *The Right to the Whole Produce of Labor;* English Translation. London; 1899.
11. *Enquiry Concerning Political Justice.*
12. *On the Effects of Civilization on the People of European States.*
13. *An Inquiry Into the Principles of the Distribution of Wealth Most Conducive to Human Happiness.*
14. Menger, op. cit., p. 56.
15. Op. cit., p. 51.
16. Cf. Menger, op. cit., pp. 62–73.

17. *Qu'est-ce que la propriété ou recherches sur al principe du droit et du gouvernment?* 1840.

18. *Zur Erkentniss unserer staatswirthschaftlichen Zustande,* 1842.

19. Cf. Polier, op. cit., pp. 352, sq.

20. *Essays in Social Justice;* especially ch. vii.

21. Op. cit., pp. 187, 188.

22. Op. cit., p. 201.

NOTES TO CHAPTER 14

1. Cf. Skelton, op. cit., p. 202; Menger, op. cit., pp. 8, sq.

2. See chapters x and xi. (Editor's Note: Chapters 6 and 7 in this edition.)

3. "The first claim of labor, which takes priority over any claim of the owners to profits, respects the right to a living wage." *The Church and Social Order,* A Statement of the Administrative Board, N.C.W.C., par. 40.

4. *Atheistic Communism,* N.C.W.C. Edition, pars. 51, 52.

5. N.C.W.C. Edition, p. 24.

6. While the statement in the text applies to *all* laborers of less than average ability, it obviously is applicable only to individual cases among those who are up to the average. These are the workers at the "margin" of the labor force in an establishment, those who could be discharged without causing the industry to shut down. If an employer would rather go out of business then pay a living wage to all his necessary laborers of average ability, he is morally free to do so; but he may not employ them at less than living wages in order to obtain interest on his capital.

7. Waggaman, *Family Allowances in Foreign Countries,* Bulletin No. 401, U.S. Bureau of Labor Statistics.

8. One of the best statements of the evil social results of low wages will be found in Webb's *Industrial Democracy,* vol. II, pp. 749–766.

9. The differences among Catholic writers on this question came to an end when Pope Pius XI issued his Encyclical, *Quadragesimo Anno,* which contained this sentence: "In the first place, the wage paid to the workingman must be sufficient for the support of himself and of this family." (N.C.W.C. Edition, p. 22.) In his Encyclical on *Atheistic Communism,* the same Pontiff referred to "the salary due in strict justice to the worker for himself and his family." (N.C.W.C. Edition, par. 31.)

10. *The Church and Social Order,* par. 40.

11. Cf. Douglas, Paul H., *Wages and the Family,* chs. i and xii.

NOTES TO CHAPTER 16

1. Fairchild, Furness, Buck, op. cit., ii, p. 217.

2. Lindley D. Clark, *Minimum Wage Laws of the United States: Construction and Operation,* Washington; 1921.

3. Op. cit., p. 48.

4. *Adkins* v. *Children's Hospital.*

5. Cf. Holcombe, *The Foundations of the Modern Commonwealth,* pp. 307–327. See also the first paper in my book, *Declining Liberty and Other Papers.* Macmillan; 1927.

6. Probably a majority of American authorities on constitutional law regarded the decision as unsound from the legal viewpoint. See *The Supreme Court and Minimum*

Wage Legislation. Comment by the Legal Profession on the District of Columbia Case. New York; 1925.

7. Cf. my pamphlet, *The Supreme Court and the Minimum Wage.* Washington; 1923.

8. Cf. Perin, Charles, *Premieres Principes d'Économie Politique,* Paris; 1896, pp. 379–391; also Vermeersch, A., *Questiones de Justitia,* No. 420.

9. *Morehead* v. *People ex rel. Joseph Tipaldo.*

10. *West Coast Hotel Company* v. *Parrish*; March 29, 1937.

11. *Minimum Wages for Women*: Opinion of the Supreme Court of the United States, March 29, 1937, p. 4.

12. Loc. cit., p. 8.

13. *Opp Cotton Mills, Inc., et al.* v. *Administrator of the Wage and Hour Division; United States* v. *Darby Lumber Company et al.*

14. Op. cit., p. 14.

15. *Hammer* v. *Dagenhart,* 1918.

16. *A Living Wage,* Macmillan, 1906, p. 313.

17. *Muller* v. *Oregon.*

18. *Lochner* v. *New York,* 1905.

19. Op. cit., pp. 6, 7.

20. For a brief but fairly comprehensive description of the project to reorganize the Supreme Court, and of the changes in the position taken by some of the justices, see my autobiography, *Social Doctrine in Action,* pp. 250–259.

NOTES TO CHAPTER 17

1. Cf. Lauck, W. J., *Political and Industrial Democracy,* New York, 1926.

2. Temporary National Economic Committee, Monograph No. 29: *The Distribution of Ownership in the 200 Largest Non-financial Corporations, passim.* "Probably in the neighborhood of half of the 8,000,000 to 9,000,000 stockholders in 1937—a year of relatively high dividend payments—received less than $100 in dividends, and not more than 2,000,000 stockholders had an annual dividend income of over $500. . . . Fewer than 75,000 persons, i.e., less than 1 percent of the number of stockholders and considerably less than one-fifth of 1 percent of the total number of income recipients, were necessary to account for one-half of all dividends received by individuals." (p. 13) "Taking common and preferred stock issues together, it appears that about 4,000,000 shareholdings, or slightly less than one-half of the total number, had a value of $500 or less." (p. 32)

3. *Forty Years After,* N.C.W.C. Edition, pp. 22, 23.

4. Ibid., pp. 25–31.

5. The remaining paragraphs of this chapter are reproduced from my book, *A Better Economic Order* (pp. 178–183), by the kind permission of the publisher, Harper & Brothers.

6. *Forty Years After,* N.C.W.C. Edition, p. 28.

NOTES TO CHAPTER 18

1. "However, if We examine matters diligently and thoroughly We shall perceive clearly that this longed-for social reconstruction must be preceded by a profound renewal of the Christian spirit, from which multitudes engaged in industry in every country have unhappily departed. Otherwise, all our endeavors will be futile, and our social edifice will be built, not upon a rock, but upon shifting sand." *Forty Years After,* N.C.W.C. Edition, p. 40.

NOTES TO CHAPTER 19

1. For an explanation of the distinction between abstract or specific and concrete or individual equality, see, Taparelli, "Droit naturel," nos. 354–363, and Naudet, "La democratie," ch. XV.

2. Cf. "Philosophia Moralis," by Julius Costa-Rosetti, 2d edition, thesis 114.

3. Cf. "The Theory of Morals," by Paul Janet, Book II, ch. IV, in which the author defends a doctrine very similar to the one just outlined, although he strangely calls a right a "responsibility."

4. See his "Methods of Ethics," Book III, chapters XIII and XIV; and Book IV, concluding chapter, 6th edition.

5. In substance this theory seems to be held by a majority of the non-Catholics of our time who write on justice and political philosophy. Not all state it in the same language nor restrict the concrete rights of the individual to the same extent, but all accept the principle that the individual has no right which society may not in certain contingencies annul for its own welfare. The sources of the theory are chiefly: (1) writers who opposed the doctrines of the French Revolution, such as, Edmund Burke in "Reflections on the Revolution in France," and Joseph de Maistre in "Essai sur le principe générateur des constitutions politiques"; (2) juristic writers who, in opposition to the Eighteenth century teaching on natural rights, endeavored to place all rights on a basis of historical facts and development, the most prominent of whom were F. C. de Savigny in "System des roemischen Rechts," and F. C. Stahl in "Philosophie des Rechts"; (3) the Hegelian conception of the State as the highest manifestation of the Universal Reason and Will, the source of all rights, and the absolute end to which the individual must subordinate his particular aims and activity; see Hegel's "Grundlinien der Philosophie des Rechts," and Lasson's "System der Rechts-philosophie"; (4) and finally, the doctrine of evolutionist utilitarianism, which emphasizes the importance of race progress at the expense of the individual.

Some indications of common points in the last two sources will be found in chapter II of Ritchie's "Darwin and Hegel," while recent statements of the general positivistic theory of rights are contained in "Natural Rights," by the same author, in Hobson's "Social Problem," and in Willoughby's "Social Justice." Good presentations of the doctrine of natural rights defended in this chapter are made by Taparelli, "Droit naturel," and Meyer, "Institutiones Juris Naturalis." Finally Hegel's general concept of personality is successfully attacked in Andrew Seth's "Hegelianism and Personality," especially on pp. 67–69 and in the concluding chapter.

6. "A Manual of Ethics," p. 296.

7. "Natural Rights," pp. 96, 97.

8. Cf. Bonar, "Philosophy and Political Economy," p. 186.

9. And the Catholic philosopher generally.

10. "Natural Rights," p. 43.

11. See Kant's "Metaphysik der Sitten," section C, and Fichte's "Science of Rights," p. 161, Kroeger's translation.

12. "Economics," section 363.

13. Gierke, "Political Theories of the Middle Age," p. 82.

RYAN'S SOURCES

The following bibliography offers publication facts for most of Ryan's book citations in this volume. The information is for the most accessible edition, printing, or translation rather than to the exact edition Ryan used, which it is often impossible to identify.

Ashley, William James. *An Introduction to English Economic History and Theory.* 2 vols. New York: G. P. Putnam's Sons, 1888, 1893.

Bonar, James. *Philosophy and Political Economy in Some of Their Historical Relations.* London: George Allen & Unwin, 1927.

Bouquillon, Thomas J. *Institutiones theologiae moralis specialis. Tractatus de virtutibus theologicis.* Bruges: Beyaert-Storie, 1890.

Burke, Edmund. "Reflections on the Revolution in France" in *The Burke-Paine Controversy: Texts and Criticism.* Edited by Ray Broadus Browne. New York: Harcourt, Brace & World, 1963.

Carver, Thomas Nixon. *Essays in Social Justice.* Cambridge, Mass.: Harvard University Press, 1915.

Castelein, Auguste, S.J. *Institutiones philosophia moralis et socialis.* Brussels: O. Scheppens, 1899.

Clark, Lindley Daniel. *Minimum Wage Laws of the United States: Construction and Operation.* Washington: Government Printing Office, 1921.

Commons, John Rogers. *The Distribution of Wealth.* New York: Macmillan, 1893.

Costa-Rosseti, Julius. *Philosophia moralis.* 2d ed. Oeniponte: Rauch, 1886.

Denzinger, Heinrich. *Enchiridion symbolorum.* 32d ed. Barcelona: Herder, 1963. See also *The Sources of Catholic Dogma.* 30th ed. Translated by Roy J. Deffarrari. St. Louis: Herder & Herder, 1957.

Devas, Charles S. *Political Economy.* 3d ed. New York: Longmans, Green, and Co., 1913.

Douglas, Paul H. *Wages and the Family.* Chicago: University of Chicago Press, 1925.

Ely, Richard T. *Property and Contract in Their Relations to the Distribution of Wealth.* 2 vols. New York: Macmillan, 1914, 1922.

———. *The Taxation of Land.* Madison, Wis.: National Tax Association, 1922.

Fairchild, Fred Rogers, Stevenson Furniss and Norman Sydney Buck. *Elementary Economics.* 2 vols. New York: Macmillan, 1926.

Fallon, Valère, S.J. *Les plus-values et l'impôt.* Brussels: P. van Fleteren, 1914.

Fichte, J. G. *The Science of Rights.* Translated by A. E. Kroeger. London: Trübner & Co., 1889.

Fillebrown, Charles Bowdoin. *A 1913 Single Tax Catechism.* 10th ed. Boston: C.B. Fillebrown, 1912.

Fisher, Irving. *Elementary Principles of Economics.* New York: Macmillan, 1928.

George, Henry. *Progress and Poverty: An Inquiry into the Cause of Industrial Depressions and of Increase of Want and with Increase of Wealth, the Remedy.* New York: Robert Schalkenbach Foundation, 1955.

Gierke, Otto Friedrich von. *Political Theories of the Middle Ages.* Translated by Frederic William Maitland. Cambridge: Cambridge University Press, 1927.

Godwin, William. *An Enquiry Concerning Political Justice,* 1793. Oxford: Woodstock Books, 1992.

Griffen, Robert. *The Growth of Capital.* New York: A.M. Kelley, 1970; reprint of 1889 ed.

Hadley, A. T. *Economics: An Account of the Relations Between Private Property and Public Welfare.* New York: G.P. Putnam's Sons, 1896.

Hall, Charles. *The Effects of Civilization on the People in European States.* 1805 ed. Reprint, New York: A.M. Kelley, 1965.

Hansen, Alvin H. *Fiscal Policy and Business Cycles.* New York: W.W. Norton & Co., 1941.

Hegel, Georg Wilhelm Friedrich. *Philosophy of Right.* Translated by M. Knox. Oxford: Clarendon Press, 1942.

Hobson, J. A. *The Economics of Distribution.* New York: Macmillan, 1900.

———. *The Evolution of Modern Capitalism: A Study of Machine Production.* New York: Charles Scribner's Sons, 1917.

———. *The Industrial System: An Inquiry into Earned and Unearned Income.* New York: Longmans, Green, and Co., 1909.

———. *The Social Problem.* New York: J. Pott, 1901.

Hohoff, Wilhelm von. *Die Bedeutung der Marxschen Kapitalkritik.* Paderborn: Bonifacius-drucerei, 1908.

Holcombe, Arthur N. *The Foundations of the Modern Commonwealth.* New York: Harper & Brothers, 1923.

Howe, Frederic Clemson. *Privilege and Democracy in America.* New York: Charles Scribner's Sons, 1912.

Janet, Paul. *The Theory of Morals.* Translated by Mary Chapman. New York: Scribner's, 1888.

Kant, Immanuel. *The Metaphysical Elements of Justice.* Part 1 of *The Metaphysics of Morals.* Translated by John Ladd. Indianapolis: Bobbs-Merrill Co., 1965.

King, Willford I. *The Wealth and Income of the People of the United States.* New York: Macmillan, 1915.

Knight, Bruce Winton. *Economic Principles in Practice.* New York: Farrar & Rhinehart, 1939.

Lassalle, Ferdinand. *What Is Capital?* Translated by F. Keddell. New York: New York Labor News, 1900.

Lasson, Adolf von. *System der Rechts-philosophie.* Berlin: J. Guttentag, 1882.

Lauck, William J. *Political and Industrial Democracy.* New York: Funk & Wagnalls, 1926.

Lehmkuhl, Augustinus. *Theologia moralis.* Freiburg: Herder, 1907; Chicago: American Theological Library Association, microfiches, 1986.

Mackenzie, John S. *A Manual of Ethics.* 4th ed. New York: Noble and Noble, 192

Maistre, Joseph de. *Essay on the Generative Principle of Political Constitutions.* 47. Reprint, Delmar, N.Y.: Scholars' Facsimiles & Reprints, 1977.

Marsh, Benjamin Clarke. *Taxation of Land Values in American Cities.* New York: n 1911.

Menger, Anton. *The Right to the Whole Produce of Labor.* Translated by M. E. Tanne New York: Macmillan, 1899.

Meyer, Theodor. *Institutiones juris naturalis.* 2 vols. Freiburg: Herder, 1885–1900.

Mill, John Stuart. *Principles of Political Economy.* Boston: C.C. Little & J. Brown, 1848.

Naudet, Paul Antoine. *La démocratie et les démocrates chrétiens.* Paris: J. Briguet, 1900.

Nell-Breuning, Oswald von, S.J. *Reorganization of Social Economy: The Social Encyclical Developed and Explained.* Translated by Bernard W. Dempsey, S.J. New York: Bruce Publishing Company, 1936–37.

Périn, Charles. *Premiers principes d'économie politique.* Paris: V. Lecoffre, 1896.

Pesch, Heinrich, S.J. *Lehrbuch der Nationaloekonomie.* 5 vols. Freiburg: Herder, 1920–26.

Polier, Léon. *L'Idée du juste salaire.* Paris: V. Giard & Bière, 1903.

Proudhon, P. J. *What Is Property?* Edited and translated by Donald R. Kelley and Bonnie Smith. Cambridge: Cambridge University Press, 1994.

Ritchie, David George. *Darwin and Hegel.* New York: Macmillan, 1893.

———. *Natural Rights: A Criticism of Some Critical and Political Conceptions.* 1952 ed. Reprint, Westport, Conn.: Hyperion Press, 1979.

Rodbertus, Karl. *Zur Erkenntniss unsrer staats-wirthschaftlichen Zustände.* Neubrandenburg: G. Barenwitz, 1942.

Roey, Joseph Ernest van. *De justo auctario ex contractu crediti.* Louvain: J. Van Linthout, 1903.

Savigny, Friedrich Karl von. *System of Modern Roman Law.* Translated by William Holloway. 1867. Reprint, Westport, Conn.: Hyperion Press, 1979.

Seligman, Edwin Robert Anderson. *Progressive Taxation in Theory and Practice.* Princeton, N.J.: American Economics Association, 1908.

———. *The Shifting and Incidence of Taxation.* 5th ed. New York: Columbia University Press, 1927.

Seth Pringle-Pattison, Andrew. *Hegelianism and Personality.* 1887. Reprint, New York: B. Franklin, 1971.

Sidgwick, Henry. *The Methods of Ethics.* Chicago: University of Chicago Press, 1962.

Skelton, Oscar D. *Socialism: A Critical Analysis.* Boston: Houghton Mifflin Co., 1911.

Stahl, Friedrich Julius. *Die Philosophie des Rechts.* Tübingen: J.C.B. Mohr, 1926.

Taparelli, d'Azeglio. *Essai théorique de droit naturel.* Translated from Italian. Microfilm. Tournai: H. Casterman, 1883.

Taussig, Frank William. *The Principles of Economics.* New York: Macmillan, 1911.

Thomas Aquinas, Saint. *Summa contra gentiles.* 4 vols. Hanover House ed. Reprint, Notre Dame, Ind.: University of Notre Dame Press, 1975.

———. *Summa theologiae.* 60 vols. New York: McGraw-Hill Book Co., 1964–1975.

Thompson, William. *An Inquiry into the Principles of Distribution of Wealth Most Conducive to Human Happiness.* Microform. London: W.S. Orr, 1850.

Vermeersch, Arthur, S.J. *Quaestiones de justitia ad usum hodierum scholasticae disputatae.* Bruges: Beyaert, 1904.

Walker, Francis A. *Land and Its Rent.* Westport, Conn.: Hyperion Press, 1979.

Watkins, George Pendleton. *The Growth of Large Fortunes: A Study of Economic Causes Affecting the Acquisition and Distribution of Property.* New York: Macmillan, 1907.

Webb, Sidney and Beatrice. *Industrial Democracy.* 1920 ed. New York: Longmans, Green, and Co., 1926.

Willoughby, W. W. *Social Justice: A Critical Essay.* New York: Macmillan, 1900.

Youngman, Anna Prichitt. *The Economic Causes of Great Fortunes.* New York: The Bankers Publishing Co., 1909.